U0084449

序 言

　　閱讀測驗是學測、指考，以及學校月期考都會考的題型，而且配分通常都很重，目前指考與學測閱讀測驗都佔有三十二分。這麼重要的題型，要參加考試的同學，一定要一而再，再而三地練習。

閱讀測驗拿滿分，其實很容易

　　閱讀測驗和詞彙題不一樣，不需要看懂每一個字，只要能大略抓住文章的重點，就能回答問題。在做閱讀測驗時，要特別注意每一段的第一句和最後一句，然後要邊讀文章，邊把重要的句子畫起來。此外，看到時間、地點、數字和人名時，也要特別注意，因為這些都是常考的重點。

　　看文章時，一定要有耐心。如果碰到看不懂的字，也不用緊張，先做個記號，然後繼續讀下去，後面一定有相關的解釋或同義字。最後，做題目時，如果有不確定的選項，一定要回頭查文章，不要憑印象亂猜，因為閱讀測驗的答案，其實都在文章裡。只要你能把握上述的重點，閱讀能力一定會大為提昇。

　　「高二英文閱讀測驗」集結了各校月期考試題的精華，全書共有四十篇閱讀測驗，每一篇都有詳盡的註釋及翻譯。各校老師精心出題，如此重要的資料，你一定要好好利用，每一篇都確實地作答和檢討。熟讀本書，閱讀測驗必將成為你搶分的最佳利器！

　　本書編校製作過程嚴謹，但仍恐有疏失之處，尚祈各界先進不吝指正。

編者　謹識

TEST 1

Read the following passage and choose the best answer for each question.

Not only graduation and wedding ceremonies but also funerals are important rites in one's life. It's said that people are born in only one way but die in various ways. Nowadays more and more people want to die at home because they think it's their origin. Many sick people decide to leave hospitals if they have a disease that can't be cured. They want to die with dignity. If they don't have a family, many of them go to places called "hospices." Hospices are small homes where about five patients can live. Nurses give them food, take them shopping and help them bathe. But they don't try to save their lives. If a patient goes home, volunteers from hospices will go to their homes and help with the chores. They even help with the funeral. The hospices stay in touch with members of the family for a year after the patient dies.

Medicine has become so advanced that many people can now be kept alive against their wishes. However, the cost of keeping them alive is very great. Most people who go to hospices have cancer, even AIDS. Many of them have no home or are rejected by their family members. But no matter what the reason is that they go to hospices, they choose not to die at hospitals.

【百齡高中】

1. What is an important rite in one's life?

   (A) Burial ceremony.

   (B) Wedding ceremony.

   (C) Graduation ceremony.

   (D) All of the above.

2. Why do sick people go to hospices?

   (A) They can die without their family.

   (B) They can die without medical advances.

   (C) They can die with dignity.

   (D) They can die at their place of origin.

3. Why do hospices NOT try to save sick people?

   (A) They don't provide any medical treatment.

   (B) They are too poor.

   (C) The patients don't pay enough money.

   (D) The patients ask to die with dignity.

4. What may be one of the problems with medicine today?

   (A) Sick people need to spend a lot of money.

   (B) People are kept alive against their wishes.

   (C) Medicine brings many side effects.

   (D) There is no cure for cancer or AIDS.

5. What do you think is the best title for this article?

   (A) Funeral Rites   (B) Medicine Today

   (C) Dying with Dignity   (D) Patients vs. Hospitals

TEST 1 詳解

Not only graduation and wedding ceremonies but also funerals are important rites in one's life. It's said that people are born in only one way but die in various ways. Nowadays more and more people want to die at home because they think it's their origin. Many sick people decide to leave hospitals if they have a disease that can't be cured. They want to die with dignity.

除了畢業典禮跟婚禮之外，葬禮也是個人生命中重要的儀式。大家都說，人們出生方式只有一種，但死去的方法卻有很多種。現在越來越多人希望在自己家裡壽終正寢，因為他們認為那是他們的根源。如果患有無法治癒的疾病時，很多病人會決定離開醫院，希望能有尊嚴地死去。

graduation〔ˌgrædʒʊˈeʃən〕*n.* 畢業典禮
wedding〔ˈwɛdɪŋ〕*n.* 婚禮 ceremony〔ˈsɛrəˌmonɪ〕*n.* 典禮；儀式
funeral〔ˈfjunərəl〕*n.* 葬禮 rite〔raɪt〕*n.* 典禮；儀式
various〔ˈvɛrɪəs〕*adj.* 各種不同的 origin〔ˈɔrədʒɪn〕*n.* 根源
cure〔kjʊr〕*v.* 治癒 dignity〔ˈdɪgnətɪ〕*n.* 尊嚴

If they don't have a family, many of them go to places called "hospices." Hospices are small homes where about five patients can live. Nurses give them food, take them shopping and help them bathe. But they don't try to save their lives. If a patient goes home, volunteers from hospices will go to their homes and help with the chores. They even help with the funeral. The hospices stay in touch with members of the family for a year after the patient dies.

如果他們無家可歸，他們其中很多人會去一個叫作「安寧病房」的地方。安寧病房是一間讓五個病患可以居住的小房子。護士會給病人們食物，帶他們購物，幫他們洗澡。但是護士們不會試著要去拯救這些病人的生命。假如病人回到家裡，安寧病房的志工們會到病人的家中協助雜務。志工們甚至會幫忙葬禮事項。病患死後，安寧病房還會跟病患家屬保持聯繫長達一年之久。

hospice〔'haspɪs〕*n.* 安寧病房；末期療養院
patient〔'peʃənt〕*n.* 病人　　bathe〔beð〕*v.* 洗澡
volunteer〔,valən'tɪr〕*n.* 自願者；志工
chore〔tʃor〕*n.* 雜務；家事　　***stay in touch with*** 和⋯保持聯絡

Medicine has become so advanced that many people can now be kept alive against their wishes. However, the cost of keeping them alive is very great. Most people who go to hospices have cancer, even AIDS. Many of them have no home or are rejected by their family members. But no matter what the reason is that they go to hospices, they choose not to die at hospitals.

　　現在醫學已經非常進步，可以違反他人意願，保持他們的生命跡象。然而，讓人活著的代價很大。很多到安寧病房的人，都是罹患癌症，甚至愛滋病。他們很多都沒有家，或是被家庭成員所排斥。但是無論他們到安寧病房的原因是什麼，他們都選擇不要在醫院裡辭世。

medicine〔'mɛdəsn̩〕*n.* 醫學　　advanced〔əd'vænst〕*adj.* 進步的
alive〔ə'laɪv〕*adj.* 活著的　　against〔ə'gɛnst〕*prep.* 違反
wish〔wɪʃ〕*n.* 願望；希望　　cost〔kɔst〕*n.* 花費
cancer〔'kænsɚ〕*n.* 癌症
AIDS〔edz〕*n.* 愛滋病【又稱「後天免疫缺乏症候群」（Acquired Immune Deficiency Syndrome）】
reject〔rɪ'dʒɛkt〕*v.* 拒絕；排斥　　***no matter~*** 無論~
choose〔tʃuz〕*v.* 選擇【三態：choose-chose-chosen】

1.(**D**) 何者是生命中重要的典禮？

    (A) 葬禮。　　(B) 婚禮。　　(C) 畢業典禮。　　(D) <u>以上皆是。</u>

    * burial〔'bɛrɪəl〕*n.* 埋葬

2.(**C**) 為什麼病人要去安寧病房？

    (A) 他們能在沒有家人在旁邊的情況下死亡。

    (B) 他們因為醫學沒有進步而死去。

    (C) <u>他們能有尊嚴地死去。</u>

    (D) 他們能在他們出生的地方死去。

    * advance〔əd'væns〕*n.* 進步

3.(**D**) 為什麼安寧病房「不」會嘗試去拯救生病的人？

    (A) 他們不提供任何醫療。

    (B) 他們太窮了。

    (C) 病人付的錢不夠多。

    (D) <u>病人要求要有尊嚴地死去。</u>

    * provide〔prə'vaɪd〕*v.* 提供
       treatment〔'tritmənt〕*n.* 治療　　*medical treatment* 醫療

4.(**B**) 下列何者可能是現代醫學的問題之一？

    (A) 病人需要花很多錢。

    (B) <u>可以在違反人們意願的情況下維持他們的生命。</u>

    (C) 藥物帶來很多副作用。

    (D) 癌症跟愛滋病沒有治療方法。

    * *side effect* 副作用　　cure〔kjur〕*n.* 治療法

5.(**C**) 你覺得何者是本文的最佳標題？

    (A) 葬禮　　　　　　　(B) 現代醫學

    (C) <u>有尊嚴地死去</u>　　　(D) 病人跟醫院

    * vs.〔'vɝsəs〕*prep.* 對抗；與～相對（= *versus*）

TEST 2

Read the following passage and choose the best answer for each question.

Sylvia Earle, a marine botanist and one of the foremost deep-sea explorers, has spent over 6,000 hours, more than seven months, underwater. From her earliest years, Earle had a fascination for marine life, and she took her first plunge into the open sea as a teenager. In the years since then she has taken part in a number of landmark underwater projects, from exploratory expeditions around the world to her well-known "Jim dive" in 1978, which was the deepest solo dive ever made without a cable connecting the diver to a support ship at the surface of the sea.

Clothed in a Jim suit, a futuristic suit of plastic and metal armor, which was secured to a manned submarine, Sylvia Earle plunged vertically into the Pacific Ocean, at times at a speed of 100 feet per minute. On reaching the ocean floor, she was released from the submarine and from that point her only connection to the sub was an 18-foot rope. For the next two and a half hours, Earle roamed the seabed taking notes, collecting specimens, and planting a U.S. flag. Having an irresistible desire to descend deeper still, in 1981 she became involved in the design and manufacture of deep-sea submersibles, one of which took her to a depth of 3,000 feet. This, however, did not end Sylvia Earle's accomplishments. 【師大附中】

1. Sylvia Earle discovered her love of the sea
   _____.
   (A) in her childhood
   (B) during her 6,000 hours underwater
   (C) after she made her deepest solo dive
   (D) well into her adulthood

2. It can be inferred from the passage that Sylvia Earle _____.
   (A) has received a very good education
   (B) is uncomfortable in the submarine
   (C) does not have technical expertise
   (D) has devoted her life to ocean exploration

3. The main purpose of this passage is _____.

   (A) to explore the botany of the ocean floor

   (B) to present an account of what Sylvia Earle did

   (C) to provide an introduction to oceanography

   (D) to show the historical importance of the Jim dive

4. Which of the following is NOT true about the Jim dive?

   (A) Sylvia Earle successfully made it in 1981.

   (B) It was performed in the Pacific Ocean.

   (C) Sylvia Earle took notes while on the ocean floor.

   (D) The submarine Sylvia Earle was connected to was manned.

5. What will the paragraph following this passage probably be about?

   (A) Sylvia Earle's early childhood.

   (B) What Sylvia Earle did in the 1980s.

   (C) How deep-sea submersibles work.

   (D) How Earle's life ended.

TEST 2 詳解

Sylvia Earle, a marine botanist and one of the foremost deep-sea explorers, has spent over 6,000 hours, more than seven months, underwater. From her earliest years, Earle had a fascination for marine life, and she took her first plunge into the open sea as a teenager.

席薇亞・厄爾是個海洋植物學家，也是最重要的深海探險者之一，她待在水面下的時間超過六千小時，也就是七個月以上。厄爾就從小對海洋生物很著迷，她在青少年時期，就第一次跳入外海。

Sylvia Earle (ˈsɪlvɪəˈɝl) *n.* 席薇亞・厄爾【美國海洋探險家】
marine (məˈrin) *adj.* 海洋的
botanist (ˈbɑtn̩ɪst) *n.* 植物學家
foremost (ˈforˌmost) *adj.* 最主要的
deep-sea (ˌdipˈsi) *adj.* 深海的
explorer (ɪkˈsplorɚ) *n.* 探險家
underwater (ˈʌndɚˌwɔtɚ) *adv.* 在水面下；在水中
fascination (ˌfæsn̩ˈeʃən) *n.* 魅力；迷戀；著迷
marine life 海洋生物　　plunge (plʌndʒ) *n.* 跳入
take the plunge into 跳入　　***the open sea*** 公海；外海
teenager (ˈtinˌedʒɚ) *n.* 青少年

In the years since then she has taken part in a number of landmark underwater projects, from exploratory expeditions around the world to her well-known "Jim dive" in 1978, which was the deepest solo dive ever made without a cable connecting the diver to a support ship at the surface of the sea.

往後幾年內,她參與多項重要的水中計畫,從遠征全世界的探索行動,到 1978 年著名的「吉米潛水」,那次是有史以來深度最深的個人潛水活動,而且潛水者跟海面上的支援船之間沒有繩索連結。

take part in 參與　*a number of* 一些;許多
landmark〔'lænd,mɑrk〕*n.* 重要事件　*adj.* 重要的;影響未來的
project〔'prɑdʒɛkt〕*n.* 計畫
exploratory〔ɪk'splorə,torɪ〕*adj.* 探險的
expedition〔,ɛkspɪ'dɪʃən〕*n.* 探險行動;遠征
well-known〔'wɛl'non〕*adj.* 著名的　　dive〔daɪv〕*n.* 潛水
Jim dive 吉米潛水【指穿著吉米潛水裝所進行的潛水活動。吉米潛水裝是一套類似太空人裝束的潛水設備,第一個使用這套裝備進行潛水活動的是吉米‧賈拉特 (Jim Jarratt),故以他為名】
solo〔'solo〕*adj.* 單獨的　　cable〔'kebl〕*n.* 繩索;纜線
connect〔kə'nɛkt〕*v.* 連結　　diver〔'daɪvə〕*n.* 潛水者
support〔sə'port〕*n.* 支援　　surface〔'sɝfɪs〕*n.* 表面;水面

Clothed in a Jim suit, a futuristic suit of plastic and metal armor, which was secured to a manned submarine, Sylvia Earle plunged vertically into the Pacific Ocean, at times at a speed of 100 feet per minute.

席薇亞‧厄爾穿著一套新潮的吉米潛水裝,由塑膠跟金屬護具製成,這套潛水裝被牢牢綁在有人操控的潛水艇上,她垂直地跳入太平洋,有時候速度高達每分鐘一百呎。

clothe〔kloð〕*v.* 使穿上
Jim suit 吉米潛水裝【一套太空衣裝扮的特殊潛水裝】
futuristic〔,fjutʃə'rɪstɪk〕*adj.* 未來的;新潮的
plastic〔'plæstɪk〕*adj.* 塑膠的　　metal〔'mɛtl〕*adj.* 金屬的
armor〔'ɑrmə〕*n.* 潛水衣;護具
secure〔sɪ'kjʊr〕*v.* 綁緊;固定

manned〔mænd〕*adj.* 由人操作的
submarine〔ˌsʌbmə'rin〕*n.* 潛水艇
plunge〔plʌndʒ〕*v.* 跳入　　　vertically〔'vɜtɪklɪ〕*adv.* 垂直地
Pacific〔pə'sɪfɪk〕*adj.* 太平洋的
the Pacific Ocean 太平洋　　*at times* 有時
feet〔fit〕*n. pl.* 呎（單數 foot）　　per〔pə〕*prep.* 每一

On reaching the ocean floor, she was released from the
submarine and from that point her only connection to the sub
was an 18-foot rope.　For the next two and a half hours, Earle
roamed the seabed taking notes, collecting specimens, and
planting a U.S. flag.

一到達海底的時候，席薇亞就與潛水艇分離，從那一刻起，她與潛水艇之間的唯一連結，就只是一條十八呎長的繩索。在接下來兩個半小時中，厄爾漫步在海底並同時記筆記、採集樣本，然後插上一面美國國旗。

on + *V-ing* 一…就　　reach〔ritʃ〕*v.* 到達
ocean floor 海底　　release〔rɪ'lis〕*v.* 釋放；使分離
point〔pɔɪnt〕*n.* 時刻　　connection〔kə'nɛkʃən〕*n.* 連結
sub〔sʌb〕*n.* 潛水艇（= *submarine*）
rope〔rop〕*n.* 繩索　　roam〔rom〕*v.* 在…漫步
seabed〔'siˌbɛd〕*n.* 海床；海底　　*take notes* 記筆記
collect〔kə'lɛkt〕*v.* 收集　　specimen〔'spɛsəmən〕*n.* 樣品；標本
plant〔plænt〕*v.* 插；放置

Having an irresistible desire to descend deeper still, in 1981
she became involved in the design and manufacture of
deep-sea submersibles, one of which took her to a depth of
3,000 feet.　This, however, did not end Sylvia Earle's
accomplishments.

懷著一股忍不住想往更深處潛的慾望，1981 年時，厄爾參與深海潛水艇的設計與製造，其中一艘就將她帶入三千呎深的海裡。但這並不是席薇亞・厄爾成就的結尾。

irresistible〔͵ɪrɪ'zɪstəbḷ〕adj. 無法抗拒的
desire〔dɪ'zaɪr〕n. 慾望　　descend〔dɪ'sɛnd〕v. 下降
still〔stɪl〕adv. 更加【強調比較級】
involve〔ɪn'vɑlv〕v. 使捲入；牽涉
be involved in 參與　　design〔dɪ'zaɪn〕n. 設計
manufacture〔͵mænjə'fæktʃɚ〕n. 製造
submersible〔sʌb'mɝsəbḷ〕n. 潛艇　　depth〔dɛpθ〕n. 深度
accomplishments〔ə'kɑmplɪʃmənts〕n. pl. 成就

1.(**A**) 席薇亞・厄爾在 ＿＿＿＿＿＿＿ 發現她對海洋的熱愛。

(A) 孩童時期　　　　　　　　(B) 水面下的六千小時之中

(C) 完成最深的獨潛之後　　　(D) 完全成年時

　* discover〔dɪ'skʌvɚ〕v. 發現
　　well〔wɛl〕adv. 相當；大大地
　　adulthood〔ə'dʌlt͵hʊd〕n. 成年時期

2.(**D**) 從本文可推論，席薇亞・厄爾 ＿＿＿＿＿＿＿。

(A) 接受過非常良好的教育

(B) 在潛水艇裡感覺不舒服

(C) 沒有技術上的專業知識

(D) 一生都致力於海洋探險

　* infer〔ɪn'fɝ〕v. 推論　　receive〔rɪ'siv〕v. 接受
　　uncomfortable〔ʌn'kʌmfɚtəbḷ〕adj. 不舒服的
　　technical〔'tɛknɪkḷ〕adj. 技術的；專門的
　　expertise〔͵ɛkspɚ'tis〕n. 專業知識；專業技術
　　devote〔dɪ'vot〕v. 奉獻；致力於 <to>
　　exploration〔͵ɛksplə'reʃən〕n. 探險

3. (**B**) 本文的主旨是 ＿＿＿＿＿＿＿＿ 。

    (A) 探索海底植物生態

    (B) <u>敘述席薇亞・厄爾所做的事</u>

    (C) 提供海洋學的介紹

    (D) 說明吉米潛水在歷史上的重要性

    * explore〔ɪkˋsplor〕v. 探險；調查
      botany〔ˋbɑtn̩ɪ〕n. 植物學；植物生態
      present〔prɪˋzɛnt〕v. 呈現；提供
      account〔əˋkaʊnt〕n. 說明；敘述
      provide〔prəˋvaɪd〕v. 提供
      introduction〔͵ɪntrəˋdʌkʃən〕n. 介紹
      oceanography〔͵oʃɪənˋɑgrəfɪ〕n. 海洋學
      historical〔hɪsˋtɔrɪkl̩〕adj. 歷史的

4. (**A**) 關於吉米潛水，下列何者不正確？

    (A) <u>席薇亞・厄爾在 1981 年時成功地完成吉米潛水。</u>

    (B) 當時是在太平洋上進行的。

    (C) 席薇亞・厄爾在海底的時候有做筆記。

    (D) 和席薇亞・厄爾相連結的潛水艇是有人操縱的。

    * successfully〔səkˋsɛsfəlɪ〕adv. 成功地
      perform〔pɚˋfɔrm〕v. 執行

5. (**B**) 本文的下一段可能是關於什麼？

    (A) 席薇亞・厄爾的童年。

    (B) <u>席薇亞・厄爾在 1980 年代做了什麼。</u>

    (C) 深海潛水艇如何運作。

    (D) 席薇亞・厄爾的生命如何結束。

    * paragraph〔ˋpærə͵græf〕n. 段落
      following〔ˋfɑloɪŋ〕prep. 接著；在…之後

TEST 3

Read the following passage and choose the best answer for each question.

Elizabeth Taylor is one of America's most popular celebrities. As a movie actress, Taylor won the hearts of millions with her role in the film *National Velvet* in 1944 when she was 12 years old. She has made over 60 films since then. But movie-making and beautiful violet eyes are not all that Taylor is known for. She is also famous for her eight marriages. Two of those marriages were to actor Richard Burton, who she married in 1964, divorced in 1974, remarried in 1975 and divorced again in 1976. For a brief time, Taylor was married to Senator John Warner. On October 6, 1991, Taylor married 40-year-old Larry Fortensky. Fortensky is a construction worker who Taylor met at a drug treatment center. (Taylor had become addicted to the painkillers that she was taking for a back injury. Fortensky was addicted to alcohol.) Taylor and Fortensky were married on the estate of Taylor's good friend, pop singer Michael Jackson. The marriage was featured in all of the supermarket tabloid newspapers. Taylor is also known as a tireless worker for AIDS research fund-raising. 【師大附中】

1. Why might people expect Taylor's marriage to Larry Fortensky to last only a few years?

   (A) Because Taylor's previous marriages often ended in divorce after a few years.

   (B) Because Fortensky is not a movie star.

   (C) Because Fortensky is younger than Taylor.

   (D) Because Taylor predicted the marriage would end.

2. Where did Taylor and Fortensky meet?

   (A) At a movie studio.

   (B) At Michael Jackson's estate.

   (C) At a drug treatment center.   (D) In the U.S. Senate.

3. What does it mean to say that Taylor is a "tireless worker for AIDS research fund-raising"?

   (A) It means Taylor has AIDS.

   (B) It means Taylor never grows tired.

   (C) It means Taylor works as a doctor with AIDS patients.

   (D) It means Taylor works very hard to collect money for the study of AIDS.

4. What is the longest period of time Taylor has been married?

   (A) Ten years.   (B) Eight years.

   (C) Since 1991.   (D) It is not stated.

5. Where did the Taylor-Fortensky wedding take place?

   (A) In Michael Jackson's home state.

   (B) In a large market.

   (C) At Jackson's home.   (D) It is not stated.

TEST 3 詳解

Elizabeth Taylor is one of America's most popular celebrities. As a movie actress, Taylor won the hearts of millions with her role in the film *National Velvet* in 1944 when she was 12 years old. She has made over 60 films since then.

伊麗莎白・泰勒是美國最受歡迎的名人之一。泰勒是一個電影女星，她在 1944 年電影「玉女神駒」中的角色，擄獲了百萬人的心，而當時她才十二歲。從那之後，她總共拍了六十多部電影。

Elizabeth Taylor 〔 ɪ'lɪzəbəθ'telə 〕 *n.* 伊麗莎白・泰勒【1932-2011，美國女演員，曾兩度獲得奧斯卡最佳女演員】

celebrity 〔 sə'lɛbrətɪ 〕 *n.* 名人　　actress 〔'æktrɪs 〕 *n.* 女演員

win the heart of *sb.* 贏得某人的喜愛　　million 〔'mɪljən 〕 *n.* 一百萬

role 〔 rol 〕 *n.* 角色　　velvet 〔'vɛlvɪt 〕 *n.* 絲絨

National Velvet 玉女神駒【電影名】

But movie-making and beautiful violet eyes are not all that Taylor is known for. She is also famous for her eight marriages. Two of those marriages were to actor Richard Burton, who she married in 1964, divorced in 1974, remarried in 1975 and divorced again in 1976. For a brief time, Taylor was married to Senator John Warner.

但泰勒之所以有名，不只是因為拍電影，和她美麗的藍紫色眼睛。她也以她的八次婚姻而聞名。其中兩次是嫁給演員理查・波頓，他們在 1964 年結婚，於 1974 年離婚；1975 年他們倆再婚，又在 1976 年二度離婚。泰勒曾短暫嫁給參議員約翰・華納。

movie-making 〔'muvɪ'mekɪŋ 〕 *n.* 拍攝電影

violet 〔'vaɪəlɪt 〕 *adj.* 紫羅蘭色的；藍紫色的

be known for 因…而有名 (= *be famous for*)

marriage 〔'mærɪdʒ 〕 *n.* 婚姻　　actor 〔'æktə 〕 *n.* 男演員

divorce 〔 də'vɔrs 〕 *v.* 離婚　　remarry 〔 ri'mærɪ 〕 *v.* 再婚

brief 〔 brif 〕 *adj.* 短暫的　　senator 〔'sɛnətə 〕 *n.* 參議員

On October 6, 1991, Taylor married 40-year-old Larry Fortensky. Fortensky is a construction worker who Taylor met at a drug treatment center. (Taylor had become addicted to the painkillers that she was taking for a back injury. Fortensky was addicted to alcohol.)

在 1991 年 10 月 6 日，泰勒嫁給當時四十歲的賴瑞‧福坦斯基。福坦斯基是泰勒在藥物治療中心認識的建築工人。（泰勒曾經對於用來治療背痛的止痛藥成癮。福坦斯基則是有酒癮。）

construction〔kən'strʌkʃən〕*n.* 建築 　　 drug〔drʌg〕*n.* 藥物
treatment〔'tritmənt〕*n.* 治療 　　 addict〔ə'dɪkt〕*v.* 使上癮
be/become addicted to 對…上癮 　　 painkiller〔'pen,kɪlɚ〕*n.* 止痛藥
injury〔'ɪndʒərɪ〕*n.* 傷害 　　 alcohol〔'ælkə,hɔl〕*n.* 酒精

Taylor and Fortensky were married on the estate of Taylor's good friend, pop singer Michael Jackson. The marriage was featured in all of the supermarket tabloid newspapers. Taylor is also known as a tireless worker for AIDS research fund-raising.

泰勒跟福坦斯基在泰勒的好友，也就是流行歌手麥可‧傑克森的莊園舉行婚禮。這場婚禮被超市中所有八卦小報大幅報導。泰勒也因為不斷地籌募愛滋病研究基金而有名。

estate〔ə'stet〕*n.*（在鄉村的）大片私有土地；莊園
pop〔pɑp〕*adj.* 流行的 　　 feature〔'fitʃɚ〕*v.* 特別報導
be featured in 在（報章雜誌上）被大篇幅報導
tabloid〔'tæblɔɪd〕*n.* 小報；八卦報紙
tireless〔'taɪrlɪs〕*adj.* 孜孜不倦的；勤奮的
AIDS〔edz〕*n.* 愛滋病（= *acquired immunodeficiency syndrome*）
research〔'risɝtʃ〕*n.* 研究 　　 fund〔fʌnd〕*n.* 基金
raise〔rez〕*v.* 籌募
fund-raising〔'fʌnd'rezɪŋ〕*n.* 籌募資金；募款

1. (**A**) 爲什麼人們會預期，泰勒跟拉瑞・福坦斯基的婚姻，只會持續幾年？
    (A) 因爲泰勒的前幾段婚姻，都是在幾年後以離婚收尾。
    (B) 因爲福坦斯基不是電影明星。
    (C) 因爲福坦斯基比泰勒年輕。　(D) 因爲泰勒預測婚姻會結束。

    * expect〔ɪkˋspɛkt〕v. 預期　　　last〔læst〕v. 持續
      previous〔ˋpriviəs〕adj. 先前的　***end in*** ~ 以~結束
      predict〔prɪˋdɪkt〕v. 預測

2. (**C**) 泰勒跟福坦斯基是在哪裡認識的？
    (A) 在電影的攝影棚裡。　　　　(B) 在麥可・傑克森的豪宅裡。
    (C) 在一個藥物治療中心。　　　(D) 在美國參議院。

    * studio〔ˋstjudɪ‚o〕n. 攝影棚　　Senate〔ˋsɛnɪt〕n. 參議院

3. (**D**) 本文提到泰勒是 "tireless worker for AIDS research fund-raising"，是什麼意思？
    (A) 意思是泰勒有愛滋病。
    (B) 意思是泰勒從來不會感到疲倦。
    (C) 意思是泰勒擔任愛滋病患者的醫生。
    (D) 意思是泰勒很努力地爲愛滋病研究籌募資金。

    * mean〔min〕v. 意思是　　　grow〔gro〕v. 變得
      work as 擔任　　　patient〔ˋpeʃənt〕n. 病人
      collect〔kəˋlɛkt〕v. 募（款）　　study〔ˋstʌdɪ〕n. 研究

4. (**D**) 泰勒最長的一段婚姻是多久？
    (A) 十年。　　　　　　　　　(B) 八年。
    (C) 從 1991 年到現在。　　　(D) 本文沒有提到。

    * period〔ˋpɪrɪəd〕n. 期間　　state〔stet〕v. 敘述；提及

5. (**C**) 泰勒跟福坦斯基的婚禮在哪裡舉行？
    (A) 在麥可・傑克森的家鄉。　(B) 在大市場裡。
    (C) 在傑克森的家。　　　　　(D) 本文沒有提到。

    * wedding〔ˋwɛdɪŋ〕n. 婚禮　　***take place*** 舉行；發生
      home〔hom〕adj. 故鄉的　　　state〔stet〕n. 州
      home state 家鄉

TEST 4

Read the following passage and choose the best answer for each question.

"AIDS" stands for Acquired Immune Deficiency Syndrome. It's a disease usually contracted by blood-contact or sexual intercourse with an infected person, and it attacks the body's immune system. So a person with AIDS easily becomes ill and within a few years may contract a second, fatal, disease.

AIDS is a serious problem in a lot of Western countries, but it's an even greater danger to the populations of Africa and South Asia. In these regions there is little public education about the disease, and medical treatment is very poor. Hence, many thousands of people are unaware that they have AIDS, and they continue to pass it on to others. For example, in Malawi, over half the population is thought to have AIDS; it's difficult to see how this small African nation can survive such a disaster. Health experts are warning that the problem is now spreading to India and Thailand. Because the AIDS epidemic is so widespread, they are calling it the modern-day plague. 【百齡高中】

1. What may happen to a person who has contracted AIDS?

   (A) He may spread to India and Thailand.

   (B) He may contract a second disease that causes his death.

   (C) He may be sent to Africa.

   (D) He may lose his blood.

2. According to the article, what may be a cause of the big problem of AIDS in Africa?

   (A) The people have little health education.

   (B) AIDS is carried by insects.

   (C) Many foreigners with AIDS move to Africa.

   (D) There is no medical treatment.

3. How can AIDS be passed between people?

   (A) Through blood donation.

   (B) Through sexual intercourse.

   (C) Through infected needles.

   (D) All of the above.

4. What percentage of people in Malawi are believed to have contracted AIDS?

   (A) 60%   (B) 10%   (C) 100%   (D) 40%

5. Why do people call AIDS "the modern-day plague?"

   (A) It is spread by infected fleas.

   (B) It originated in Western countries.

   (C) It affects people all over the world.

   (D) New medicine has been invented to overcome it.

TEST 4 詳解

"AIDS" stands for Acquired Immune Deficiency Syndrome. It's a disease usually contracted by blood-contact or sexual intercourse with an infected person, and it attacks the body's immune system. So a person with AIDS easily becomes ill and within a few years may contract a second, fatal, disease.

「愛滋病」代表「後天免疫缺乏症候群」，這種疾病通常是因為跟已受到感染的人，有血液接觸或性交而傳染的，它會侵襲人體的免疫系統。所以得到愛滋病的人很容易會變得虛弱，在幾年之內就會感染到第二種絕症。

AIDS〔edz〕*n.* 愛滋病　　***stand for*** 代表
acquired〔əˋkwaɪrd〕*adj.* 獲得的；後天養成的
immune〔ɪˋmjun〕*adj.* 免疫的　　deficiency〔dɪˋfɪʃənsɪ〕*n.* 缺乏
syndrome〔ˋsɪn͵drom〕*n.* 症候群　　contract〔kənˋtrækt〕*v.* 感染
blood〔blʌd〕*n.* 血液　　contact〔ˋkɑntækt〕*n.* 接觸
sexual〔ˋsɛkʃuəl〕*adj.* 性的　　intercourse〔ˋɪntɚ͵kors〕*n.* 性交
sexual intercourse 性交　　infected〔ɪnˋfɛktɪd〕*adj.* 受感染的
attack〔əˋtæk〕*v.* 侵襲　　***immune system*** 免疫系統
ill〔ɪl〕*adj.* 生病的；虛弱的　　fatal〔ˋfetḷ〕*adj.* 致命的
fatal disease 不治之症；絕症

AIDS is a serious problem in a lot of Western countries, but it's an even greater danger to the populations of Africa and South Asia. In these regions there is little public education about the disease, and medical treatment is very poor. Hence, many thousands of people are unaware that they have AIDS, and they continue to pass it on to others. For example, in Malawi, over

half the population is thought to have AIDS; it's difficult to see
how this small African nation can survive such a disaster. Health
experts are warning that the problem is now spreading to India
and Thailand. Because the AIDS epidemic is so widespread, they
are calling it the modern-day plague.

愛滋病在很多西方國家是個嚴重的問題，但對於非洲跟南亞居民來
說，更是個巨大的威脅。在這些地區，關於這種疾病的公共教育很缺乏，
醫療也不足。因此，成千上萬的人不知道自己有愛滋病，而且繼續把疾病
傳染給他人。例如，一般認為在馬拉威有超過一半人口罹患愛滋病，很難
理解這個非洲小國要怎麼從這場災難中存活。健康專家警告，這個問題現
在正向印度以及泰國擴散。因為愛滋傳染病是如此普遍，人們稱它為現代
黑死病。

serious (ˈsɪrɪəs) *adj.* 嚴重的　　western (ˈwɛstən) *adj.* 西方的
Western countries 西方國家【指歐洲、美國等先進國家】
population (ˌpɑpjəˈleʃən) *n.* 居民；人口總數
Africa (ˈæfrɪkə) *n.* 非洲　　Asia (ˈeʒə , ˈeʃə) *n.* 亞洲
South Asia 南亞　　region (ˈridʒən) *n.* 地區
treatment (ˈtritmənt) *n.* 治療
medical treatment 醫療　　hence (hɛns) *adv.* 因此
unaware (ˌʌnəˈwɛr) *adj.* 不知情的；未察覺的
pass (pæs) *v.* 傳播
Malawi (məˈlɑwɪ) *n.* 馬拉威【非洲東南部國家】
African (ˈæfrɪkən) *adj.* 非洲的　　survive (səˈvaɪv) *v.* 生存
disaster (dɪzˈæstə) *n.* 災難　　expert (ˈɛkspɝt) *n.* 專家
warn (wɔrn) *v.* 警告　　spread (sprɛd) *v.* 傳播；蔓延
India (ˈɪndɪə) *n.* 印度　　Thailand (ˈtaɪlənd) *n.* 泰國
epidemic (ˌɛpəˈdɛmɪk) *n.* 傳染病
widespread (ˈwaɪdˌsprɛd) *adj.* 普遍的；廣泛流傳的
modern-day (ˈmɑdənˈde) *adj.* 現代的
plague (pleg) *n.* 黑死病

1. (**B**) 一個感染愛滋病的人可能會發生什麼事情？

    (A) 他可能會散佈疾病到印度跟泰國。

    (B) <u>他可能會感染到導致他死亡的第二種疾病。</u>

    (C) 他可能會被送到非洲。   (D) 他可能會失血。

    * cause〔kɔz〕v. 導致；造成

2. (**A**) 根據本文，愛滋病在非洲成為廣大問題的原因可能是何者？

    (A) <u>人們很少接受健康教育。</u>

    (B) 愛滋病由昆蟲傳染。

    (C) 很多有愛滋病的外國人搬到非洲。

    (D) 那裡沒有醫療。

    * cause〔kɔz〕n. 原因   carry〔'kærɪ〕v. 傳送；傳播

    insect〔'ɪnsɛkt〕n. 昆蟲

3. (**D**) 愛滋病如何在人與人之間傳染？

    (A) 透過捐血。   (B) 透過性交。

    (C) 透過受感染的針頭。   (D) <u>以上皆是。</u>

    * donation〔do'neʃən〕n. 捐獻

    blood donation 捐血   needle〔'nidl〕n. 針頭

4. (**A**) 一般認為馬拉威人口中，有多少比例已經受到愛滋病感染？

    (A) <u>百分之六十</u>   (B) 百分之十

    (C) 百分之百   (D) 百分之四十

    * percentage〔pə'sɛntɪdʒ〕n. 百分比；比率

5. (**C**) 為什麼人們稱愛滋病為「現代黑死病」？

    (A) 它是由受到感染的跳蚤所傳播。

    (B) 它起源於西方國家。   (C) <u>它影響了全世界的人。</u>

    (D) 已經發明新的藥物來打敗這個疾病。

    * flea〔fli〕n. 跳蚤   originate〔ə'rɪdʒə,net〕v. 起源

    invent〔ɪn'vɛnt〕v. 發明

    overcome〔,ovə'kʌm〕v. 克服；打敗

TEST 5

Read the following passage and choose the best answer for each question.

Protests against the use of animals in research have played a frightening part in the attempted murder of two British scientists with pre-planted car-bombs. The scientific research community will rightly pay full attention to <u>this development</u>, which has its purposes — to arouse public attention and to frighten people working with experiments on animals. Two days after the incident, the Defense Research Society took the practical step of offering a reward of 10,000 pounds to anyone who could identify those responsible for the crime. However, the result has not been encouraging and the police are faced with the problem of searching for a needle in a haystack.

That is why the research community in Britain must act more vigorously in its own defense. Organizations with the aim of safeguarding the interests of animals have been asked to declare their attitude toward the violent car-bombing incident. And it will not be enough for the chairpersons of these organizations to utter placatory statements on behalf of their members. These members are also called upon to give their word that they will take no part in any acts of violence against scientific researchers. Although people may lie and promises are sometimes hard to keep, at least these declarations show some willingness to continue the dialogue with the research community about the rights of animals in experiments. 【景美女中】

1. What does "this development" (Para. 1) most probably refer to?

    (A) The use of animals in research.

    (B) The act of violence against scientists.

    (C) The technique of planting bombs in cars.

    (D) The establishment of new animal rights organizations.

2. Which of the following is TRUE according to the passage?

    (A) The public sympathized with the murderer.

    (B) The police found and arrested the bombers.

    (C) The bombers escaped with the help of their organizations.

    (D) The attempted murder caused great anxiety among British scientists.

3. According to the passage, what have animal rights organizations been asked to do?

    (A) To stop experimenting with animals.

    (B) To promise no violence against scientists.

    (C) To continue the dialogue with the scientific community.

    (D) To help to find those responsible for the attempted murder.

4. What problem do the police currently face?

(A) The criminals have hidden themselves in a rural area.

(B) They have not been able to narrow their search for the criminals.

(C) They have not been able to identify the needle used in the attack.

(D) They must find more money in order to increase the reward.

5. What is implied in the last paragraph?

(A) Some animal rights organizations may make insincere statements.

(B) Animal rights activists have been unwilling to talk with researchers.

(C) Scientific researchers must promise to safeguard the interests of animals.

(D) Activists and the scientific community are in agreement on the rights of animals.

TEST 5 詳解

Protests against the use of animals in research have played a frightening part in the attempted murder of two British scientists with pre-planted car-bombs. The scientific research community will rightly pay full attention to <u>this development</u>, which has its purposes — to arouse public attention and to frighten people working with experiments on animals. Two days after the incident, the Defense Research Society took the practical step of offering a reward of 10,000 pounds to anyone who could identify those responsible for the crime. However, the result has not been encouraging and the police are faced with the problem of searching for a needle in a haystack.

反對做動物研究的抗議聲浪，在一件用預先安裝的汽車炸彈，謀殺兩位英國科學家未遂的案件中，扮演令人恐懼的角色。科學研究社群當然會充分留意這件案子的發展，案件的目的是要引起公衆注意，並讓那些做動物實驗的人們感到驚慌。事件發生後兩天，國防研究協會採取實際的行動，提供一萬英鎊作爲報酬，給任何能夠指認造成這起罪行的人。然而，結果並不樂觀，警方面臨著大海撈針的問題。

protest (ˈprotɛst) *n.* 抗議　　research (ˈrisɜtʃ) *n.* 研究
frightening (ˈfraɪtnɪŋ) *adj.* 令人恐懼的
play a(n) ~ part 扮演～的角色；起～的作用
attempted (əˈtɛmptɪd) *adj.* 未遂的；意圖的
murder (ˈmɝdə) *n.* 謀殺案　　***attempted murder*** 殺人未遂案
British (ˈbrɪtɪʃ) *adj.* 英國的　　plant (plænt) *v.* 安裝
pre-planted (ˈpriˈplæntɪd) *adj.* 預先安裝好的
bomb (bɑm) *n.* 炸彈　　car-bomb (ˈkɑrˈbɑm) *n.* 汽車炸彈
scientific (ˌsaɪənˈtɪfɪk) *adj.* 科學的
community (kəˈmjunətɪ) *n.* 社群
rightly (ˈraɪtlɪ) *adv.* 確實地；當然　　full (ful) *adj.* 充分的
attention (əˈtɛnʃən) *n.* 注意力　　***pay attention to*** 留意；注意

development〔dɪ'vɛləpmənt〕*n.* 發展　　purpose〔'pɝpəs〕*n.* 目的
arouse〔ə'rauz〕*v.* 喚醒；激起　　frighten〔'fraɪtn̩〕*v.* 使驚嚇
experiment〔ɪk'spɛrəmənt〕*n.* 實驗　　incident〔'ɪnsədənt〕*n.* 事件
defense〔dɪ'fɛns〕*n.* 防衛　　society〔sə'saɪətɪ〕*n.* 協會；團體
the Defense Research Society 國防研究協會
practical〔'præktɪkl̩〕*adj.* 實際的　　step〔stɛp〕*n.* 步驟；措施
offer〔'ɔfɚ〕*v.* 提供　　reward〔rɪ'wɔrd〕*n.* 獎賞；報酬
identify〔aɪ'dɛntə,faɪ〕*v.* 指認
be responsible for 該為⋯負責的；造成⋯
crime〔kraɪm〕*n.* 犯罪；罪行
encouraging〔ɪn'kɝdʒɪŋ〕*adj.* 令人鼓舞的；激勵的
be faced with 面臨；面對　　needle〔'nidl̩〕*n.* 針
haystack〔'he,stæk〕*n.* 乾草堆
search/look for a needle in a haystack 大海撈針

That is why the research community in Britain must act more
vigorously in its own defense.　Organizations with the aim of
safeguarding the interests of animals have been asked to declare
their attitude toward the violent car-bombing incident.　And it will
not be enough for the chairpersons of these organizations to utter
placatory statements on behalf of their members.　These members
are also called upon to give their word that they will take no part in
any acts of violence against scientific researchers.　Although people
may lie and promises are sometimes hard to keep, at least these
declarations show some willingness to continue the dialogue with
the research community about the rights of animals in experiments.

　　這就是為什麼英國的研究社群，必須採取更有力的行動來保護自己。以
保護動物權利為目標的組織，被要求對這起汽車炸彈暴力事件表態。這些
組織的主席們，只是代表成員做出安撫懷柔的陳述還不夠。這些組織的成
員，也被要求承諾，他們不會參與任何反對科學研究者的暴力行動。雖然
人們可能會說謊，而且諾言有時候很難被遵守，但至少這些宣言，關於實
驗的動物之權利，展現了一些他們的意願，要持續與研究社群對話。

Britain〔'brɪtn̩〕*n.* 英國　　act〔ækt〕*v.* 採取行動
vigorously〔'vɪgərəslɪ〕*adv.* 有力地；猛烈地
organization〔͵ɔrgənə'zeʃən〕*n.* 組織　　aim〔em〕*n.* 目的
safeguard〔'sef͵gard〕*v.* 保護　　interest〔'ɪntərɪst〕*n.* 利益
declare〔dɪ'klɛr〕*v.* 宣布；聲明　　attitude〔'ætə͵tjud〕*n.* 態度
violent〔'vaɪələnt〕*adj.* 暴力的　　chairperson〔'tʃɛr͵pɝsn̩〕*n.* 主席
utter〔'ʌtɚ〕*v.* 說出　　placatory〔'plekə͵torɪ〕*adj.* 懷柔的；安撫的
statement〔'stetmənt〕*n.* 陳述　　behalf〔bɪ'hæf〕*n.* 代表
on behalf of 代表　　***call upon*** 要求
give *one's* ***word*** 承諾；答應　　***take part in*** 參與
violence〔'vaɪələns〕*n.* 暴力　　lie〔laɪ〕*v.* 說謊
promise〔'pramɪs〕*n.* 諾言　　***keep a promise*** 遵守諾言
at least 至少　　declaration〔͵dɛklə'reʃən〕*n.* 宣言
willingness〔'wɪlɪŋnɪs〕*n.* 意願　　dialogue〔'daɪə͵lɔg〕*n.* 對話
right〔raɪt〕*n.* 權利

1. (**B**) 第一段的 "this development" 最可能指什麼？

   (A) 用動物做研究。　　(B) <u>對科學家的暴力行動。</u>

   (C) 把炸彈安裝到車子裡的技術。

   (D) 新動物權利組織的建立。

   * ***refer to*** 指；表示　　technique〔tɛk'nik〕*n.* 技術
   　　establishment〔ə'stæblɪʃmənt〕*n.* 設立

2. (**D**) 根據本文，下列何者為真？

   (A) 公眾同情兇手。　　(B) 警察找到並逮捕炸彈客。

   (C) 在組織的協助下，炸彈客逃走了。

   (D) <u>謀殺未遂案件，引起英國科學界廣大不安。</u>

   * sympathize〔'sɪmpə͵θaɪz〕*v.* 同情 < *with* >
   　　murderer〔'mɝdərɚ〕*n.* 兇手
   　　arrest〔ə'rɛst〕*v.* 逮捕　　bomber〔'bamɚ〕*n.* 炸彈客
   　　escape〔ə'skep〕*v.* 逃走
   　　anxiety〔æŋ'zaɪətɪ〕*n.* 焦慮；不安

3. (**B**) 根據本文，動物人權組織被要求做什麼？

(A) 停止做動物實驗。

(B) <u>保證不會對科學家採取暴力行動。</u>

(C) 持續跟科學界對話。

(D) 協助找到應該對這起謀殺未遂案件負責的人。

4. (**B**) 目前警方面臨什麼問題？

(A) 犯人藏身在鄉間。

(B) <u>警方無法縮小搜尋犯罪者的範圍。</u>

(C) 警方無法指認在攻擊事件中所使用的針頭。

(D) 警方爲了提高報酬，必須募集更多資金。

* currently〔ˈkɜəntlɪ〕*adv.* 目前；現在
criminal〔ˈkrɪmənḷ〕*n.* 犯罪者
rural〔ˈrʊrəl〕*adj.* 鄉村的
narrow〔ˈnæro〕*v.* 縮小範圍　　***in order to V.*** 爲了~

5. (**A**) 最後一段暗示什麼？

(A) <u>有些動物人權組織會做出不誠懇的陳述。</u>

(B) 動物權利激進份子一直都不願意與研究者對話。

(C) 科學研究者必須要承諾保護動物的利益。

(D) 激進份子跟科學社群對動物的權利達成共識。

* insincere〔ˌɪnsɪnˈsɪr〕*adj.* 不誠實的；虛僞的
activist〔ˈæktəvɪst〕*n.* 激進份子；行動主義者
agreement〔əˈgrimənt〕*n.* 協議；一致的意見

TEST 6

Read the following passage and choose the best answer for each question.

The disaster that would give Johnstown, Pennsylvania, a place in history began when it started to rain on the evening of May 30, 1889. All through the night and continuing all the next day the rain poured down, swelling creeks and rivers and filling the reservoir behind the South Fork Dam to overflowing.

At three o'clock in the afternoon, the Reverend Brown noticed the first break on the side of the old earthen dam and cried, "God have mercy on the people below!" The break quickly widened, and the swollen lake of water in the reservoir behind the dam hurled itself into the valley below. The collapse of the dam was so sudden that the water surged downhill in a wall 30-40 feet high, crushing and carrying along trees, boulders, buildings, railroad cars — everything in its path. When the flood hit a stone bridge 15 miles downstream in Johnstown, the mass of wreckage jammed into a pile about 700 feet high, creating a dangerous new dam that caused the water racing behind it to rise and spread <u>debris</u> over 30 acres of land. Mercifully, most of the local residents went to their deaths quickly. They never had the slightest chance to escape a watery fate.

More than 2,000 people were killed in the Johnstown flood and thus it became the worst flood disaster in North American history — a record no one wants to see surpassed. 【新店高中】

1. The passage is primarily about
   (A) a Memorial Day celebration.
   (B) dam safety measures.
   (C) unusually heavy rainfall.
   (D) a terrible flood.

2. The Johnstown flood is famous because of
   (A) the number of lives that were lost.
   (B) the size of the dam.
   (C) the date on which it happened.
   (D) the speed at which the flood moved.

3. What is the most likely reason that no flood has taken so many lives since 1889?
   (A) People no longer live near dams.
   (B) There are fewer heavy rainfalls.
   (C) Dams are being built more carefully.
   (D) Towns are not built to survive floods.

4. The writer quotes the Reverend Brown in order to
   (A) supply all the facts.
   (B) add emotional impact.
   (C) reveal his own bias.
   (D) support his argument.

5. <u>Debris</u> is
   (A) chaos.   (B) disease.
   (C) terror.   (D) wreckage.

TEST 6 詳解

The disaster that would give Johnstown, Pennsylvania, a place in history began when it started to rain on the evening of May 30, 1889. All through the night and continuing all the next day the rain poured down, swelling creeks and rivers and filling the reservoir behind the South Fork Dam to overflowing.

讓賓州的約翰斯頓城在歷史上留名的那場災禍，開始於 1889 年五月三十日，傍晚開始下雨。五月三十日整夜，以及隔天一整天，大雨持續傾盆而下，使得溪水跟河水高漲，也使位於南叉水壩後方的蓄水池滿溢而氾濫。

disaster〔dɪz'æstə〕*n.* 災難

Johnstown〔'dʒɑnz,taun〕*n.* 約翰斯頓城【美國賓州的城市，位於山谷底部，每年都有輕微水患，但以 1889 年的約翰斯頓水災災情最慘重】

Pennsylvania〔,pɛnsl'venɪə〕*n.* 賓夕凡尼亞州【位於美國東部，簡稱賓州】

a place in history 在歷史上有地位

pour〔por〕*v.* 倒；灌；雨傾盆而下 < *down* >

swell〔swɛl〕*v.* 使（河水）漲高　　creek〔krik〕*n.* 溪流；小溪

fill〔fɪl〕*v.* 使充滿　　reservoir〔'rɛzə,vɔr〕*n.* 蓄水池；水庫

fork〔fɔrk〕*n.* 叉狀物；叉子　　dam〔dæm〕*n.* 水壩

South Fork Dam 南叉水壩【位於賓州約翰斯頓城上游的水壩，1852 年完工。1889 年五月底，約翰斯頓暴雨不止，水庫蓄水池水位高漲，洪水溢出沖垮水壩，造成約兩千多人死亡，是美國史上最嚴重的水患】

overflow〔,ovə'flo〕*v.* 溢流；氾濫

At three o'clock in the afternoon, the Reverend Brown noticed the first break on the side of the old earthen dam and cried, "God have mercy on the people below!" The break quickly widened, and the swollen lake of water in the reservoir behind the dam hurled itself into the valley below. The collapse of the dam was so sudden that the water surged downhill in a wall 30-40 feet high, crushing and carrying along trees, boulders, buildings, railroad cars — everything in its path. When the flood hit a stone bridge 15 miles downstream in Johnstown, the mass of wreckage jammed into a pile about 700 feet high, creating a dangerous new dam that caused the water racing behind it to rise and spread <u>debris</u> over 30 acres of land. Mercifully, most of the local residents went to their deaths quickly. They never had the slightest chance to escape a watery fate.

當天下午三點，布朗牧師注意到土製水壩邊上的第一道裂縫，他大喊：「主啊，請憐憫地上的人們吧！」裂縫很快地變寬，水壩後方蓄水池裡暴漲的湖水猛烈撲向下方的山谷。水壩倒塌地太突然，大水以三、四十呎高的水牆，向下坡洶湧奔騰，壓垮並沖走了樹木、巨礫、建築物、鐵路車輛等等 —— 它所經之路上的所有物品。當洪水撞擊約翰斯頓下游約十五哩的一座石橋時，大塊的殘骸阻塞堆到約七百呎高，造成一座危險的新水壩，使得後方奔騰的水流上漲，瓦礫碎片散布在約三十英畝的土地上。幸虧大部分當地居民在瞬間死去。他們完全沒有一丁點的機會，逃脫溺死的命運。

reverend (ˈrɛvrənd) *adj.* 牧師的　　***the Reverend*** 牧師【敬稱】
notice (ˈnotɪs) *v.* 注意；發覺　　break (brek) *n.* 裂縫
earthen (ˈɝθən) *adj.* 土製的　　cry (kraɪ) *v.* 叫喊；大叫
mercy (ˈmɝsɪ) *n.* 慈悲　　***have mercy on*** 對⋯發慈悲；垂憐⋯
below (bəˈlo) *adv.* 在下方；在下游　　widen (ˈwaɪdən) *v.* 變寬
swollen (ˈswolən) *adj.* 漲大的　　hurl (hɝl) *v.* 猛撲；猛撞
valley (ˈvælɪ) *n.* 山谷　　collapse (kəˈlæps) *n.* 倒塌；坍塌
sudden (ˈsʌdṇ) *adj.* 突然的　　surge (sɝdʒ) *v.* 洶湧而至
downhill (ˈdaʊnˌhɪl) *adv.* 向下坡　　feet (fit) *n. pl.* 呎（單數 foot）
crush (krʌʃ) *v.* 壓碎；壓垮　　boulder (ˈboldɚ) *n.* 沖刷後的巨礫

building〔'bɪldɪŋ〕*n.* 建築物　　railroad〔'rel,rod〕*adj.* 鐵路的

path〔pæθ〕*n.* 路徑　　flood〔flʌd〕*n.* 洪水

downstream〔'daʊn,strim〕*adv.* 在下游　　mass〔mæs〕*n.* 大塊

wreckage〔'rɛkɪdʒ〕*n.* 碎片；殘骸　　jam〔dʒæm〕*v.* 堵塞

pile〔paɪl〕*n.* 堆；堆積物　　cause〔kɔz〕*v.* 導致；造成

race〔res〕*v.* 快跑；競速　　spread〔sprɛd〕*v.* 散布

debris〔də'bri〕*n.* 瓦礫；岩石碎片　　acre〔'ekə〕*n.* 英畝

mercifully〔'mɜsɪfəlɪ〕*adv.* 仁慈地；幸虧

local〔'lokḷ〕*adj.* 當地的　　resident〔'rɛzədənt〕*n.* 居民

slight〔slaɪt〕*adj.* 一點也（沒有）；輕微的

escape〔ə'skep〕*v.* 逃脫　　watery〔'wɔtərɪ〕*adj.* 水中的；溺死的

fate〔fet〕*n.* 命運；死亡

More than 2,000 people were killed in the Johnstown flood
and thus it became the worst flood disaster in North American
history — a record no one wants to see surpassed.

　　超過兩千人在約翰斯頓大洪水中死亡，因此這場災難成為北美史上最
嚴重的水患——沒有人希望看到這項紀錄被超越。

Johnstown flood 約翰斯頓大洪水　　***North American*** 北美的
record〔'rɛkəd〕*n.* 紀錄　　surpass〔sə'pæs〕*v.* 超越；凌駕

1.(**D**) 本文主要是有關於 ＿＿＿＿＿＿ 。

　　(A) 美國陣亡將士紀念日儀式　　(B) 水壩安全措施

　　(C) 不尋常地大量降雨　　(D) <u>一場可怕的洪水</u>

　　* primarily〔'praɪ,mɛrəlɪ〕*adv.* 主要地
　　　memorial〔mə'morɪəl〕*adj.* 紀念的
　　　the Memorial Day （美國）陣亡將士紀念日【五月最後一個星期一】
　　　celebration〔,sɛlə'breʃən〕*n.* 儀式；慶祝會
　　　measure〔'mɛʒə〕*n.* 措施
　　　unusually〔ʌn'judʒʊəlɪ〕*adv.* 異常地
　　　rainfall〔'ren,fɔl〕*n.* 降雨量　　terrible〔'tɛrəbḷ〕*adj.* 可怕的

2. (**A**) 約翰斯頓大洪水之所以有名是因為 _____。

    (A) <u>水災中的死亡人數</u>   (B) 水壩的尺寸

    (C) 水災發生的日期   (D) 洪水移動的速度

3. (**C**) 何者最有可能是從 1889 年以後，洪水沒有奪走這麼多人命的

    原因？

    (A) 人們不再居住在水壩附近。

    (B) 大量降雨比較少了。

    (C) <u>水壩被更謹慎地建造。</u>

    (D) 為了從洪水中生還，就不建立城鎮了。

    * *no longer* 不再   survive (sə'vaɪv) v. 從～中生還

4. (**B**) 作者引用布朗牧師的話是為了 _____。

    (A) 補充所有事實   (B) <u>加進情感的影響力</u>

    (C) 顯示自己的偏見   (D) 支持自己的論點

    * quote (kwot) v. 引用（人、實例、話語）

    supply (sə'plaɪ) v. 補充

    emotional (ɪ'moʃənḷ) adj. 情感的

    impact ('ɪmpækt) n. 影響   reveal (rɪ'vil) n. 透露；顯示

    bias ('baɪəs) n. 偏見   support (sə'port) v. 支持

    argument ('ɑrgjəmənt) n. 論點；主張

5. (**D**) "debris" 是 _____。

    (A) 混亂   (B) 疾病

    (C) 恐怖   (D) <u>殘骸</u>

    * chaos ('keɑs) n. 混亂   terror ('tɛrə) n. 恐怖

TEST 7

Read the following passage, and choose the best answer for each question.

For most of the 20th century, happiness was largely seen as a denial or delusion. Psychologists were busy healing sick minds, not bettering healthy ones. Today, however, a growing body of psychologist is taking the mystery out of happiness. They focus on humanity's strengths, rather than its weaknesses, and seek to help people move toward happiness and fulfillment. Contrary to the common belief that good income, intelligence or fame or sunny weather may bring happiness, psychologists now emphasize that family ties, friendships, strong marriages or spirituality will predict happiness.

Although some studies suggest that about half of one's potential for happiness is inherited, there are still some effective ways to increase our happiness. For example, setting and pursuing the right goals will make people happier. Besides, cultivating positive emotions such as gratitude and hope also brings happiness. Some researchers found that people who wrote down five things for which they were grateful in daily journals were more joyful, less stressed, and more likely to help others.

Finally, the ability to concentrate is also connected to the feeling of happiness. When doing anything that is challenging and demands full attention, we are likely to feel happy and contented. That is why athletes, artists, and scientists often look cheerful and contented. Will people work to learn happiness? Positive psychologists think that **if they can tease out the best in people, happiness will follow.** To psychologist Martin Seligman, happiness is "the emotion that arises when we do something that stems from our strengths and virtues." And those, anyone can cultivate. 【松山高中】

1. What is the best title for this passage?
   (A) Some Misconceptions about Happiness
   (B) How to Bring Real Joy to Your Life
   (C) How to Bring Happiness to Others
   (D) Some Stories About Happy People

2. According to psychologists nowadays, what are the main factors of happiness?
   (A) fame and good weather
   (B) intelligence and income
   (C) friendships and spirituality
   (D) educational background and career

3. According to the passage, one's potential for happiness _____.

   (A) is completely inherited

   (B) is partly inherited, but we can still work to learn happiness

   (C) has nothing to do with one's family background

   (D) is not an important issue

4. According to the passage, which of the following is not one of the ways to increase happiness?

   (A) cultivating positive emotions

   (B) developing the ability to concentrate

   (C) setting some proper goals for your life

   (D) having a good income

5. Which of the following sentences is closer in meaning to the sentence "if they can tease out the best in people, happiness will follow"?

   (A) It is difficult to find out the true meaning of life.

   (B) We may make people happy by teasing them and telling jokes.

   (C) If people can be inspired to show the best part of themselves, they will feel happy.

   (D) We should not play up the importance of happiness.

TEST 7 詳解

For most of the 20th century, happiness was largely seen as a denial or delusion. Psychologists were busy healing sick minds, not bettering healthy ones. Today, however, a growing body of psychologist is taking the mystery out of happiness. They focus on humanity's strengths, rather than its weaknesses, and seek to help people move toward happiness and fulfillment. Contrary to the common belief that good income, intelligence or fame or sunny weather may bring happiness, psychologists now emphasize that family ties, friendships, strong marriages or spirituality will predict happiness.

二十世紀的大部分時間，快樂多半都被否定或被視爲幻覺。心理學家們忙著治療生病的心靈，而不是改善健康的心靈。然而今日，有越來越多心理學家，正解開快樂的迷團。他們專注於人性的優點，而非缺點，並試著幫助人們走向幸福跟滿足。和人們普遍的想法相反的是，認爲高收入、聰明才智、聲望、或是晴朗的天氣，能帶來快樂，心理學家現在強調，家庭聯繫、友誼、穩固的婚姻或心智，能預言快樂的到來。

happiness (ˈhæpɪnɪs) *n.* 幸福；快樂　　largely (ˈlɑrdʒlɪ) *adv.* 大多
be seen as 被視爲　　denial (dɪˈnaɪəl) *n.* 否定；拒絕接受
delusion (dɪˈluʒən) *n.* 幻覺；妄想
psychologist (saɪˈkɑlədʒɪst) *n.* 心理學家　　heal (hil) *v.* 治療
better (ˈbɛtɚ) *v.* 改善　　growing (ˈgroɪŋ) *adj.* 增大的；發展中的
body (ˈbɑdɪ) *n.* 一群；大部分　　*a growing body of* 越來越多的
mystery (ˈmɪstərɪ) *n.* 謎　　focus (ˈfokəs) *v.* 聚焦；集中注意力
focus on 專注於　　humanity (hjuˈmænətɪ) *n.* 人性
strength (strɛŋθ) *n.* 優點　　*rather than* 而不是
weakness (ˈwiknɪs) *n.* 缺點　　seek (sik) *v.* 嘗試
fulfillment (fulˈfɪlmənt) *n.* 實現；完成；滿足
contrary (ˈkɑntrɛrɪ) *adj.* 相反的　　*contrary to* 與～相反

income〔'ɪn,kʌm〕*n.* 收入
intelligence〔ɪn'tɛlədʒəns〕*n.* 智力；知識　　fame〔fem〕*n.* 名聲
emphasize〔'ɛmfə,saɪz〕*v.* 強調　　tie〔taɪ〕*n.* 關係
family tie 家族關係　　marriage〔'mærɪdʒ〕*n.* 婚姻
spirituality〔,spɪrɪtʃʊ'ælətɪ〕*n.* 心靈；靈性；精神
predict〔prɪ'dɪkt〕*v.* 預告

Although some studies suggest that about half of one's
potential for happiness is inherited, there are still some effective
ways to increase our happiness.　For example, setting and pursuing
the right goals will make people happier.　Besides, cultivating
positive emotions such as gratitude and hope also brings
happiness.　Some researchers found that people who wrote down
five things for which they were grateful in daily journals were
more joyful, less stressed, and more likely to help others.

儘管有些研究指出，人類快樂的潛能，有一半是來自遺傳，但還是
有些有效的方法，能增加快樂。例如，設定並追求正確的目標，能讓人們
更快樂。除此之外，培養正面的情緒，例如感激與期待，也能帶來快樂。
有些研究者發現，每天在日記中，寫下五件值得感激的事情的人會比較快
樂，比較不會覺得有壓力，而且更可能會幫助他人。

suggest〔səg'dʒɛst〕*v.* 暗示；指出　　potential〔pə'tɛnʃəl〕*n.* 潛力
inherit〔ɪn'hɛrɪt〕*v.* 遺傳　　effective〔ɪ'fɛktɪv〕*adj.* 有效的
increase〔ɪn'kris〕*v.* 增加　　set〔sɛt〕*v.* 設定
pursue〔pə'su〕*v.* 追求　　goal〔gol〕*n.* 目標
cultivate〔'kʌltə,vet〕*v.* 培養　　positive〔'pazətɪv〕*adj.* 樂觀的
emotion〔ɪ'moʃən〕*n.* 情感　　gratitude〔'grætə,tjud〕*n.* 感激
grateful〔'gretfəl〕*adj.* 感激的　　daily〔'delɪ〕*adj.* 每日的
journal〔'dʒɝnl〕*n.* 日記　　joyful〔'dʒɔɪfəl〕*adj.* 高興的
stressed〔strɛst〕*adj.* 感到有壓力的；緊張的
be likely to V. 可能～

Finally, the ability to concentrate is also connected to the feeling of happiness. When doing anything that is challenging and demands full attention, we are likely to feel happy and contented. That is why athletes, artists, and scientists often look cheerful and contented. Will people work to learn happiness? Positive psychologists think that **if they can tease out the best in people, happiness will follow**. To psychologist Martin Seligman, happiness is "the emotion that arises when we do something that stems from our strengths and virtues." And those, anyone can cultivate.

最後，專注力也跟快樂的感覺有關。做有挑戰性，並需要全神貫注的事情時，我們可能會感到快樂和滿足。這就是為什麼運動員、藝術家跟科學家，常常看起來快樂又滿足。人們能努力學習快樂嗎？樂觀的心理學家認為，如果能夠釋放人們最好的那一面，那麼快樂也將隨之到來。對心理學家馬丁・塞利格曼來說，快樂是「當我們出於自己的能力跟美德，做某些事情的時候，所產生的情緒。」而這是任何人都可以培養的。

ability (ə'bɪlətɪ) *n.* 能力　　concentrate ('kɑnsn̩‚tret) *v.* 集中；專心
connect (kə'nɛkt) *v.* 連結　　***be connected to*** 跟…有關
challenging ('tʃælɪndʒɪŋ) *adj.* 有挑戰性的
demand (dɪ'mænd) *v.* 要求　　attention (ə'tɛnʃən) *n.* 注意力
contented (kən'tɛntɪd) *adj.* 滿足的　　athlete ('æθlit) *n.* 運動員
cheerful ('tʃɪrfəl) *adj.* 快樂的　　tease (tiz) *v.* 取笑；揶揄
tease out 釋放；鬆開　　***the best in people*** 人們最好的一面
arise (ə'raɪz) *v.* 發生；產生　　stem (stɛm) *v.* 起源於 *< from >*
virtue ('vɝtʃʊ) *n.* 美德

1. (**B**) 本篇文章的最佳標題是什麼？
  (A) 一些關於快樂的錯誤觀念
  (B) <u>如何將眞正的快樂帶進你的生活</u>
  (C) 如何將快樂帶給他人
  (D) 關於快樂的人的一些故事
  * misconception (‚mɪskən'sɛpʃən) *n.* 錯誤觀念；誤解

2. (**C**) 根據現代心理學家的說法，快樂的主要因素是什麼？

    (A) 名聲和好天氣　　　　　(B) 聰明才智和收入

    (C) <u>友誼和靈性</u>　　　　　　(D) 教育背景和職業

    * main〔men〕*adj.* 主要的　　factor〔'fæktɚ〕*n.* 因素
        background〔'bæk,graʊnd〕*n.* 背景
        career〔kə'rɪr〕*n.* 職業

3. (**B**) 依照本文，一個人快樂的潛能 _____ 。

    (A) 完全是遺傳而來

    (B) <u>部分是遺傳，但我們仍可以努力學會快樂</u>

    (C) 跟個人家庭背景無關

    (D) 並不是個重要的議題

    * completely〔kəm'plitlɪ〕*adv.* 完全地
      have nothing to do with 和…無關
      issue〔'ɪʃʊ〕*n.* 問題；議題

4. (**D**) 根據本文，下列何者不是增進快樂的方法？

    (A) 培養正面情緒　　　　　(B) 培養專注的能力

    (C) 設定一些正確的生活目標 (D) <u>有很好的收入</u>

    * develop〔dɪ'vɛləp〕*v.* 發展；培養
      proper〔'prɑpɚ〕*adj.* 適當的；正確的

5. (**C**) 下列何者最接近 "if they can tease out the best in people, happiness will follow" 這句話的意思？

    (A) 要找到人生真正的意義很難。

    (B) 我們可以藉由挪揄別人和說笑話，來讓其他人開心。

    (C) <u>如果人們能夠被啟發而展現出自己最好的一面，他們就會覺得快樂。</u>

    (D) 我們不應該大肆渲染快樂的重要性。

    * joke〔dʒok〕*n.* 笑話　　inspire〔ɪn'spaɪr〕*v.* 鼓舞；激勵
      play up 大肆渲染；強調

TEST 8

Read the following passage and choose the best answer for each question.

A unique and memorable slogan that summarizes and highlights your firm's special capabilities can strengthen the impact of your message and increase your firm's name recognition. An effective slogan can also act as a powerful closer or summary statement for your advertisement.

Moreover, a distinctive and attractive logo can enhance your firm's image and communicate something about the personality of your firm and the nature of your corporate environment. Some firms like to portray a traditional, highly formal image; others like to convey the idea that their firm's culture is rather informal and somewhat more casual.

Like your slogan and logo, the type and layout that is selected for your advertisement should reflect your firm's personality and the image you want to project to existing clients, potential clients, your employees, and the general public. In most instances, you will want to utilize a simple layout that is direct and to the point. A busy and chaotic layout can make people feel that your firm is poorly organized and inefficient. 【大同高中】

1. Which of the following words can replace "memorable" as used to describe a slogan?

   (A) special   (B) modest

   (C) creative   (D) catchy

2. Which of the following effects of a logo is not mentioned in the article?

   (A) improving a company's reputation

   (B) increasing a company's income

   (C) communicating a company's nature

   (D) communicating a company's culture

3. What did the author mean by "chaotic"?

   (A) neat   (B) ordered

   (C) equivalent   (D) disorganized

4. What does the passage mainly discuss?

   (A) Different types of corporate culture.

   (B) How to create a good corporate environment.

   (C) How to effectively represent your firm.

   (D) Various types of logos.

5. According to the passage, why are simple layouts preferable?

   (A) They appeal to more customers.

   (B) They communicate orderliness and competence.

   (C) They are less expensive to produce.

   (D) They allow more room for a good slogan.

TEST 8 詳解

A unique and memorable slogan that summarizes and highlights your firm's special capabilities can strengthen the impact of your message and increase your firm's name recognition. An effective slogan can also act as a powerful closer or summary statement for your advertisement.

一句獨特且令人難忘，概略陳述並強調你公司特性的標語，能強化訊息的影響力，並增加你公司的知名度。有效的標語，也可以作爲你的廣告中有說服力的結尾，或是摘要陳述。

unique〔juˋnik〕*adj.* 獨特的　　memorable〔ˋmɛmərəb!〕*adj.* 難忘的
slogan〔ˋslogən〕*n.* 標語　　summarize〔ˋsʌmə͵raɪz〕*v.* 概括地說
highlight〔ˋhaɪ͵laɪt〕*v.* 強調　　firm〔fɝm〕*n.* 公司
capability〔͵kepəˋbɪlətɪ〕*n.* 才能；特性
strengthen〔ˋstrɛŋθən〕*v.* 加強
impact〔ˋɪmpækt〕*n.* 影響力　　increase〔ɪnˋkris〕*v.* 增加
recognition〔͵rɛkəgˋnɪʃən〕*n.* (對事物的) 認識；認出
name recognition 姓名識別；知名度
effective〔ɪˋfɛktɪv〕*adj.* 有效的　　***act as*** 作爲
powerful〔ˋpauɚfəl〕*adj.* 強有力的；(論點) 有說服力的
closer〔ˋklozɚ〕*n.* 結束者　　summary〔ˋsʌmərɪ〕*adj.* 摘要的
statement〔ˋstetmənt〕*n.* 陳述
advertisement〔͵ædvɚˋtaɪzmənt〕*n.* 廣告

Moreover, a distinctive and attractive logo can enhance your firm's image and communicate something about the personality of your firm and the nature of your corporate environment. Some firms like to portray a traditional, highly formal image; others like to convey the idea that their firm's culture is rather informal and somewhat more casual.

此外，獨特、有吸引力的商標，能增進公司的形象，並傳達你公司的特性，以及公司環境的特質。有些公司喜歡描述自己傳統、非常正式的形象；有些公司則喜歡傳達自己的公司文化，是稍微非正式，而有點隨性這樣的理念。

distinctive〔dɪ'stɪŋktɪv〕*adj.* 獨特的
attractive〔ə'træktɪv〕*adj.* 有吸引力的
logo〔'lɔgo〕*n.* 商標　　enhance〔ɪn'hæns〕*v.* 增進
image〔'ɪmɪdʒ〕*n.* 形象
communicate〔kə'mjunəˌket〕*v.* 傳達
personality〔ˌpɝsṇ'ælətɪ〕*n.* 個性；魅力
nature〔'netʃɚ〕*n.* 特質　　corporate〔'kɔrpərɪt〕*adj.* 公司的
portray〔por'tre〕*v.* 描寫　　formal〔'fɔrml〕*adj.* 正式的
convey〔kən've〕*v.* 傳達　　rather〔'ræðɚ〕*adv.* 稍微；相當
informal〔ɪn'fɔrml〕*adj.* 非正式的
somewhat〔'sʌmˌhwɑt〕*adv.* 略微；有點
casual〔'kæʒʊəl〕*adj.* 隨性的；非正式的

Like your slogan and logo, the type and layout that is selected for your advertisement should reflect your firm's personality and the image you want to project to existing clients, potential clients, your employees, and the general public. In most instances, you will want to utilize a simple layout that is direct and to the point. A busy and chaotic layout can make people feel that your firm is poorly organized and inefficient.

就像你的標語跟商標，你所選的廣告樣式跟版面設計，也應該要能反映公司的特性，以及你希望傳達給現有客戶、潛在客戶、公司員工、以及一般大眾的形象。在大多數情況下，你會想採用簡單的版面，既直接又適切。繁複而且混亂的版面，會讓人們覺得，你的公司組織很差，而且沒有效率。

type〔taɪp〕*n.* 樣式　　layout〔'le,aʊt〕*n.* 版面設計

select〔sə'lɛkt〕*v.* 選擇　　reflect〔rɪ'flɛkt〕*v.* 反映；表達

project〔prə'dʒɛkt〕*v.* 投射；傳達（思想）

existing〔ɪg'zɪstɪŋ〕*adj.* 現存的　　client〔'klaɪənt〕*n.* 客戶

potential〔pə'tɛnʃəl〕*adj.* 潛在的

employee〔,ɛmplɔɪ'i〕*n.* 員工　　general〔'dʒɛnərəl〕*adj.* 一般的

the general public 一般大眾

instance〔'ɪnstəns〕*n.* 例子；實證　　utilize〔'jutḷ,aɪz〕*v.* 利用

direct〔də'rɛkt〕*adj.* 直接的　　***to the point*** 適切的；扼要的

busy〔'bɪzɪ〕*adj.* 過份複雜的　　chaotic〔ke'ɑtɪk〕*adj.* 混亂的

poorly〔'pʊrlɪ〕*adv.* 差勁地

organized〔'ɔrgən,aɪzd〕*adj.* 有組織的

inefficient〔,ɪnə'fɪʃənt〕*adj.* 沒有效率的

1.(**D**) 下列哪個字能夠取代 "memorable"，被用來描述標語？

    (A) 特別的　　　　　　(B) 謙虛的

    (C) 有創意的　　　　　(D) 引人注意的

    * replace〔rɪ'ples〕*v.* 取代

      describe〔dɪ'skraɪb〕*v.* 描述

      modest〔'mɑdɪst〕*adj.* 謙虛的

      creative〔krɪ'etɪv〕*adj.* 有創意的

      catchy〔'kætʃɪ〕*adj.* 引人注意的；動人的

2.(**B**) 下列哪一種商標的效果在文章中沒有提到？

    (A) 增進公司的聲望。　　(B) 增加公司的收入。

    (C) 傳達公司的特質。　　(D) 傳達公司的文化。

    * effect〔ɪ'fɛkt〕*n.* 效果　　mention〔'mɛnʃən〕*v.* 提到

      reputation〔,rɛpjə'teʃən〕*n.* 名聲

      income〔'ɪn,kʌm〕*n.* 收入

3. (**D**) 作者提到 "chaotic" 的意思是什麼？

    (A) 整潔的   (B) 井然有序的

    (C) 相等的   (D) <u>雜亂無章的</u>

   * neat〔nit〕*adj.* 整潔的；乾淨俐落的
     ordered〔'ɔrdəd〕*adj.* 整齊的；有秩序的
     equivalent〔ɪ'kwɪvələnt〕*adj.* 相等的
     disorganized〔dɪs'ɔrgəˌnaɪzd〕*adj.* 雜亂無章的

4. (**C**) 這篇文章主要在討論什麼？

    (A) 不同形式的公司文化。

    (B) 如何創造好的公司環境。

    (C) <u>如何有效地呈現你的公司。</u>

    (D) 許多不同種類的商標。

   * mainly〔'menlɪ〕*adv.* 主要地
     effectively〔ə'fɛktɪvlɪ〕*adv.* 有效地
     present〔prɪ'zɛnt〕*v.* 呈現   various〔'vɛrɪəs〕*adj.* 各種的

5. (**B**) 根據本文，為什麼簡單的版面比較好？

    (A) 簡單的版面能吸引更多顧客。

    (B) <u>簡單的版面能傳達紀律，跟公司的能力。</u>

    (C) 簡單的版面比較便宜。

    (D) 簡單的版面能留更多空間給好的標語。

   * preferable〔'prɛfrəbl̩〕*adj.* 較好的；更可取的
     appeal〔ə'pil〕*v.* 吸引 < *to* >
     orderliness〔'ɔrdəlɪnɪs〕*n.* 紀律；有秩序
     competence〔'kɑmpətəns〕*n.* 能力；資格
     allow〔ə'lau〕*v.* 允許   room〔rum〕*n.* 空間

TEST 9

Read the following passage and choose the best answer for each question.

Ramadan, the ninth month of the Islamic calendar, is the holiest month for Muslims. It is a special period in which over one billion Muslims all over the world practice compulsory **fasting**, one of their most widely used forms of worship.

Fasting may be difficult but it gives those who practice it many special benefits. The greatest advantage is learning self-control. During this whole month, Muslims do not eat from dawn to sunset. They can prepare food for themselves only before dawn and after sunset every day. Besides that, they cannot drink nor smoke. They believe that getting rid of the anxiety of looking for satisfaction in food can lift up one's spiritual nature and lets them get closer to their God, Allah.

Besides, it is a way of experiencing hunger and developing sympathy for the unlucky ones, and learning to be grateful and appreciate what they get from God. Therefore, during fasting, Muslims worship Allah by reading their holy book, the Koran. They also need to purify their mind and behavior by giving others a helping hand.

Although fasting is compulsory during Ramadan, the sick, travelers and women in certain conditions, for example, pregnancy, will be excused. But, because this is a holy period, they are still encouraged to participate if they can.

At the end of Ramadan, Muslims celebrate the end of fasting with the celebration of "Eid-ul-Fitr". Family, relatives and friends get together to pray in groups for prosperity and peace in the following years. 【延平高中】

1. What is the topic of this passage?
   (A) Muslims' holy month.
   (B) Muslims' God.
   (C) Muslims' calendar.
   (D) Muslims' holy book.

2. In this passage, fasting is _____.
   (A) a celebration in the Muslim family
   (B) a protest in which people refuse to eat
   (C) a common form of worship for Muslims all over the world
   (D) the days when Allah has a celebration with Muslims

3. During Ramadan, most Muslims are required to practice fasting _____.

   (A) all night long

   (B) from midnight to noon

   (C) during the night

   (D) from dawn to sunset

4. Which of the following statements about Muslims is NOT true?

   (A) Fasting enables them to be closer to their God, Allah.

   (B) When rid of the anxiety of wanting food, they gain spiritual growth.

   (C) Anyone who does not want to fast may be excused.

   (D) Helping those in need can purify their minds and behavior.

5. We can infer from this passage that Muslims practice fasting for _____.

   (A) religious reasons

   (B) political reasons

   (C) medical reasons

   (D) economic reasons

TEST 9 詳解

Ramadan, the ninth month of the Islamic calendar, is the holiest month for Muslims. It is a special period in which over one billion Muslims all over the world practice compulsory **fasting**, one of their most widely used forms of worship.

齋戒月是伊斯蘭曆法中第九個月，對回教徒而言是最神聖的月份。在這段特別期間內，全世界超過十億名回教徒會實行強制性禁食，這也是回教徒最廣泛使用的禮拜儀式之一。

> Ramadan〔͵ræmə'dɑn〕*n.*（回教的）齋戒月【回曆的九月，整個月從日出到日落都必須禁食】
> Islamic〔ɪs'læmɪk〕*adj.* 伊斯蘭教的；回教的
> calendar〔'kæləndɚ〕*n.* 曆法　　holy〔'holɪ〕*adj.* 神聖的
> Muslim〔'mʌzlɪm〕*n.* 回教徒　　billion〔'bɪljən〕*n.* 十億
> ***all over*** 遍及　　practice〔'præktɪs〕*v.* 實行；實踐
> compulsory〔kəm'pʌlsərɪ〕*adj.* 強制的
> fast〔fæst〕*v.* 禁食；齋戒　　worship〔'wɝʃəp〕*n.* 禮拜儀式

Fasting may be difficult but it gives those who practice it many special benefits. The greatest advantage is learning self-control. During this whole month, Muslims do not eat from dawn to sunset. They can prepare food for themselves only before dawn and after sunset every day. Besides that, they cannot drink nor smoke. They believe that getting rid of the anxiety of looking for satisfaction in food can lift up one's spiritual nature and lets them get closer to their God, Allah.

禁食也許很困難，但它帶給實踐者很多特殊好處。最大的好處就是學習自律。在整個齋戒月裡，回教徒們從日出到日落都不能吃東西。他們每天只能在日出前，或是日落後幫自己準備食物。除此之外，他們不能喝酒也不能抽煙。回教徒相信，擺脫從食物中找尋滿足的焦慮，能提升每個人的心靈本質，並且讓他們更接近他們的真神阿拉。

benefit〔'bɛnəfɪt〕*n.* 好處；利益

advantage〔əd'væntɪdʒ〕*n.* 好處；益處

self-control〔,sɛlfkən'trol〕*n.* 自律

whole〔hol〕*adj.* 整個的

dawn〔dɔn〕*n.* 黎明　　sunset〔'sʌn,sɛt〕*n.* 日落

get rid of 擺脫；免除

anxiety〔æŋ'zaɪətɪ〕*n.* 焦慮　***look for*** 尋找

satisfaction〔,sætɪs'fækʃən〕*n.* 滿足　***lift up*** 提升

spiritual〔'spɪrɪtʃʊəl〕*adj.* 精神的；心靈的

nature〔'netʃɚ〕*n.* 天性；特質

Allah〔'ælə,'ɑlə〕*n.* 阿拉【回教唯一真神】

Besides, it is a way of experiencing hunger and developing sympathy for the unlucky ones, and learning to be grateful and appreciate what they get from God. Therefore, during fasting, Muslims worship Allah by reading their holy book, the Koran. They also need to purify their mind and behavior by giving others a helping hand.

　　而且，禁食也是一種方法，能體驗飢餓，並且培養對不幸的人的同情心，學會感恩，並珍視從眞神那裡得來之物。所以在禁食期間，回教徒藉著讀他們的聖書──可蘭經，來敬拜阿拉眞主。回教徒也必須藉由幫助別人，來淨化心靈跟舉止。

experience〔ɪk'spɪrɪəns〕*v.* 體驗　　hunger〔'hʌŋgɚ〕*n.* 飢餓

develop〔dɪ'vɛləp〕*v.* 培養

sympathy〔'sɪmpəθɪ〕*n.* 同情心　　unlucky〔ʌn'lʌkɪ〕*adj.* 不幸的

grateful〔'gretfəl〕*adj.* 感激的　　appreciate〔ə'priʃɪ,et〕*v.* 珍視

worship〔'wɝʃəp〕*v.* 崇拜　　holy〔'holɪ〕*adj.* 神聖的

Koran〔ko'rɑn〕*n.* 可蘭經【回教的聖典】

purify〔'pjʊrə,faɪ〕*v.* 淨化　　mind〔maɪnd〕*n.* 心靈；精神

behavior〔bɪ'hevjɚ〕*n.* 行為舉止

give/lend sb. a helping hand 幫助某人

Although fasting is compulsory during Ramadan, the sick, travelers and women in certain conditions, for example, pregnancy, will be excused. But, because this is a holy period, they are still encouraged to participate if they can.

雖然在齋戒月中，禁食是強制的行為，但是生病的人、旅行者，跟處於某些情況下的女人，例如孕婦，可以被免除禁食。但因為這是一段神聖的日子，如果可以的話，這些人還是被鼓勵參與禁食。

> ***the sick*** 病人　　certain〔'sɜtn̩〕*adj.* 某些
> condition〔kən'dıʃən〕*n.* 情況；狀況
> pregnancy〔'prɛgnənsı〕*n.* 懷孕
> excuse〔ık'skjuz〕*v.* 免除（義務）；原諒
> encourage〔ın'kɜıdʒ〕*v.* 鼓勵　　participate〔par'tısə‚pet〕*v.* 參與

At the end of Ramadan, Muslims celebrate the end of fasting with the celebration of "Eid-ul-Fitr". Family, relatives and friends get together to pray in groups for prosperity and peace in the following years.

在齋戒月結束時，回教徒會用「開齋節」的慶典，來慶祝禁食結束。家人、親戚、朋友們團聚，集體祈禱接下來幾年的豐收跟平安。

> end〔ɛnd〕*n.* 結束　　celebrate〔'sɛlə‚bret〕*v.* 慶祝
> celebration〔‚sɛlə'breʃən〕*n.* 慶祝儀式；慶典
> ***Eid-ul-Fitr*** 開齋節【齋戒月的最後一天，回教徒們早上祈禱後就可以恢復進食，象徵齋戒月結束。然後出去團拜，和朋友親戚互相擁抱問候，是快樂和平的日子】
> relative〔'rɛlətıv〕*n.* 親戚　　pray〔pre〕*v.* 祈禱
> prosperity〔pras'pɛrətı〕*n.* 繁榮　　following〔'faloıŋ〕*adj.* 接下來的

1.（**A**）本文的主題是什麼？

　　(A) 回教的聖月。　　　　　(B) 回教的真神。
　　(C) 回教的曆法。　　　　　(D) 回教的聖經。

2. (**C**)　在本文中，"fasting" 是 ＿＿＿＿＿＿。

(A) 在回教家庭中的慶祝活動

(B) 人們拒絕進食的一種抗議活動

(C) 一種全世界回教徒之中常見的敬拜儀式

(D) 阿拉與回教徒舉辦慶典的日子

* protest〔ˋprotɛst〕*n.* 抗議

common〔ˋkɑmən〕*adj.* 常見的；普遍的

3. (**D**)　在齋戒月之中，大部分的回教徒必須 ＿＿＿＿＿＿ 實行禁食。

(A) 整個晚上　　　　　(B) 從午夜到正午

(C) 在夜間　　　　　　(D) 從日出到日落

* require〔rɪˋkwaɪr〕*v.* 要求　　***be required to V.* 必須…**

midnight〔ˋmɪd͵naɪt〕*n.* 午夜　　noon〔nun〕*n.* 正午

4. (**C**)　下列關於回教徒的敘述何者為非？

(A) 禁食讓回教徒更接近他們的真主阿拉。

(B) 當擺脫渴望食物的焦慮，他們就能獲得心靈成長。

(C) 無論誰不想參加禁食活動，都能被原諒。

(D) 幫助貧困的人，能夠淨化他們的心靈跟行為舉止。

* statement〔ˋstetmənt〕*n.* 敘述

enable〔ɪnˋeb!〕*v.* 使（人）能夠　　gain〔gen〕*v.* 獲得

growth〔groθ〕*n.* 成長　　***in need* 貧困的**

5. (**A**)　我們可以從文章中推論，回教徒奉行禁食是因為 ＿＿＿＿＿＿。

(A) 宗教因素　　　　　(B) 政治因素

(C) 醫療因素　　　　　(D) 經濟因素

* infer〔ɪnˋfɝ〕*v.* 推論　　religious〔rɪˋlɪdʒəs〕*adj.* 宗教的

political〔pəˋlɪtɪk!〕*adj.* 政治的

medical〔ˋmɛdɪk!〕*adj.* 醫療的；醫學的

economic〔͵ikəˋnɑmɪk〕*adj.* 經濟的

TEST 10

Read the following passage and choose the best answer for each question.

Born in Germany in 1879, Einstein received his early education in Munich. In 1900, he graduated as a teacher of mathematics and physics but had trouble finding a teaching position at a university. After teaching in private schools for a while, he took a job in a patent office in Bern, Switzerland. He worked there from 1902 to 1909, during which time he became a citizen of Switzerland.

1905 was a very big year for Einstein. It is known as Einstein's "miracle year." It was during this year that he developed the special theory of relativity and the quantum theory of light and gave us what is probably the most famous equation in physics: $E = mc^2$.

Einstein continued to make other big scientific discoveries for over twenty years. In 1932, he took a temporary position at Princeton University. The Nazis came to power in Germany soon after that and Einstein made his stay in the United States permanent. In 1940, he became an American citizen. He continued to work for world peace and scientific awareness until his death in 1955.

How did Einstein do all of this? What made him such a genius? Well, no one knows for sure, but a group of Canadian researchers who examined Einstein's brain after his death discovered that it was a little different from that of most people. The part of the brain that deals with mathematical thought was larger than normal in Einstein, and the connections between his frontal and temporal lobes were shorter than normal. However, this sheds light on only one aspect of Einstein. Many other things about the man remain a mystery. One thing that is certain, however, is that the importance of Albert Einstein and his ideas remain unmatched in modern science. 【延平高中】

1. Einstein was born in Germany, but he was also a citizen of _____.
   (A) Switzerland and England
   (B) Switzerland and the US
   (C) England and America
   (D) France and Holland

2. Which of the following events did NOT take place in Einstein's "miracle year"?
   (A) He developed the theory of relativity.
   (B) He developed the quantum theory of light.
   (C) He figured out the most famous equation in physics.
   (D) He was awarded the Nobel Prize for his achievement in physics.

3. A group of Canadian researchers examined Einstein's brain _____.

    (A) and found his brain was abnormally larger than any other person's

    (B) but found nothing special about it

    (C) and finally found out the cause of his death

    (D) and found the connections between his frontal and temporal lobes were shorter than normal

4. Why did Einstein stay in the United States permanently?

    (A) Because he got married there.

    (B) Because he had no money to go back to Germany.

    (C) Because the Nazis came to power in Germany.

    (D) It is not mentioned in the article.

5. How long did Einstein live in the United States?

    (A) Most of his life.

    (B) More than two decades.

    (C) Fifteen years.

    (D) Until 1940.

TEST 10 詳解

Born in Germany in 1879, Einstein received his early education in Munich. In 1900, he graduated as a teacher of mathematics and physics but had trouble finding a teaching position at a university. After teaching in private schools for a while, he took a job in a patent office in Bern, Switzerland. He worked there from 1902 to 1909, during which time he became a citizen of Switzerland.

1879 年愛因斯坦在德國出生，他在慕尼黑接受早期教育。1900 年時，他以數學跟物理學的教師資格畢業，但是卻很難在大學中找到教職。在私立學校教了幾年書之後，他找到一個在瑞士柏恩專利辦公室的工作。他從 1902 年到 1909 年都在此工作，這段時間內他也成爲瑞士公民。

Germany〔ˈdʒɝmənɪ〕n. 德國
Einstein〔ˈaɪnstaɪn〕n. 愛因斯坦【1879-1955，全名亞伯特・愛因斯坦
　　（Albert Einstein），生於德國的美國籍物理學家，相對論的提出者】
receive〔rɪˈsiv〕v. 接受（教育、訓練等）
Munich〔ˈmjunɪk〕n. 慕尼黑【德國地名】
graduate〔ˈgrædʒʊˌet〕v. 畢業　　mathematics〔ˌmæθəˈmætɪks〕n. 數學
physics〔ˈfɪzɪks〕n. 物理學　　have trouble + V-ing 做～有困難
position〔pəˈzɪʃən〕n. 職位　　university〔ˌjunəˈvɝsətɪ〕n. 大學
private〔ˈpraɪvɪt〕adj. 私人的　　private school 私立學校
for a while 一段時間；一會兒　　patent〔ˈpætn̩t〕n. 專利權
Bern〔bɝn〕n. 柏恩【瑞士首都】　　Switzerland〔ˈswɪtsələnd〕n. 瑞士
citizen〔ˈsɪtəzn̩〕n. 公民

1905 was a very big year for Einstein. It is known as Einstein's "miracle year." It was during this year that he developed the special theory of relativity and the quantum theory of light and gave us what is probably the most famous equation in physics: $E = mc^2$.

1905 年對愛因斯坦來說是非常重要的一年。這一年被稱爲愛因斯坦的「奇蹟之年」。在這一年當中，他發展出狹義相對論，跟光的量子理論，並帶給我們或許是物理學中最有名的等式：$E = mc^2$（能量轉換公式）。

be known as 被稱為　　miracle〔'mɪrəkl̩〕*n.* 奇蹟
develop〔dɪ'vɛləp〕*v.* 發展　　special〔'spɛʃəl〕*adj.* 獨特的
theory〔'θiərɪ〕*n.* 理論
relativity〔ˌrɛlə'tɪvətɪ〕*n.* 相對性；（大寫）相對論
the special theory of relativity 特殊相對論；狹義相對論
　　【將牛頓的時空觀念加以修正，相對於廣義相對論：General Theory
　　　of Relativity】
quantum〔'kwɑntəm〕*n.* 量子【物理學】
the quantum theory 量子理論
equation〔ɪ'kweʒən〕*n.* 等式；方程式　　$E = mc^2$ 質能轉換公式

Einstein continued to make other big scientific discoveries
for over twenty years. In 1932, he took a temporary position at
Princeton University. The Nazis came to power in Germany soon
after that and Einstein made his stay in the United States permanent.
In 1940, he became an American citizen. He continued to work for
world peace and scientific awareness until his death in 1955.

超過二十年的歲月中，愛因斯坦持續完成其他重要科學發現。1932
年，他在普林斯敦大學擔任短暫教職。在那之後不久，納粹在德國掌權，
愛因斯坦就長住美國。1940 年他成為美國公民。直到 1955 年他去世之前，
他一直都為了世界和平，以及科學認知而努力。

continue〔kən'tɪnju〕*v.* 繼續
temporary〔'tɛmpəˌrɛrɪ〕*adj.* 暫時的
Princeton University 普林斯敦大學【位於美國紐澤西州的私立大學】
Nazi〔'nɑtsɪ〕*n.* 納粹【全名：國家社會主義德意志工人黨。由希特勒
　　領導，在二次大戰時屠殺猶太人。愛因斯坦身為猶太人，當納粹執政時
　　他剛好在美國任教，他為了自保所以決定留在美國。Nazi 是德文
　　Nationalsozialist 的簡寫】
power〔'pauɚ〕*n.* 權力；勢力　　**come to power** 掌權；得勢
stay〔ste〕*n.* 停留　　permanent〔'pɜmənənt〕*adj.* 永久的
awareness〔ə'wɛrnɪs〕*n.* 認識；認知

How did Einstein do all of this? What made him such a genius? Well, no one knows for sure, but a group of Canadian researchers who examined Einstein's brain after his death discovered that it was a little different from that of most people. The part of the brain that deals with mathematical thought was larger than normal in Einstein, and the connections between his frontal and temporal lobes were shorter than normal. However, this sheds light on only one aspect of Einstein. Many other things about the man remain a mystery. One thing that is certain, however, is that the importance of Albert Einstein and his ideas remain unmatched in modern science.

愛因斯坦是怎麼做到這一切的呢？是什麼讓他成為這樣一位天才？沒有人確實知道，但一群加拿大研究人員，在愛因斯坦死後仔細檢查他的大腦，發現他的腦部跟一般人有一點不一樣。愛因斯坦腦部處理數學思維的部份，比正常的要大，而且連結前腦跟顳的腦葉的地方，比正常的短。然而，這項發現只說明了愛因斯坦的其中一面而已。關於這個人的很多其他事情都還是個謎。但有一件事是肯定的，亞伯特・愛因斯坦與他的思想的重要性，在現代科學中依然無人可匹敵。

genius〔'dʒinjəs〕*n.* 天才　　***for sure*** 確實；確定
Canadian〔kə'nedɪən〕*adj.* 加拿大（人）的
examine〔ɪg'zæmɪn〕*v.* 檢查　　brain〔bren〕*n.* 大腦
deal with 處理；應付
mathematical〔ˌmæθə'mætɪkl̩〕*adj.* 數學的
thought〔θɔt〕*n.* 思維　　normal〔'nɔrml̩〕*adj.* 正常的
connection〔kə'nɛkʃən〕*n.* 連結
frontal〔'frʌntl̩〕*adj.* 正面的；前額的
temporal〔'tɛmpərəl〕*adj.* 太陽穴的；顳的
lobe〔lob〕*n.* （腦、肺的）葉片　　shed〔ʃɛd〕*v.* 發出（光）
shed light on 照亮；闡明；解釋清楚
aspect〔'æspɛkt〕*n.* 方面　　remain〔rɪ'men〕*v.* 仍然是
mystery〔'mɪstrɪ〕*n.* 謎　　certain〔'sɝtn̩〕*adj.* 確定的
unmatched〔ʌn'mætʃt〕*adj.* 無可匹敵的

1. (**B**) 愛因斯坦在德國出生，但他也是 ＿＿＿＿＿＿＿＿＿ 的公民。

    (A) 瑞士跟英國   (B) <u>瑞士跟美國</u>

    (C) 英國跟美國   (D) 法國跟荷蘭

    * England ('ɪŋglənd) *n.* 英國

      France (fræns) *n.* 法國   Holland ('hɑlənd) *n.* 荷蘭

2. (**D**) 下列哪件事並非發生在愛因斯坦的「奇蹟之年」？

    (A) 他發展出相對論。   (B) 他發展出光的量子理論。

    (C) 他想出物理學中最有名的等式。

    (D) <u>他因爲物理學的成就而獲頒諾貝爾獎。</u>

    * event (ɪ'vɛnt) *n.* 事件   *take place* 發生

     figure out 想出   award (ə'wɔrd) *v.* 頒發

     prize (praɪz) *n.* 獎   *the Nobel Prize* 諾貝爾獎

     achievement (ə'tʃivmənt) *n.* 成就；功績

3. (**D**) 一群加拿大研究人員檢視愛因斯坦的大腦，＿＿＿＿＿＿＿＿。

    (A) 發現他的大腦跟其他人比起來異常地大

    (B) 但是沒有發現任何特別之處

    (C) 終於找到他的死因

    (D) <u>發現前腦跟顳的腦葉之間的連結比正常的短</u>

    * abnormally (æb'nɔrmḷɪ) *adv.* 不正常地；異常地

     cause (kɔz) *n.* 起因

4. (**C**) 爲什麼愛因斯坦後來永久在美國居留？

    (A) 因爲他在美國結婚。   (B) 因爲他沒有錢可以回去德國。

    (C) <u>因爲納粹在德國掌權。</u>   (D) 文章中沒有提到。

    * marry ('mærɪ) *v.* 結婚   mention ('mɛnʃən) *v.* 提到

5. (**B**) 愛因斯坦在美國住了多久？

    (A) 大半輩子。   (B) <u>超過二十年。</u>

    (C) 十五年。   (D) 直到 1940 年。

    * decade ('dɛked) *n.* 十年

TEST 11

Read the following passage and choose the best answer for each question.

About 16 major languages and several hundred dialects are spoken in India. As a result, the Indian government has enormous trouble trying to knit together as a nation the many different tribal and religious groups in India.

Different radio networks broadcast the news in 14 different languages, yet there are many people in India who don't understand any of them. While India was a part of the British Empire, English was the official language of the government, but only about 2 percent of the Indian people spoke this language. When India gained its independence in 1947, the country's leaders wanted to stop using English. They chose Hindi, which is understood by about 50 percent of the people. However, the other 50 percent resented this choice. Bloody riots were started by groups that wanted to continue using their own languages.

In 1957, the Indian government announced a plan for reorganizing India's 27 states into 14 new states. These new states corresponded roughly to India's major language areas. Each state could adopt its own major language for official use within the state. In 1967, the government voted to continue using English as an "associate" language along with Hindi for official business. Indian children would learn three languages. Today, most educated Indians speak English, so until Indians can agree on a common language, English may serve as a link to bind them together. 【內湖高中】

1. On the whole, this article is about
   (A) reorganizing official business in Hindi.
   (B) the problem Indians have in knitting.
   (C) the confusion of languages in India.
   (D) independence from the British Empire.

2. Why were another 50 percent of the Indians angry about the choice of Hindi?
   (A) They preferred to speak in Swahili.
   (B) It sounded too much like English.
   (C) Their religion forced them to do it.
   (D) Most of them did not understand it.

3. While it is not directly stated, the article suggests that

   (A) language is sometimes a barrier among the people of India.

   (B) everyone in India can speak and understand English.

   (C) it is hard for the Indian people to learn Hindi.

   (D) Hindi has served as a link to bind Indians together.

4. Which statement is true according to the article?

   (A) Indian children are expected to learn English, Hindi, and the official language of their state.

   (B) The Indian government is less interested in using a common language.

   (C) Indians feel all their problems can be solved by the English language.

   (D) The Hindi-speaking people started riots to gain their independence from British.

5. Why has English retained its importance in India?

   (A) India is still a close ally of the British Empire.

   (B) English is understood by most people in business and government.

   (C) It is the official state language of 14 out of 16 states.

   (D) Around 50 percent of the population can speak it.

TEST 11 詳解

About 16 major languages and several hundred dialects are spoken in India. As a result, the Indian government has enormous trouble trying to knit together as a nation the many different tribal and religious groups in India.

在印度，大概有十六種主要語言，以及上百種方言被人們所使用。結果造成印度政府要把印度很多不同的部落，以及宗敎團體，整合成一個國家有很大的困難。

major〔'medʒɚ〕adj. 主要的　　dialect〔'daɪə,lɛkt〕n. 方言
India〔'ɪndɪə〕n. 印度　　*as a result* 結果
Indian〔'ɪndɪən〕adj. 印度的
have trouble + *V-ing* 很難～
enormous〔ɪ'nɔrməs〕adj. 巨大的　　knit〔nɪt〕v. 使結合；編織
tribal〔'traɪbḷ〕adj. 部落的　　religious〔rɪ'lɪdʒəs〕adj. 宗敎的

Different radio networks broadcast the news in 14 different languages, yet there are many people in India who don't understand any of them. While India was a part of the British Empire, English was the official language of the government, but only about 2 percent of the Indian people spoke this language. When India gained its independence in 1947, the country's leaders wanted to stop using English. They chose Hindi, which is understood by about 50 percent of the people. However, the other 50 percent resented this choice. Bloody riots were started by groups that wanted to continue using their own languages.

　　不同的無線電聯播網，用十四種語言播送新聞，但還有很多印度民眾，完全不懂這些語言。當印度還隸屬於大英帝國的時候，英語曾是政府的官方語言，但是只有大約百分之二的印度民眾會說英語。當印度在1947 年獲得獨立時，國家領導者希望能停止使用英語。他們選擇了能被大約百分之五十的人民聽懂的印地語。然而，另外百分之五十的民眾對這個選擇相當不滿。族群間發生血腥暴動，因為人們希望能繼續使用自己的語言。

radio〔ˈredɪ͵o〕*n.* 無線電廣播　　network〔ˈnɛt͵wɝk〕*n.* 聯絡網
broadcast〔ˈbrɔd͵kæst〕*v.* 廣播　　British〔ˈbrɪtɪʃ〕*adj.* 英國的
empire〔ˈɛmpaɪr〕*n.* 帝國　　***the British Empire*** 大英帝國
official〔əˈfɪʃəl〕*adj.* 官方的　　gain〔gen〕*v.* 獲得
independence〔͵ɪndɪˈpɛndəns〕*n.* 獨立
leader〔ˈlidɚ〕*n.* 領導者
choose〔tʃuz〕*v.* 挑選；選擇【三態：choose-chose-chosen】
Hindi〔ˈhɪndɪ〕*n.* 印地語【印度北部方言】
resent〔rɪˈzɛnt〕*v.* 對…感到生氣
bloody〔ˈblʌdɪ〕*adj.* 血腥的；殘忍的
riot〔ˈraɪət〕*n.* 暴動

In 1957, the Indian government announced a plan for reorganizing India's 27 states into 14 new states. These new states corresponded roughly to India's major language areas. Each state could adopt its own major language for official use within the state. In 1967, the government voted to continue using English as an "associate" language along with Hindi for official business. Indian children would learn three languages. Today, most educated Indians speak English, so until Indians can agree on a common language, English may serve as a link to bind them together.

在 1957 年，印度政府宣布一項計畫，將 27 個州重組為 14 個州，新的州界大致跟印度主要語言區域一致。每個州在州界內，都可以採用自己的主要語言作為官方語言。在 1967 年，政府表決繼續使用英語作為「連結的」語言，而印地語作為官方企業的語言。印度的孩子要學習三種語言。而今，大部分受過教育的印度人都說英語，而直到印度人一致同意共通語言是什麼之前，英語還是作為將他們連結在一起的環節。

announce〔əˈnaʊns〕v. 宣布；發表
reorganize〔riˈɔrgəˌnaɪz〕v. 重組；整頓
state〔stet〕n. 州　　correspond〔ˌkɔrəˈspɑnd〕v. 符合；一致 < to >
roughly〔ˈrʌflɪ〕adv. 粗略地　　adopt〔əˈdɑpt〕v. 採取；批准
within〔wɪðˈɪn〕prep. 在…範圍之中
vote〔vot〕v. 投票；表決　　associate〔əˈsoʃɪɪt〕adj. 聯合的
along with 與…一起　　business〔ˈbɪznɪs〕n. 企業
educated〔ˈɛdʒəˌketɪd〕adj. 受過教育的　　agree〔əˈgri〕v. 意見一致
common〔ˈkɑmən〕adj. 共同的　　*serve as* 作為
link〔lɪŋk〕n. 連繫物；環節　　bind〔baɪnd〕v. 綑綁；連結

1.(**C**) 整體來說，本篇文章是關於 ＿＿＿＿＿＿＿＿。

(A) 用印地語重整官方企業

(B) 印度編織工藝所面臨的問題

(C) 印度語言混亂　　　　　(D) 脫離大英帝國獨立

* *on the whole* 大體上；整體而言
knitting〔ˈnɪtɪŋ〕n. 編織工藝
confusion〔kənˈfjuʒən〕n. 混亂

2.(**D**) 為什麼另外百分之五十的人，對於選擇印地語感到生氣？

(A) 他們偏好說史瓦希里語。　　(B) 印地語聽起來太像英語。

(C) 他們的宗教迫使他們這樣做。

(D) 他們大部分都不懂這個語言。

* prefer〔prɪˈfɝ〕v. 比較喜歡　　*prefer to V.* 偏好～
Swahili〔swɑˈhilɪ〕n. 史瓦希里語
religion〔rɪˈlɪdʒən〕n. 宗教　　force〔fors〕v. 強迫

3. (**A**) 即使不是直接地陳述，本文暗指 ＿＿＿＿＿＿ 。

(A) 對於印度人來說，語言有時候是一種隔閡

(B) 在印度的每個人都會說英語，也懂英語

(C) 對於印度人來說，學習印地語很困難

(D) 印地語是作爲將印度人連結在一起的環節

* suggest〔səg'dʒɛst〕*v.* 暗示；建議
barrier〔'bærɪə〕*n.* 障礙物；隔閡

4. (**A**) 根據本文，下列何者敘述爲眞？

(A) 印度的孩子被期望要學習英語、印地語，跟州的官方
語言。

(B) 印度政府對於使用共通語言不感興趣。

(C) 印度人認爲，他們所有的問題都會因使用英語而得到
解決。

(D) 說印地語的人發起暴動，以脫離英國而獨立。

* expect〔ɪk'spɛkt〕*v.* 預期；期望
be interested in 對⋯感興趣
solve〔salv〕*v.* 解決

5. (**B**) 爲什麼英語在印度仍然很重要？

(A) 印度跟英國還是親近的同盟。

(B) 在政府部門跟商業活動中，英語還是最廣爲使用的
語言。

(C) 在 16 個州中，有 14 州將英語當作官方州立語言。

(D) 大約百分之五十的人口能夠說英語。

* ally〔'ælaɪ〕*n.* 盟友　　retain〔rɪ'ten〕*v.* 保持
population〔,papjə'leʃən〕*n.* 人口

TEST 12

Read the following passage and choose the best answer for each question.

William Shakespeare (1564-1616)
Sonnet 18

Shall I compare thee to a summer's day?

Thou art more lovely and more temperate.

Rough winds do shake the darling buds of May,

And summer's leave hath all too short a date:

Sometimes too hot the eye of heaven shines,

And often is his gold complexion dimmed;

And every fair from fair sometime declines,

By chance, or nature changing course, untrimmed;

But thy eternal summer shall not fade

Nor lose possession of that fair thou owest,

Nor shall Death brag thou wand'rest in his shade

When in eternal lines to time thou grow'st.

So long as men can breathe or eyes can see

So long lives this, and gives life to thee.

Notes:

1. Thou 為第二人稱單數主格之古語，所有格 thy，受格 thee

2. Hath 為 has 之古語

3. owest 為現代英語之 own 　　　【成淵高中】

1. Which of the following lines is *__a metaphor__*?

   (A) Shall I compare thee to a summer's day?

   (B) Sometimes too hot the eye of heaven shines,

   (C) Nor lose possession of that fair thou owest,

   (D) So long as men can breathe or eyes can see

2. In the line "Sometimes too hot the eye of heaven shines,"
   the phrase "the eye of heaven shines" means _____.

   (A) the sky   (B) the moon

   (C) the sun   (D) the eyes of a person

3. Which of the following statements is *__not an idea__*
   __expressed in this poem__?

   (A) Shakespeare compares the "you" to a summer's day.

   (B) The "you" will leave as the summer goes away.

   (C) But the "you" will not fade away.

   (D) The "you" will live so long as men can breathe.

4. When does Death brag that one "wand'rest in his shade?"

   (A) When one is tired to death.

   (B) When one has died.

   (C) When death has been overcome.

   (D) When one enters hell.

5. What does the word "fair" mean in the context of this
   sonnet?

   (A) just   (B) pale

   (C) market   (D) beauty

TEST 12 詳解

William Shakespeare (1564-1616)
Sonnet 18

Shall I compare thee to a summer's day?

Thou art more lovely and more temperate.

Rough winds do shake the darling buds of May,

And summer's lease hath all too short a date:

Sometimes too hot the eye of heaven shines,

And often is his gold complexion dimmed;

And every fair from fair sometime declines,

By chance, or nature changing course, untrimmed;

But thy eternal summer shall not fade

Nor lose possession of that fair thou owest,

Nor shall Death brag thou wand'rest in his shade

When in eternal lines to time thou grow'st.

So long as men can breathe or eyes can see

So long lives this, and gives life to thee.

威廉・莎士比亞（**1564-1616**）
十四行詩第十八首

我怎麼能夠把你比作夏天？
你不僅比它可愛，也更溫和。
狂風吹搖五月所珍寵的花蕊，
而夏日的租賃期只有一天未免短暫；
有時天堂之眼閃閃發亮，
有時它耀眼的金色容顏又黯淡，
所有美人的容顏總會凋零腐敗，
因機緣或自然的代謝而凌亂。
但是你永恆的夏日不會逝去，

你擁有的美貌紅顏也不會褪去，
也不會有死神說你在他的陰府裡遊蕩，
當在永恆的詩句裡，你與時間共存，
只要人們還能呼吸，還能看見，
這詩將永遠存在，並給你生命。

William Shakespeare (ˈwɪljəmˈʃekˌspɪr) *n.* 威廉・莎士比亞
【1564-1616，英國詩人以及劇作家】

sonnet (ˈsɑnɪt) *n.* 十四行詩【源於義大利民間的抒情短詩，於文藝復興
時期盛行於歐洲。莎士比亞的十四行詩結構爲前三段每段四行，最後一
段爲兩行，每行十個音節】　　compare (kəmˈpɛr) *v.* 比較；比喻

compare A to B 將 A 比擬爲 B

thee (ðɪ) *pron.* 你【古語 thou 的受格】

thou (ðaʊ) *pron.* 你；汝【古語第二人稱單數的主格，表 you】

art (ɑt) *v.* 古語中跟第二人稱單數連用的 be 動詞【thou art = you are】

lovely (ˈlʌvlɪ) *adj.* 可愛的　　temperate (ˈtɛmpərɪt) *adj.* 溫和的

rough (rʌf) *adj.* 粗暴的　　shake (ʃek) *v.* 搖動

darling (ˈdɑrlɪŋ) *adj.* 寵愛的；鍾愛的

bud (bʌd) *n.* 花苞；花蕾　　lease (lis) *n.* 租賃期

hath (hæθ) *v.* 有；是【古詩中第三人稱現在式所連用的 has】

date (det) *n.* 日期　　shine (ʃaɪn) *v.* 發光；照耀

complexion (kəmˈplɛkʃən) *n.* 臉色

dim (dɪm) *v.* 變黯淡；使模糊　　fair (fɛr) *n.* 美麗的女子

decline (dɪˈklaɪn) *v.* 下降；衰退　　***by chance*** 偶然地

nature (ˈnetʃə) *n.* 自然　　course (kors) *n.* 過程；發展

untrimmed (ʌnˈtrɪmd) *adj.* 未經修剪的

thy (ðaɪ) *adj.* 你的【古語 thou 的所有格，後面接子音爲首的名詞】

eternal (ɪˈtɜnḷ) *adj.* 永恆的；不朽的

fade (fed) *v.* (花) 凋謝；(美貌) 衰退

possession (pəˈzɛʃən) *n.* 擁有物　　owest (ˈoɪst) *v.* 擁有【古語的 own】

Death (dɛθ) *n.* 死神【大寫】　　brag (bræg) *v.* 自誇；吹噓

wanderest (ˈwɑndəˌrɪst) *v.* 漂泊；流浪【古語的 wander】

shade (ʃed) *n.* 陰影【the shade 可指陰府】

line (laɪn) *n.* (詩的) 一行

grow'st (grost) *v.* 生長；存在【古語的 grow】

breathe (brið) *v.* 呼吸

1.(**B**) 下列哪一個句子是個「隱喻」？

(A) 我怎麼能夠把你比作夏天？

(B) <u>有時天堂之眼閃閃發亮，</u>

(C) 你擁有的美貌紅顏也不會褪去，

(D) 只要人們還能呼吸，還能看見

  * metaphor〔ˈmɛtəfə〕*n.* 隱喻；暗喻

2.(**C**) 在「有時天堂之眼閃閃發亮，」這一句中，"the eye of heaven shines" 指的是 ＿＿＿＿＿＿＿。

(A) 天空　　(B) 月亮　　(C) <u>太陽</u>　　(D) 人的眼睛

  * phrase〔frez〕*n.* 措辭；說法　　mean〔min〕*v.* 意指

3.(**B**) 下列哪一個敘述 ***不是本詩所表達的概念***？

(A) 莎士比亞將「你」比喻成夏日。

(B) <u>「你」將會隨著夏天的離去而遠離。</u>

(C) 但是「你」將不會凋零。

(D) 只要人類還有氣息，「你」就能存活。

  * idea〔aɪˈdiə〕*n.* 念頭；構想；概念
    express〔ɪkˈsprɛs〕*v.* 表達　　poem〔ˈpoɪm〕*n.* 詩

4.(**B**) 什麼時候死神會吹噓有人 "wand'rest in his shade"？

(A) 當某個人疲累到快要死去的時候。

(B) <u>當有人死亡的時候。</u>

(C) 當死亡被征服的時候。　　(D) 當有人進入地獄的時候。

  * overcome〔ˌovəˈkʌm〕*v.* 征服；打敗
    hell〔hɛl〕*n.* 地獄

5.(**D**) "fair" 這個字在這首十四行詩的上下文中的意義是什麼？

(A) 正直的　　(B) 蒼白的　　(C) 市場　　(D) <u>美人</u>

  * context〔ˈkɑntɛkst〕*n.* 上下文
    just〔dʒʌst〕*adj.* 正直的　　pale〔pel〕*adj.* 蒼白的
    market〔ˈmɑrkɪt〕*n.* 市場　　beauty〔ˈbjutɪ〕*n.* 美人

TEST 13

Read the following passage and choose the best answer for each question.

Educational psychologists in Germany say that bullying is a group phenomenon and that students and teachers should stand up to school bullies and show support for victims. Children bully other children because they hope it will gain the attention and admiration of the group. Students who are higher in the social hierarchy find bullying amusing, and those with lower social standing join in because they fear that if they do not do so, they will become victims themselves.

Once bullying has started, it may be difficult to stop. Some victims may try to become the teacher's pet for protection. Other victims try to play the class clown, which causes other students to believe that the victims deserve the bullying.

Children who are bullied are in great danger of losing self-confidence and may even become ill. Bullies are more likely to become criminals. To prevent this from happening, teachers must stop bullying immediately. Students can help by standing together against bullies. As Dr. Brian Shaifer, a psychologist at Munich University, explained, bullying does not work without other group members. "Those who simply look on are just as responsible," the psychologist said. 【成淵高中】

1. What is the passage about?

    (A) How bullies may change a student's life.

    (B) How a teacher may stop bullies at school.

    (C) School bullies and the way to stop them.

    (D) How students like being the victims of bullies.

2. The meaning of the word "criminals" in line 15 is

    (A) lawbreakers.   (B) lawmakers.

    (C) respectful of the law.   (D) lawyers.

3. According to the passage, why would children bully their schoolmates?

    (A) To express happiness.   (B) To get attention.

    (C) To carry out justice.   (D) To set things straight.

4. Which of the following is NOT a reason for school bullying?

    (A) Some students think bullying is amusing.

    (B) Bullying sometimes helps students get admiration from the group.

    (C) Some victims deserve the punishment.

    (D) Students join in to avoid becoming the victims.

5. What is the best description of bullying?

    (A) It is a common phenomenon at summer camp.

    (B) It is a popular sport for children.

    (C) It is a punishment teachers give students.

    (D) It is when students are bothered or hurt by their schoolmates.

TEST 13 詳解

Educational psychologists in Germany say that bullying is a group phenomenon and that students and teachers should stand up to school bullies and show support for victims. Children bully other children because they hope it will gain the attention and admiration of the group. Students who are higher in the social hierarchy find bullying amusing, and those with lower social standing join in because they fear that if they do not do so, they will become victims themselves.

德國的教育心理學家說，霸凌是一種集體現象，而學生跟老師應該一起對抗校園惡霸，展現對受害者的支持。孩子欺負其他小孩，希望這樣能受到注意，以及團體欽佩。處在較高社會階層的學生，覺得霸凌很有趣，而其他社會地位較低的學生加入欺壓的行列，是怕自己如果不這樣做，就會變成受害者。

educational〔͵ɛdʒə'keʃənḷ〕 *adj.* 教育的
psychologist〔saɪ'kɑlədʒɪst〕 *n.* 心理學家
German〔'dʒɝmən〕 *n.* 德國
bullying〔'bulɪɪŋ〕 *n.* 強欺弱的行為；霸凌
phenomenon〔fə'nɑmə͵nɑn〕 *n.* 現象　　***stand up to*** 抵禦；對抗
bully〔'bulɪ〕 *n.* 惡霸；流氓　　support〔sə'port〕 *n.* 支持
victim〔'vɪktɪm〕 *n.* 受害者　　bully〔'bulɪ〕 *v.* 欺凌；強欺弱
gain〔gen〕 *v.* 獲得　　attention〔ə'tɛnʃən〕 *n.* 注意力
admiration〔͵ædmə'reʃən〕 *n.* 欽佩；讚賞
hierarchy〔'haɪə͵rɑrkɪ〕 *n.* 階層；階級
amusing〔ə'mjuzɪŋ〕 *adj.* 有趣的　　standing〔'stændɪŋ〕 *n.* 地位
join〔dʒɔɪn〕 *v.* 參加　　fear〔fɪr〕 *v.* 害怕

Once bullying has started, it may be difficult to stop. Some victims may try to become the teacher's pet for protection. Other victims try to play the class clown, which causes other students to believe that the victims deserve the bullying.

霸凌一旦開始，就很難停止。有些受害者試著成爲老師的寵兒來尋求保護，其他受害者試著扮演課堂上的丑角，但這也讓其他學生相信，受害者會被欺凌是活該。

pet〔pɛt〕*n.* 寵物；受寵之人　　protection〔prəˋtɛkʃən〕*n.* 保護

cause〔kɔz〕*v.* 引起；造成　　clown〔klaʊn〕*n.* 丑角

class clown 班上的搞笑人物【指某些故意扮成傻瓜，讓人覺得很好笑的學生】　　deserve〔dɪˋzɝv〕*v.* 應得

Children who are bullied are in great danger of losing self-confidence and may even become ill. Bullies are more likely to become criminals. To prevent this from happening, teachers must stop bullying immediately. Students can help by standing together against bullies. As Dr. Brian Shaifer, a psychologist at Munich University, explained, bullying does not work without other group members. "Those who simply look on are just as responsible," the psychologist said.

被欺壓的孩子，有很大的危險會失去自信心，可能甚至會生病。而惡霸很可能會變成犯罪者。爲了防止事件發生，老師必須立即阻止霸凌。學生們也可以藉著團結，來幫助對抗惡霸。就像慕尼黑大學的心理學博士，布萊恩‧夏佛解釋，如果沒有其他團體成員，霸凌就無法起作用。「那些只是觀看的學生也有責任，」這位心理學家說到。

in danger of 有…的危險

self-confidence〔ˏsɛlfˋkɑnfədəns〕*n.* 自信心

ill〔ɪl〕*adj.* 生病的　　***be likely to V.*** 可能~

criminal〔ˋkrɪmənl〕*n.* 犯罪者　　prevent〔prɪˋvɛnt〕*v.* 防止；預防

immediately〔ɪˋmidɪɪtlɪ〕*adv.* 立刻

Munich〔ˋmjunɪk〕*n.* 慕尼黑【德國地名】

explain〔ɪkˋsplen〕*v.* 解釋　　***look on*** 旁觀；觀看

responsible〔rɪˋspɑnsəbl〕*adj.* 應負責的

1. (**C**) 本文是關於什麼？
   (A) 霸凌如何改變學生的生活。
   (B) 教師如何阻止校園惡霸。　　(C) 校園惡霸以及如何阻止他們。
   (D) 學生喜歡成爲校園惡霸的受害者。

2. (**A**) 第十五行的"criminals"這個字的意思是 ＿＿＿＿＿＿＿
   (A) 犯法者。　　(B) 立法者。　(C) 尊敬法律。　(D) 律師。
   * lawbreaker〔'lɔ͵brekɚ〕*n.* 犯法者
     lawmaker〔'lɔ͵mekɚ〕*n.* 立法者
     respectful〔rɪ'spɛktfəl〕*adj.* 尊敬的
     lawyer〔'lɔjɚ〕*n.* 律師

3. (**B**) 根據本文，爲什麼孩子們會欺壓同學？
   (A) 爲了表達快樂。　　　　　(B) 爲了得到注意。
   (C) 爲了實踐正義。　　　　　(D) 爲了把事情弄清楚。
   * schoolmate〔'skul͵met〕*n.* 同學
     express〔ɪk'sprɛs〕*v.* 表達　　*carry out* 實現；實踐
     justice〔'dʒʌstɪs〕*n.* 正義　　*set sth. straight* 把事情弄清楚

4. (**C**) 下列何者「不」是校園欺壓事件的原因？
   (A) 有些學生覺得欺壓別人很有趣。
   (B) 有時候欺壓別人可以讓學生得到團體敬佩。
   (C) 有些受害者活該被處罰。
   (D) 學生加入欺壓行動以避免成爲受害者。
   * punishment〔'pʌnɪʃmənt〕*n.* 處罰；懲罰
     avoid〔ə'vɔɪd〕*v.* 避免

5. (**D**) 對於霸凌行爲最佳的敘述是什麼？
   (A) 在夏令營中是常見的現象。
   (B) 對於學生來說是受歡迎的運動。
   (C) 是教師給學生的處罰。
   (D) 是學生被其他同學所打擾或傷害。
   * description〔dɪ'skrɪpʃən〕*n.* 描述
     common〔'kamən〕*adj.* 常見的　　*summer camp* 夏令營
     bother〔'baðɚ〕*v.* 困擾　　hurt〔hɝt〕*v.* 傷害

TEST 14

Read the following passage and choose the best answer for each question.

Like most people in the past, the Kauwerak of western Alaska preserved their history by storytelling. One tragic story they've told for over two centuries is that of the summer that didn't come. It tells of a summer hunting season that never began, leaving most of the people in the region starving. This story has now been confirmed by scientists. The Kauwerak relied on the short hunting season to gather food for the winter. One June, however, just as the weather was warming up, it suddenly turned cold again. Dark clouds covered the sky, bringing the bitter cold early. The hunting season never started and people had no food for the coming winter. As a result, many people died of starvation.

Now, scientists have confirmed the story and discovered why that summer never came. It was 1783, the year when a huge volcano erupted in Iceland. The eruption destroyed twenty villages and killed some ten thousand people — 20 percent of the country's population. Researchers have found that the volcano sent clouds of ash into the sky, and thus the sun was blocked. Winds brought the clouds to the northern tip of Canada and Alaska, and even as far as Japan. There it was also said that summer never came that year. Historians would have called the story legend. Science, however, has proved it to be true and shown that we must look more seriously at such tales. 【中正高中】

1. The main idea of this passage is that _____.
   (A) a scientific reason has been found that explains a legend
   (B) air pollution is getting more and more serious in Alaska
   (C) there are always legends about the disasters in Alaska
   (D) science has proved that a volcano erupted in 1783

2. How and when did people in Alaska get food?
   (A) By fishing in summer.
   (B) By hunting in summer.
   (C) By farming in winter.
   (D) By starving in winter.

3. Which was NOT an effect of having no summer that year?

(A) People had no food for the coming winter.

(B) The death of many people.

(C) Many people no longer made a living by hunting.

(D) The winter cold began unusually early.

4. What might be the reason for the sudden disappearance of summer that year?

(A) Strong winds melted the ice at the northern tip of Canada.

(B) It was the greenhouse effect destroying the natural environment.

(C) A volcano erupted and caused the temperature to drop suddenly.

(D) The sky was covered with volcanic ash, which blocked the sun.

5. The story "The Summer That Never Came" _____.

(A) is unbelievable now

(B) is no longer a mystery

(C) is a made-up story that serves as a warning

(D) has changed the attitude of historians

TEST 14 詳解

Like most people in the past, the Kauwerak of western Alaska preserved their history by storytelling. One tragic story they've told for over two centuries is that of the summer that didn't come. It tells of a summer hunting season that never began, leaving most of the people in the region starving. This story has now been confirmed by scientists. The Kauwerak relied on the short hunting season to gather food for the winter. One June, however, just as the weather was warming up, it suddenly turned cold again. Dark clouds covered the sky, bringing the bitter cold early. The hunting season never started and people had no food for the coming winter. As a result, many people died of starvation.

就像古時候多數人類一樣，住在西部阿拉斯加的庫維拉克人，用說故事來保存歷史。兩個多世紀以來，他們傳頌著一則「夏天消失」的悲劇。這個故事是訴說某年夏季，狩獵季節沒有展開，讓這個地區的大部分人都處於飢餓的狀態。這則故事現在已經被科學家證實了。庫維拉克人仰賴短暫的狩獵季節，採集食物以度過冬天。然而，有一年六月，正當天氣逐漸變暖，突然間卻又再度變回寒冷。黑色的雲覆蓋天空，提早帶來酷寒。狩獵季節從來沒有展開，人們沒有食物可以度過即將到來的冬天，結果很多人餓死。

Kauwerak ('kuwɪ,ræk) *n.* 庫維拉克族【西部阿拉斯加的一個民族】
western ('wɛstən) *adj.* 西部的
Alaska (ə'læskə) *n.* 阿拉斯加【美國西北部在極圈內的一州】
preserve (prɪ'zɝv) *v.* 保存
storytelling ('storɪ,tɛlɪŋ) *n.* 說故事

tragic〔'trædʒɪk〕*adj.* 悲劇的　　***hunting season*** 狩獵季節
leave *sb.* ***V-ing*** 使（人）處於～的狀態
region〔'ridʒən〕*n.* 地區
starve〔starv〕*v.* 飢餓　　　confirm〔kən'fɝm〕*v.* 證實
rely〔rɪ'laɪ〕*v.* 依靠＜*on*＞
gather〔'gæðɚ〕*v.* 採集　　　***warm up*** 變暖；暖化
suddenly〔'sʌdṇlɪ〕*adv.* 突然間
cloud〔klaʊd〕*n.* 雲　　　cover〔'kʌvɚ〕*v.* 覆蓋；遮蔽
bitter〔'bɪtɚ〕*adj.* 猛烈的；嚴酷的　　　cold〔kold〕*n.* 寒冷
coming〔'kʌmɪŋ〕*adj.* 即將來臨的　　　***as a result*** 因此；結果
starvation〔star'veʃən〕*n.* 飢餓

Now, scientists have confirmed the story and discovered why that summer never came. It was 1783, the year when a huge volcano erupted in Iceland. The eruption destroyed twenty villages and killed some ten thousand people — 20 percent of the country's population. Researchers have found that the volcano sent clouds of ash into the sky, and thus the sun was blocked. Winds brought the clouds to the northern tip of Canada and Alaska, and even as far as Japan. There it was also said that summer never came that year. Historians would have called the story legend. Science, however, has proved it to be true and shown that we must look more seriously at such tales.

現在，科學家證實了這個故事，也發現為什麼那年的夏天沒有來。那時候 1783 年，當時冰島有一座大型火山爆發。火山爆發摧毀了二十個村莊，大約有一萬個人死亡——佔當時該國人口的五分之一。研究人員發現，火山將火山灰雲送往天空，因此太陽就被遮蔽了。風把雲帶往加拿大北端以及阿拉斯加，甚至遠至日本。而那些地方據說那一年的夏天也沒有到來。歷史學家或許把這些故事稱爲神話，但科學已經證明這是事實，而且顯示我們必須更認眞地看待這些故事。

discover〔dɪˋskʌvɚ〕v. 發現
volcano〔vɑlˋkeno〕n. 火山
erupt〔ɪˋrʌpt〕v.（火山）爆發
Iceland〔ˋaɪslənd〕n. 冰島　　eruption〔ɪˋrʌpʃən〕n. 爆發
destroy〔dɪˋstrɔɪ〕v. 催毀　　village〔ˋvɪlɪdʒ〕n. 村莊
population〔͵pɑpjəˋleʃən〕n. 人口
ash〔æʃ〕n. 灰燼　　block〔blɑk〕v. 阻塞
northern〔ˋnɔrðɚn〕adj. 北部的　　tip〔tɪp〕n. 尖端
Canada〔ˋkænədə〕n. 加拿大　　*as far as* 遠及
Japan〔dʒəˋpæn〕n. 日本
historian〔hɪsˋtorɪən〕n. 歷史學家
legend〔ˋlɛdʒənd〕n. 傳說　　prove〔pruv〕v. 證明
seriously〔ˋsɪrɪəslɪ〕adv. 認眞地
tale〔tel〕n. 故事

1.（**A**）本文的主旨是 ＿＿＿＿＿。
(A) 找到可以解釋傳說的科學原因
(B) 阿拉斯加的空氣污染越來越嚴重
(C) 在阿拉斯加總有災難傳說
(D) 科學已經證實有一座火山在 1783 年爆發
* pollution〔pəˋluʃən〕n. 污染
serious〔ˋsɪrɪəs〕adj. 嚴重的
disaster〔dɪzˋæstɚ〕n. 災難

2.（**B**）阿拉斯加的人在何時，用什麼方法取得食物？
(A) 在夏天時釣魚。　　(B) 在夏天時打獵。
(C) 在冬天時耕作。　　(D) 在冬天時挨餓。

3. (**C**) 下列何者「不」是那一年沒有夏天的影響？

(A) 人們沒有食物可以度過即將到來的冬天。

(B) 很多人死去。

(C) 很多人不再靠打獵維生。

(D) 冬季嚴寒比往常更早來到。

* *make a living by~* 靠～維生
unusually〔ʌn'juʒʊəlɪ〕*adv.* 稀罕地；特別地

4. (**D**) 下列何者可能是那一年夏季突然消失的原因？

(A) 強風融化了加拿大北端的冰層。

(B) 溫室效應摧毀大自然環境。

(C) 火山爆發，造成氣溫突然下降。

(D) 天空被火山灰所遮蔽，也擋住陽光。

* sudden〔'sʌdn̩〕*adj.* 突然的
disappearance〔͵dɪsə'pɪrəns〕*n.* 消失
melt〔mɛlt〕*v.* 融化 greenhouse〔'grin͵haʊs〕*n.* 溫室
greenhouse effect 溫室效應 cause〔kɔz〕*v.* 引起；導致
drop〔drɑp〕*v.* 突然下降
volcanic〔vɑl'kænɪk〕*adj.* 火山的 ***volcanic ash*** 火山灰

5. (**B**) 「夏天沒有來」這個故事 ＿＿＿＿＿＿＿。

(A) 現在看來不可置信

(B) 再也不是個謎

(C) 是個作爲警告的虛構故事

(D) 改變了歷史學家的態度

* unbelievable〔͵ʌnbə'livəbl̩〕*adj.* 難以置信的
mystery〔'mɪstrɪ〕*n.* 謎 made-up〔'med'ʌp〕*adj.* 虛構的
serve as 作爲 warning〔'wɔrnɪŋ〕*n.* 警告
attitude〔'ætə͵tjud〕*n.* 態度

TEST 15

Read the following passage and choose the best answer for each question.

According to ancient Chinese tradition, the entire seventh month of the lunar calendar is the month of ghosts. The gates of Hell are opened on the first day of this month. At that time, the spirits of the dead are released from the world of the dead and they wander around the world of the living for the whole month.

To avoid anything unpleasant caused by the ghosts, the living postpone or do in advance important activities and events, such as moving house, getting married, opening shops, starting projects, or buying cars. Many activities are done to please the wandering spirits during this month: banquets, operas, parades, chanting and the burning of sacrificial paper money. Most of these activities are religious and are centered on temples, with tall bamboo poles inviting and guiding the ghost to the feasts. Besides, lanterns are placed near the water to show the way for those spirits who have drowned. Ghost month activities reach a <u>climax</u>

on the 15th day, the date of the Taoist Chungyuan Festival. Huge displays of food and drinks area placed in the yards or outside the front doors of both private homes and modern business buildings to feed the ghosts. 【陽明高中】

1. This passage is mainly about _____.
   (A) the origin of the ghost month
   (B) the customs people observe in the ghost month and their variations
   (C) how celebrations for the ghost month have become less popular over the years
   (D) how superstitious people become during the ghost month

2. What does the word "climax" mean in the second paragraph?
   (A) The low point of an event.
   (B) The turning point of an event.
   (C) The most exciting and important point of an event.
   (D) The unpredictable point of the event.

3. According to the passage, what would people NOT do during the ghost month?

   (A) Get a driver's license.

   (B) Sing a song.

   (C) Find a new boyfriend/girlfriend.

   (D) Move.

4. Where can offerings to wandering ghosts be seen?

   (A) Weddings, funerals, and temples.

   (B) Temples, shops, and homes.

   (C) Cars, restaurants, and new stores.

   (D) Private homes, churches, and the gates of Hell.

5. Why are lanterns placed near water?

   (A) To guide thirsty ghosts.

   (B) The spirits of drowned ghosts stay in the water.

   (C) Some ghosts were blinded when they died.

   (D) To lead the ghosts back to hell.

TEST 15 詳解

According to ancient Chinese tradition, the entire seventh month of the lunar calendar is the month of ghosts. The gates of Hell are opened on the first day of this month. At that time, the spirits of the dead are released from the world of the dead and they wander around the world of the living for the whole month.

根據中國古代傳統，整個農曆七月都是鬼月。地獄之門會在七月第一天打開，在那時候，亡魂會從冥界被釋放，它們整個七月都在人間四處遊蕩。

ancient〔'enʃənt〕*adj.* 古代的；自古以來的
tradition〔trə'dıʃən〕*n.* 傳統　　entire〔ın'taır〕*adj.* 整個的
lunar〔'lunɚ〕*adj.* 月亮的　　*lunar calendar* 農曆；陰曆
ghost〔gost〕*n.* 鬼　　gate〔get〕*n.* 大門
Hell〔hɛl〕*n.* 地獄　　spirit〔'spırıt〕*n.* 靈魂
the world of the dead 亡魂的世界；冥界
release〔rı'lis〕*v.* 釋放　　wander〔'wɑndɚ〕*v.* 遊蕩；漂泊
wander around 四處遊蕩
the world of the living 人界；人世間

To avoid anything unpleasant caused by the ghosts, the living postpone or do in advance important activities and events, such as moving house, getting married, opening shops, starting projects, or buying cars. Many activities are done to please the wandering spirits during this month: banquets, operas, parades, chanting and the burning of sacrificial paper money.

Most of these activities are religious and are centered on temples, with tall bamboo poles inviting and guiding the ghost to the feasts.

爲了避免鬼魂引發的任何不愉快的事，活著的人會延後或事先完成重要活動，例如搬家、結婚、開店、開始新計畫，或買車。在這個月當中會舉辦很多活動，來取悅遊蕩的鬼魂，像是宴會、歌劇、遊行、詠唱，以及燒供奉的紙錢等。這些活動很多都具有宗教意義，而且集中在寺廟裡面舉行，會有高高的竹竿邀請及帶領鬼魂到宴會地點。

avoid〔əˋvɔɪd〕v. 避免

unpleasant〔ʌnˋplɛznt〕adj. 令人不愉快的

cause〔kɔz〕v. 引起　　postpone〔postˋpon〕v. 延後；延期

in advance 預先　　activity〔ækˋtɪvətɪ〕n. 活動

event〔ɪˋvɛnt〕n. 事件；大型活動

project〔ˋprɑdʒɛkt〕n. 計畫　　please〔pliz〕v. 取悅

wandering〔ˋwɑndrɪŋ〕adj. 徘徊的；漂泊的；流浪的

banquet〔ˋbæŋkwɪt〕n. 盛宴　　opera〔ˋɑpərə〕n. 歌劇演出

parade〔pəˋred〕n. 遊行　　chant〔tʃænt〕v. 詠唱

sacrificial〔ˌsækrəˋfɪʃəl〕adj. 供品的；奉獻的

paper money 紙錢　　religious〔rɪˋlɪdʒəs〕adj. 宗教的

center〔ˋsɛntɚ〕v. 集中　　temple〔ˋtɛmpl〕n. 寺廟

bamboo〔bæmˋbu〕n. 竹子　　pole〔pol〕n. 竿

invite〔ɪnˋvaɪt〕v. 邀請　　guide〔gaɪd〕v. 引領

feast〔fist〕n. 盛宴

Besides, lanterns are placed near the water to show the way for those spirits who have drowned. Ghost month activities reach a <u>climax</u> on the 15th day, the date of the Taoist Chungyuan Festival. Huge displays of food and drinks area placed in the yards or outside the front doors of both private homes and modern business buildings to feed the ghosts.

此外，在水邊設有燈籠，爲溺死的亡靈照亮路途。鬼月活動在道教中元節七月十五日這天到達高峰。無論在私人住家，或是現代商業大樓的院子或門前，都會擺滿許多食物跟飲料來餵養這些鬼魂。

besides〔bɪˋsaɪdz〕*prep.* 此外   lantern〔ˋlæntən〕*n.* 燈籠
place〔ples〕*v.* 放置   drown〔draʊn〕*v.* 淹死；溺水
climax〔ˋklaɪmæks〕*n.* 頂點；高潮
Toaist〔ˋtaoɪst〕*adj.* 道教（徒）的
festival〔ˋfɛstəvḷ〕*n.* 節慶
Taoist Chungyuan Festival 道教中元節
huge〔hjudʒ〕*adj.* 巨大的
display〔dɪˋsple〕*n.* 展示；陳列
yard〔jɑrd〕*n.* 院子   private〔ˋpraɪvɪt〕*adj.* 私人的
modern〔ˋmɑdən〕*adj.* 現代的
building〔ˋbɪldɪŋ〕*n.* 大樓；建築物   feed〔fid〕*v.* 餵食

1. (**B**) 這篇文章主要是關於 _____ 。

    (A) 鬼月的起源

    (B) <u>人們在鬼月遵守的習俗以及習俗的變化</u>

    (C) 鬼月慶祝活動爲什麼逐年變得不受歡迎

    (D) 人們在鬼月變得有多迷信

    * origin〔ˋɔrədʒɪn〕*n.* 起源   custom〔ˋkʌstəm〕*n.* 習俗
       observe〔əbˋzɝv〕*v.* 遵守；觀察
       variation〔ˌvɛrɪˋeʃən〕*n.* 改變；變化
       celebration〔ˌsɛləˋbreʃən〕*n.* 慶祝活動
       superstitious〔ˌsupəˋstɪʃəs〕*adj.* 迷信的

2. (**C**) 第二段 "climax" 這個字的意思是什麼？

    (A) 事件的低點。

    (B) 事件的轉捩點。

    (C) <u>事件中最刺激、也是最重要的時間點。</u>

    (D) 事件中不可預期的重點。

* point〔pɔɪnt〕*n.* 階段；（程度的）點；重點
  turning point 轉捩點
  exciting〔ɪk'saɪtɪŋ〕*adj.* 令人興奮的；刺激的
  unpredictable〔͵ʌnprɪ'dɪktəbḷ〕*adj.* 不能預期的

3. (**D**) 根據本文，鬼月的時候人們「不」會做下列哪一件事？

　　(A) 去考駕照。　　　　　　(B) 唱歌。

　　(C) 交新的男/女朋友。　　(D) 搬家。

　　* license〔'laɪsṇs〕*n.* 執照　　***driver's license*** 駕照

4. (**B**) 下列哪些地方能看到給漂泊鬼魂的祭品？

　　(A) 婚禮、喪禮、寺廟。

　　(B) 寺廟、商店、家裡。

　　(C) 車子裡、餐廳裡、新的商店。

　　(D) 私人住家、教堂、地獄之門。

　　* offering〔'ɔfərɪŋ〕*n.* 供品；祭品
　　　wedding〔'wɛdɪŋ〕*n.* 婚禮
　　　funeral〔'fjunərəl〕*n.* 葬禮

5. (**B**) 為什麼燈籠被設置在水邊？

　　(A) 引導口渴的鬼魂。

　　(B) 因為溺死的靈魂留在水裡。

　　(C) 有些鬼魂在死的時候是看不見的。

　　(D) 帶領鬼魂回到地獄。

　　* thirsty〔'θɝstɪ〕*adj.* 口渴的
　　　blind〔blaɪnd〕*adj.* 瞎的；失明的
　　　lead〔lid〕*v.* 帶領

TEST 16

Read the following passage and choose the best answer for each question.

Before the first book about Harry Potter was published in 2001, the single most popular fantasy series for children was C. S. Lewis's books about Narnia. The seven novels, set in the imaginary country of Narnia, can be enjoyed individually, but be warned: the more of them you read, the harder it is to stop! Even though they were written fifty years ago, they are still frequently named by critics as the best children's books ever written.

C. S. Lewis was a close friend of J. R. R. Tolkien, who wrote the Lord of the Rings series of books. It is probably the success of the Lord of the Rings movies that has brought the Narnia novels back into the spotlight. Indeed, the first movie in the series, based on the novel, *The Lion, the Witch, and the Wardrobe*, was released in 2005.

However, the Narnia books have much more in common with the Harry Potter books than with the Lord of the Rings books, which explore a totally imaginary world and tell the story of an epic journey. The Narnia books are set partly in the real world, and the heroes are all children. In Narnia, as in the Harry Potter books, the familiar meets the unfamiliar in continually surprising ways. 【中正高中】

1. The Narnia books _____.
   (A) are the most popular children's books after the Harry Potter books
   (B) can only be understood by reading from the first one to the last one
   (C) are no longer read because they are out of date
   (D) are still named as the best children's books ever written

2. The author's warning that "the more of them you read, the harder it is to stop" suggests that _____.
   (A) the stories in the Narnia books are fascinating
   (B) it is difficult to read the Narnia books
   (C) reading the Narnia books is time-consuming
   (D) readers should not read too much at a time when reading the Narnia books

3. The Narnia books and the Harry Potter books are similar in that _____.

   (A) their stories both involve the story of an epic journey
   (B) their characters are mythological heroes
   (C) their settings combine real and imaginary worlds
   (D) they were written at around the same time

4. According to the passage, _____.

   (A) the Harry Potter movies are more popular than the Lord of the Rings movies
   (B) the success of the Lord of the Rings movies probably made people notice the Narnia books again
   (C) no movie companies plan to film the Narnia books again
   (D) J. R. R. Tolkien turned the Narnia books into movies

5. What is true about the Narnia series?

   (A) It is one book divided into seven chapters.
   (B) Each of the books has been made into its own movie.
   (C) The books must be read in order to be understood.
   (D) *The Lion, the Witch, and the Wardrobe* was the first book written.

TEST 16 詳解

Before the first book about Harry Potter was published in 2001, the single most popular fantasy series for children was C. S. Lewis's books about Narnia. The seven novels, set in the imaginary country of Narnia, can be enjoyed individually, but be warned: the more of them you read, the harder it is to stop! Even though they were written fifty years ago, they are still frequently named by critics as the best children's books ever written.

在 2001 年第一本哈利波特書出版之前，最受歡迎的兒童奇幻文學系列，是 C. S. 路易斯所寫的納尼亞傳奇。這套七本小說場景設在虛構的納尼亞王國裡的，可以被個別閱讀，但要注意：「讀了越多本，就越難停下來！」即使它們是在五十年前寫的，但還是時常被評論家指名爲是有史以來最好的兒童讀物。

Harry Potter〔'hærɪ'patə〕*n.* 哈利・波特【英國作家 J. K. Rowling 所寫的奇幻文學小説，一系列共七冊，是史上最暢銷的系列小説】

publish〔'pʌblɪʃ〕*v.* 出版　　single〔'sɪŋgl〕*adj.* 單一的；獨一的

fantasy〔'fæntəsɪ〕*n.* 幻想的文學作品

series〔'sɪrɪz〕*n.* 系列刊物；叢書

C. S. Lewis〔'si'ɛs'luɪs〕*n.* C. S. 路易斯【1898-1963，納尼亞傳奇的作者，全名 Civil Staples Lewis】

Narnia〔'nɑr,nɪɑ〕*n.* 納尼亞傳奇【一套七冊的奇幻兒童文學，由英國作家 C. S. Lewis 在 1950 年代所著，故事中用不同的人物及動物角色，隱喻或譬喻聖經故事】

set〔sɛt〕*v.* 將（故事）定於（時代、國家）< *in* >

imaginary〔ɪ'mædʒə,nɛrɪ〕*adj.* 虛構的；想像的

individually〔,ɪndə'vɪdʒʊəlɪ〕*adv.* 個別地；單獨地

warn〔wɔrn〕*v.* 警告；提醒　　***even though*** 即使

frequently〔'frikwəntlɪ〕*adv.* 經常　　name〔nem〕*v.* 提名

critic〔'krɪtɪk〕*n.* 評論家；批評家

C. S. Lewis was a close friend of J. R. R. Tolkien, who wrote the Lord of the Rings series of books. It is probably the success of the Lord of the Rings movies that has brought the Narnia novels back into the spotlight. Indeed, the first movie in the series, based on the novel, *The Lion, the Witch, and the Wardrobe*, was released in 2005.

C. S. 路易斯是魔戒系列作者 J. R. R. 托爾金的摯友。很可能是因為魔戒電影成功,而將納尼亞傳奇帶回鎂光燈之下。的確,以小說為基礎的系列電影首部曲〈獅子、女巫、魔衣櫥〉,已在 2005 年上映。

close〔klos〕*adj.* 親密的
J. R. R. Tolkien〔'dʒe'ar'ar'tolkin〕*n.* J. R. R. 托爾金【1892-1973;
　　英國作家跟語言學家,全名 John Ronald Reuel Tolkien】
lord〔lɔrd〕*n.* 君主
the Lord of the Rings 魔戒【J. R. R. 托爾金所著的奇幻文學史詩三部
　　曲,1954 年出版第一冊之後大受歡迎,使得奇幻文學體裁迅速發展】
probably〔'prɑbəblɪ〕*adv.* 可能
spotlight〔'spɑt,laɪt〕*n.* 聚光燈;焦點　　indeed〔ɪn'did〕*adv.* 的確
film〔fɪlm〕*v.*(把小說)拍成電影　　witch〔wɪtʃ〕*n.* 女巫
wardrobe〔'wɔrd,rob〕*n.* 衣櫥
The Lion, the Witch, and the Wardrobe 獅子、女巫、魔衣櫥
　　【納尼亞傳奇系列的第一集】
release〔rɪ'lis〕*v.* 放映

However, the Narnia books have much more in common with the Harry Potter books than with the Lord of the Rings books, which explore a totally imaginary world and tell the story of an epic journey. The Narnia books are set partly in the real world, and the heroes are all children. In Narnia, as in the Harry Potter books, the familiar meets the unfamiliar in continually surprising ways.

　　然而，跟魔戒系列比較起來，納尼亞傳奇跟哈利波特系列有較多相似之處。魔戒是探險完全虛構的世界，訴說史詩般的長途歷程；納尼亞傳奇書中的場景部分設置在眞實世界，而書中英雄都是小孩。在納尼亞系列書中，就像哈利波特系列一樣，我們所熟知的跟未知的事物，不斷地以令人驚訝的方式交會。

> common〔ˋkɑmən〕*n.* 共同之處
>
> A *have much in common with* B　A 和 B 有很多相似之處
>
> explore〔ɪkˋsplor〕*v.* 探險　　totally〔ˋtotl̩ɪ〕*adv.* 完全地
>
> epic〔ˋɛpɪk〕*n.* 敘事詩般的長篇作品　　journey〔ˋdʒɝnɪ〕*n.* 旅程
>
> partly〔ˋpɑrtlɪ〕*adv.* 部分地　　familiar〔fəˋmɪljɚ〕*adj.* 熟悉的
>
> meet〔mit〕*v.* 遇見　　unfamiliar〔ˌʌnfəˋmɪljɚ〕*adj.* 不熟悉的
>
> continually〔kənˋtɪnjʊəlɪ〕*adv.* 持續地
>
> surprising〔səˋpraɪzɪŋ〕*adj.* 令人驚訝的

1. (**D**) 納尼亞系列書籍 ＿＿＿＿＿＿。

   (A) 是繼哈利波特叢書之後最受歡迎的童書

   (B) 從第一本讀到最後一本才能理解

   (C) 因爲過時所以不再被閱讀

   (D) 還是能被指名爲有史以來最棒的兒童讀物

   * *no longer* 不再　　*out of date* 過時的

2. (**A**) 作者警告：「你讀越多本，就越難停下來」暗示 ＿＿＿＿＿＿。

   (A) 納尼亞傳奇系列叢書很有吸引力

   (B) 納尼亞傳奇的書很不好讀

   (C) 看納尼亞傳奇的書很費時

   (D) 閱讀納尼亞傳奇時，不能一次讀太多篇幅

   * author〔ˋɔθɚ〕*n.* 作者　　warning〔ˋwɔrnɪŋ〕*n.* 警告
     suggest〔səgˋdʒɛst〕*v.* 暗示
     fascinating〔ˋfæsn̩ˌetɪŋ〕*adj.* 迷人的；很吸引人的
     consume〔kənˋsum〕*v.* 消耗　　*time-consuming* 費時的
     at a time 一次

3. (**C**) 納尼亞傳奇跟哈利波特書裡很相似因為 ＿＿＿＿＿＿＿＿＿。

    (A) 兩者故事都是關於一段史詩般的長途旅程

    (B) 兩者的角色都是神話般的英雄

    (C) 兩者的場景結合了現實跟虛構世界

    (D) 兩者都在大約相同的時間寫成

    * *in that* 因為   involve〔ɪnˈvɑlv〕*v.* 牽涉；與…有關
       character〔ˈkærɪktɚ〕*n.* 角色
       mythological〔ˌmɪθəˈlɑdʒɪkl̩〕*adj.* 神話般的
       setting〔ˈsɛtɪŋ〕*n.* 場景；背景
       combine〔kəmˈbaɪn〕*v.* 結合

4. (**B**) 根據本文，＿＿＿＿＿＿＿＿＿。

    (A) 哈利波特電影比魔戒電影更受歡迎

    (B) 魔戒電影的成功可能讓人們再次注意到納尼亞傳奇

    (C) 沒有電影公司計畫要再次拍攝納尼亞傳奇

    (D) J. R. R. 托爾金讓納尼亞傳奇的書變成電影

    * notice〔ˈnotɪs〕*v.* 注意   company〔ˈkʌmpənɪ〕*n.* 公司
    turn A ***into*** B 把 A 變成 B

5. (**D**) 關於納尼亞系列，何者為真？

    (A) 是一本被分為七個章節的書。

    (B) 每一本都各自被拍成電影。

    (C) 必須照順序讀才看得懂。

    (D) 第一本是《獅子、女巫、魔衣櫥》。

    * divide〔dɪˈvaɪd〕*v.* 分割；分開
       chapter〔ˈtʃæptɚ〕*n.* 章節
       order〔ˈɔrdɚ〕*n.* 順序   ***in order*** 按照順序

TEST 17

Read the following passage, and choose the best answer for each question.

Beware of those who use the truth to **deceive**. When someone tells you something that is true, but leaves out important information that should be included, he can create a false impression. For example, someone might say, "I just won a hundred dollars on the lottery. I took that dollar ticket back to the store and turned it in for one hundred dollars!" However, we then discover that he bought two hundred tickets, only one of which was a winner. He didn't say anything false, but he deliberately omitted important information. That's called a half-truth. Half-truths are not technically lies, but they are just as dishonest.

Untrustworthy candidates for political office often use this tactic. Let's say that during Governor Smith's last term, her state lost one million jobs and gained three million jobs. Then she seeks another term. One of her opponents runs an ad saying, "During Governor Smith's term, the state lost one million jobs!" That's true. However, an honest statement would have been, "During Governor Smith's term, the state had a net gain of two million jobs."

Advertisers will sometimes use half-truths. It's against the law to make false claims, so they try to mislead you with the truth. An ad might boast, "Nine out of ten doctors recommend Yucky Pills to cure nose pimples." It fails to mention that they only asked ten doctors and nine of them work for the Yucky Corporation.

This kind of deception happens too often. It's a sad fact of life: Lies are lies, and sometimes the truth can lie as well. 【師大附中】

1. Which statement is true according to the article?

(A) You can't trust gamblers.

(B) Whenever people tell the truth, they are really lying.

(C) All political figures lie to get elected.

(D) The truth can be used in dishonest ways.

2. What does the word "deceive" mean?

(A) persuade   (B) mislead

(C) ignore   (D) advise

3. What is the best title for the article?

(A) The Cure for Nose Pimples

(B) Lie to Survive

(C) Lying with the Truth

(D) People Lie by Nature

4. According to the article, when is a statement a half-truth?

(A) When it includes a lie.

(B) When it is a white lie.

(C) When it does not include all the facts.

(D) When someone misinterprets it.

5. What does the author imply in the last paragraph?

(A) Employees of a corporation are likely to have a favorable opinion of its products.

(B) The Yucky Corporation tested its pills on its own employees.

(C) The doctors at Yucky Corporation are not real doctors.

(D) There is no cure for nose pimples.

TEST 17 詳解

Beware of those who use the truth to **deceive**. When someone tells you something that is true, but leaves out important information that should be included, he can create a false impression. For example, someone might say, "I just won a hundred dollars on the lottery. I took that dollar ticket back to the store and turned it in for one hundred dollars!" However, we then discover that he bought two hundred tickets, only one of which was a winner. He didn't say anything false, but he deliberately omitted important information. That's called a half-truth. Half-truths are not technically lies, but they are just as dishonest.

要小心那些用眞相來欺騙別人的人。當有人告訴你眞實的事情,但是遺漏應該被包含在內的重要資訊,他可以創造出假象。例如,有人可能說:「我剛剛彩券贏了一百美金。我拿那張彩券到店裡,然後兌現了一百美金!」然而,我們後來發現他買了兩百張彩券,其中只有一張中獎。他沒有說假話,但他故意刪去了重要資訊。這就叫做部分眞相。部分眞相在嚴格來說並不算謊言,但也一樣不誠實。

beware〔bɪ'wɛr〕v. 小心;注意 < of >
truth〔truθ〕n. 眞相;事實　　deceive〔dɪ'siv〕v. 欺騙
leave out 略去;遺漏
information〔͵ɪnfɚ'meʃən〕n. 資訊;情報
include〔ɪn'klud〕v. 包含　　create〔krɪ'et〕v. 創造
false〔fɔls〕adj. 虛假的;錯誤的
impression〔ɪm'prɛʃən〕n. 印象;模糊的想法
lottery〔'lɑtərɪ〕n. 彩券　　ticket〔'tɪkɪt〕n. 票券;彩券
turn sth. **in** 將~提出交換 < for >　　discover〔dɪ'skʌvɚ〕v. 發現
winner〔'wɪnɚ〕n. 得獎者(物品)

deliberately〔dɪˈlɪbərɪtlɪ〕*adv.* 故意地
omit〔oˈmɪt〕*v.* 刪除
half-truth〔ˈhæfˈtruθ〕*n.* 半眞半假的陳述；部分眞相
technically〔ˈtɛknɪklɪ〕*adv.* 技術上地；嚴格來說
dishonest〔dɪsˈɑnɪst〕*adj.* 不誠實的；欺騙的

Untrustworthy candidates for political office often use this tactic. Let's say that during Governor Smith's last term, her state lost one million jobs and gained three million jobs. Then she seeks another term. One of her opponents runs an ad saying, "During Governor Smith's term, the state lost one million jobs!" That's true. However, an honest statement would have been, "During Governor Smith's term, the state had a net gain of two million jobs."

　　不值得信賴的政治候選人，經常使用這樣的策略。例如說在史密斯州長最後的任期之內，她的州裡少了一百萬個工作機會，但多了三百萬個工作機會，而她正尋求連任。她其中的一個敵手登廣告說：「在史密斯州長的任期內，州裡少了一百萬個工作機會！」這是正確的。然而誠實的說法應該是：「在史密斯州長的任期內，州裡總共獲得兩百萬個工作機會。」

untrustworthy〔ʌnˈtrʌst‚wɝðɪ〕*adj.* 不可信賴的；不可靠的
candidate〔ˈkændə‚det〕*n.* 候選人
political〔pəˈlɪtɪkl̩〕*adj.* 政治的　　office〔ˈɔfɪs〕*n.* 官職；公職
tactic〔ˈtæktɪk〕*n.* 策略；戰術　　*let's say* 假定；舉例來說
Governor〔ˈgʌvənɚ〕*n.* 州長
term〔tɝm〕*n.* 任期　　state〔stet〕*n.* 州
million〔ˈmɪljən〕*n.* 一百萬　　gain〔gen〕*v.* 獲得　*n.* 增加；獲得
opponent〔əˈponənt〕*n.* 對手；敵手　　run〔rʌn〕*v.* 刊登
ad〔æd〕*n.* 廣告　　honest〔ˈɑnɪst〕*adj.* 誠實的
statement〔ˈstetmənt〕*n.* 陳述；敘述
net〔nɛt〕*adj.* 淨的…；最終的

Advertisers will sometimes use half-truths. It's against the law to make false claims, so they try to mislead you with the truth. An ad might boast, "Nine out of ten doctors recommend Yucky Pills to cure nose pimples." It fails to mention that they only asked ten doctors and nine of them work for the Yucky Corporation.

廣告商有時會使用部分真相。謊報是違法的,所以廣告商試著用事實誤導你。廣告可能會自誇:「十位醫師中有九位都推薦優奇藥丸來治療鼻頭粉刺。」廣告中沒有提到說,他們只詢問了十位醫師,而其中九位是替優奇藥廠工作。

advertiser〔ˈædvɚˌtaɪzɚ〕*n.* 刊登廣告者　　claim〔klem〕*n.* 宣稱
mislead〔mɪsˈlid〕*v.* 誤導　　boast〔bost〕*v.* 自誇
recommend〔ˌrɛkəˈmɛnd〕*v.* 推薦　　pill〔pɪl〕*n.* 藥丸;藥品
Yucky Pill 優奇藥丸【藥名】　　cure〔kjur〕*v.* 治療;醫治
nose〔noz〕*n.* 鼻子　　pimple〔ˈpɪmpl̩〕*n.* 青春痘;粉刺
fail to V. 未能~　　mention〔ˈmɛnʃən〕*v.* 提到
corporation〔ˌkɔrpəˈreʃən〕*n.* 有限公司

This kind of deception happens too often. It's a sad fact of life: Lies are lies, and sometimes the truth can lie as well.

這類欺騙行為太常發生。生活中令人難過的事實是,謊言終歸是謊言,但有時真相也會說謊。

deception〔dɪˈsɛpʃən〕*n.* 欺騙;欺瞞　　*as well* 同樣地

1. (**D**) 關於本篇文章,下列敘述何者為真?
    (A) 你不可以相信投機商人。
    (B) 每當人們說真話時,他們其實是在說謊。
    (C) 所有政治人物都為了當選而說謊。
    (D) <u>真相能以不誠實的方法被使用。</u>

    * gambler〔ˈgæmblɚ〕*n.* 賭徒;投機商人
      figure〔ˈfɪgjɚ〕*n.* 人物　　elect〔ɪˈlɛkt〕*v.* 選舉

2. (**B**)　"deceive" 這個字的意思是什麼？

　　(A) 說服　　　(B) <u>誤導</u>　　　(C) 忽略　　　(D) 建議

　　* persuade〔pɚ'swed〕v. 說服
　　　ignore〔ɪg'nor〕v. 忽略
　　　advise〔əd'vaɪz〕v. 勸告

3. (**C**)　本篇文章最佳的標題是什麼？

　　(A) 鼻頭粉刺的療法　　　　(B) 說謊才能生存
　　(C) <u>用真相說謊</u>　　　　　(D) 人們天生會說謊

　　* survive〔sə'vaɪv〕v. 生存　　　lying〔'laɪɪŋ〕n. 說謊
　　　by nature 天性；天生

4. (**C**)　根據本文，何種情況是部分真實的敘述？

　　(A) 當敘述包含謊言。
　　(B) 當敘述是善意的謊言。
　　(C) <u>當敘述裡沒有囊括所有事實。</u>
　　(D) 當人誤解了這個敘述。

　　* ***white lie*** 善意的謊言　　　misinterpret〔ˌmɪsɪn'tɝprɪt〕v. 誤解

5. (**A**)　在最後一段，作者暗指什麼？

　　(A) <u>公司的雇員可能會對自家產品有好評。</u>
　　(B) 優奇公司在自己的員工身上試驗藥丸。
　　(C) 優奇公司的醫生不是真的醫生。
　　(D) 鼻頭粉刺沒有療法。

　　* imply〔ɪm'plaɪ〕v. 暗指；暗示
　　　employee〔ˌɛmplɔɪ'i〕n. 雇員　　　***be likely to V.*** 可能會~
　　　favorable〔'fevrəbḷ〕adj. 有利的；贊成的
　　　opinion〔ə'pɪnɪən〕n. 意見　　　test〔tɛst〕v. 做試驗

TEST 18

Read the following passage and choose the best answer for each question.

The quest for food has shaped the development of our society. In his search for sustenance, man has influenced population growth and urban expansion, has dictated economic and political theory, and has inspired wars. Food and the science of food touch our lives in numerous ways. Many religions follow strict dietary laws. Some of the earliest observations in the world of chemistry came from the preparation and cooking of food. Food has influenced technology, too. The water wheel, developed for the milling of grain, became a primary tool during the Industrial Revolution. Even class distinctions in some societies are determined by what foods are put on the table.

The necessity for convenience foods during travel fostered their development in the 1700s. Sea travel posed special problems, since ships needed to carry men, cargo and ammunition, in addition to food and water. The staple food item was the sea biscuit, made with flour and water, but the biscuits proved inedible to all but the weevils that took up residence in them. The dried, salted meats that were offered to the sailors were inedible, but proved to be the perfect substance for carving intricate trinkets and snuff boxes.

After months of sea travel, without any fresh fruits or vegetables, an epidemic of scurvy developed on most ships. This disease was characterized by bleeding and swollen gums, and many died of starvation. Although the treatment was soon discovered, it took many years for officials to approve fresh fruit and vegetable rations, deeming them too expensive. By the 1700's, the British navy accepted the notion that citrus could prevent and treat scurvy, and lemon and lime juice rations were added to the diet.

The Industrial Revolution changed the availability, distribution and production of food like never before. The 19th century brought with it huge growth in towns (the population of New York multiplied 80 times between 1800 and 1900), and expansion of roads and railways. Interestingly, this period also brought the first food **adulteration**. With a rapidly increasing population, the food industry had a difficult time dealing with shortages of materials and, in an effort to keep costs down, bulked up food items with questionable additional substances. Tea was a particular target for adulteration because the taxes were so high — street cleaners collected used tea leaves from restaurant trash bins, and the leaves were dried, stiffened with a gum solution, and then dyed with black lead.

These days we are hard pressed to imagine life without a variety of foods, preservatives, transportation, tools, and microwaves. In addition, we are now offered new sweeteners, new fat substitutes, juice boxes, aseptic meat packages, freeze dried items and "functional foods". Manufacturers and food technologists are scrambling to provide what consumers want most — taste, cost, and convenience. No doubt, the technological explosion will continue to affect why we eat what we eat. 【北一女中】

1. Which of the following statements **didn't** affect the production of food during the Industrial Revolution?
   (A) The rapid growth of the population.
   (B) The delicate packaging of tea leaves.
   (C) The desire to lower food prices.
   (D) The improvement of transportation systems.

2. The article says that food technologists and manufacturers seek to provide consumers with

   _____.

   (A) satisfaction, warmth, and hospitality
   (B) sweeteners, fat substitutes and juice boxes
   (C) preservatives, microwaves, and canned foods
   (D) cost, taste, and convenience

3. What is the passage about?

   (A) The important role of the diet in sea travel.

   (B) The relationship between civilization and food.

   (C) Primary tools of different eras.

   (D) The influence of manufacturers on consumption habits.

4. According to the passage, what should sailors eat to avoid developing scurvy?

   (A) water

   (B) muffins

   (C) bacon

   (D) oranges

5. As used in paragraph 3, line 4, the word "adulteration" refers to _____.

   (A) raising the value of the product

   (B) improving the flavor of the food

   (C) adding impurities to food

   (D) avoiding high taxes

TEST 18 詳解

The quest for food has shaped the development of our society. In his search for sustenance, man has influenced population growth and urban expansion, has dictated economic and political theory, and has inspired wars. Food and the science of food touch our lives in numerous ways. Many religions follow strict dietary laws. Some of the earliest observations in the world of chemistry came from the preparation and cooking of food. Food has influenced technology, too. The water wheel, developed for the milling of grain, became a primary tool during the Industrial Revolution. Even class distinctions in some societies are determined by what foods are put on the table.

對食物的追尋,形塑了我們社會的發展。人類找尋食物的過程,影響了人口成長以及都市擴張,提出經濟跟政治理論,也激發戰爭。食物跟食品科技在很多方面,都與我們的生活有所接觸。許多宗教遵循嚴格的飲食戒律。某些化學界最早期的發現,來自於準備跟烹調食物。食物也影響了科技。為了輾磨穀物所發明的水車,成為工業革命時期的主要工具。甚至某些社會中的階級分野,同樣由桌上的食物所決定。

quest〔kwɛst〕*n.* 追求;探求　　shape〔ʃep〕*v.* 塑造
development〔dɪ'vɛləpmənt〕*n.* 發展　　society〔sə'saɪətɪ〕*n.* 社會
search〔sɝtʃ〕*n.* 搜尋　　***in the search for*** 尋找…;尋求…
sustenance〔'sʌstənəns〕*n.* 食物;維持生命的東西;營養物
man〔mæn〕*n.* 人類　　population〔ˌpɑpjə'leʃən〕*n.* 人口
growth〔groθ〕*n.* 成長　　urban〔'ɝbən〕*adj.* 都市的
expansion〔ɪk'spænʃən〕*n.* 擴張
dictate〔'dɪktet〕*v.* 強制規定;決定
economic〔ˌikə'nɑmɪk〕*adj.* 經濟的
political〔pə'lɪtɪkḷ〕*adj.* 政治的　　theory〔'θiərɪ〕*n.* 理論
inspire〔ɪn'spaɪr〕*v.* 激發;激勵　　touch〔tʌtʃ〕*v.* 接觸

numerous〔'njumrəs〕*adj.* 許多的　　religion〔rɪ'lɪdʒən〕*n.* 宗教
follow〔'falo〕*v.* 遵守　　strict〔strɪkt〕*adj.* 嚴格的
dietary〔'daɪə,tɛrɪ〕*adj.* 飲食的　　law〔lɔ〕*n.* 戒律
observation〔,ɑbzɚ'veʃən〕*n.* 觀察；觀測結果
world〔wɝld〕*n.* …界　　chemistry〔'kɛmɪstrɪ〕*n.* 化學
come from 來自於　　preparation〔,prɛpə'reʃən〕*n.* 準備
cooking〔'kʊkɪŋ〕*n.* 烹調　　technology〔tɛk'nɑlədʒɪ〕*n.* 科技
water wheel 灌溉用水車　　milling〔'mɪlɪŋ〕*n.* 磨製成粉
grain〔gren〕*n.* 穀物　　primary〔'praɪ,mɛrɪ〕*adj.* 主要的
industrial〔ɪn'dʌstrɪəl〕*adj.* 工業的
revolution〔,rɛvə'luʃən〕*n.* 革命
the Industrial Revolution 工業革命　　class〔klæs〕*n.* 階級
distinction〔dɪ'stɪŋkʃən〕*n.* 區別；特性
determine〔dɪ't3mɪn〕*v.* 決定

The necessity for convenience foods during travel fostered their development in the 1700s. Sea travel posed special problems, since ships needed to carry men, cargo and ammunition, in addition to food and water. The staple food item was the sea biscuit, made with flour and water, but the biscuits proved inedible to all but the weevils that took up residence in them. The dried, salted meats that were offered to the sailors were inedible, but proved to be the perfect substance for carving intricate trinkets and snuff boxes.

　　對旅行中的便利食品的需求，在 1970 年代加速了這些食品的發展。海上的旅行引起特殊的問題，因為船隻需要載運人、貨物、軍火，除此之外還有食物跟水。海上主食是由麵粉跟水作成，可以長久保存的硬麵包，但是硬麵包被證實，除了住在裡面的象鼻蟲之外，對所有人來說，都是不可食用的。供給水手的鹹肉乾雖然不能吃，但被證實是用來雕刻複雜的小飾品，或鼻煙盒的絕佳物品。

necessity〔nə'sɛsətɪ〕*n.* 必要；需要
convenience food 便利食品【冷凍或是真空包裝的簡單速食】
foster〔'fɔstɚ〕*v.* 促進；助長　　pose〔poz〕*v.* 引起（問題）

cargo〔ˈkɑrgo〕*n.* 貨物　　ammunition〔ˌæmjəˈnɪʃən〕*n.* 軍火；彈藥
in addition to 除了…之外還有　　staple〔ˈstepḷ〕*adj.* 主要的
staple food 主食　　item〔ˈaɪtəm〕*n.* 項目；品目
biscuit〔ˈbɪskɪt〕*n.* 餅乾；小甜麵包
sea biscuit （可以永久儲藏的）硬麵包　　flour〔flaʊr〕*n.* 麵粉
prove〔pruv〕*v.* 證實（為…）；（結果）成為
inedible〔ɪnˈɛdəbḷ〕*adj.* 不能吃的　　weevil〔ˈwivḷ〕*n.* 象鼻蟲
take up 佔用（地方）　　residence〔ˈrɛzədəns〕*n.* 居住
dried〔draɪd〕*adj.* 乾燥的　　salted〔ˈsɔltɪd〕*adj.* 用鹽調味的
offer〔ˈɔfɚ〕*v.* 提供　　sailor〔ˈselɚ〕*n.* 水手
substance〔ˈsʌbstəns〕*n.* 物質　　carve〔kɑrv〕*v.* 雕刻
intricate〔ˈɪntrəkɪt〕*adj.* 複雜的　　trinket〔ˈtrɪŋkɪt〕*n.* 小飾品
snuff〔snʌf〕*n.* 鼻煙　　***snuff box*** 鼻煙盒

After months of sea travel, without any fresh fruits or vegetables, an epidemic of scurvy developed on most ships. This disease was characterized by bleeding and swollen gums, and many died of starvation. Although the treatment was soon discovered, it took many years for officials to approve fresh fruit and vegetable rations, deeming them too expensive. By the 1700's, the British navy accepted the notion that citrus could prevent and treat scurvy, and lemon and lime juice rations were added to the diet.

在海上航行數個月後，因為缺乏新鮮蔬菜跟水果，幾乎每艘船上都出現一種具傳染性的壞血病。這種疾病的特徵是會流血，及牙齦腫脹，而且很多人死於飢餓。即使治療方法很快就被發現，政府官員認為蔬菜水果價格高昂，所以很多年以後，才同意蔬菜跟水果的海上糧食配給。到了十八世紀，英國海軍接受了柑橘類食物可以預防並治療壞血病的觀念，把檸檬跟萊姆汁等配糧加進飲食中。

epidemic〔ˌɛpəˈdɛmɪk〕*adj.* 流行（病）的；傳染的
scurvy〔ˈskɝvɪ〕*n.* 壞血病　　develop〔dɪˈvɛləp〕*v.*（症狀）顯現
be characterized by 以…為特徵；特色是…
bleeding〔ˈblidɪŋ〕*n.* 放血；流血　　swollen〔ˈswolən〕*adj.* 腫大的
gum〔gʌm〕*n.* 牙齦　　starvation〔stɑrˈveʃən〕*n.* 飢餓

treatment〔'tritmənt〕*n.* 治療法　　official〔ə'fɪʃəl〕*n.* 政府官員
approve〔ə'pruv〕*v.* 同意；贊成
ration〔'ræʃən〕*n.* 配給　　deem〔dim〕*v.* 認為
British〔'brɪtɪʃ〕*adj.* 英國的　　navy〔'nevɪ〕*n.* 海軍
notion〔'noʃən〕*n.* 觀念
citrus〔'sɪtrəs〕*n.* 柑橘類植物　　prevent〔prɪ'vɛnt〕*v.* 預防
treat〔trit〕*v.* 治療　　lemon〔'lɛmən〕*n.* 檸檬
lime〔laɪm〕*n.* 萊姆　　***add* A *to* B** 把 A 加在 B 之上

The Industrial Revolution changed the availability, distribution
and production of food like never before. The 19th century brought
with it huge growth in towns (the population of New York multiplied
80 times between 1800 and 1900), and expansion of roads and
railways. Interestingly, this period also brought the first food
adulteration. With a rapidly increasing population, the food
industry had a difficult time dealing with shortages of materials
and, in an effort to keep costs down, bulked up food items with
questionable additional substances. Tea was a particular target
for adulteration because the taxes were so high — street cleaners
collected used tea leaves from restaurant trash bins, and the leaves
were dried, stiffened with a gum solution, and then dyed with black
lead.

　　工業革命前所未有地改變了食品的可得性、分配跟生產。十九世紀帶
來了城市大幅的成長（紐約的人口在 1800 年到 1900 年之間，增加了八十
倍），和道路、鐵路的擴張。有趣的是，這段期間也首次出現食物劣質品。
隨著人口的迅速增加，食品工業很難去處理材料短缺的問題，為了努力降
低成本，所以用有問題的添加物，來增大食品體積。茶葉是劣質食品中，
格外顯著的目標，因為茶葉稅非常地高。清道夫會從餐廳垃圾桶裡，蒐集
已經使用過的茶葉，將它烘乾，用膠質溶液使它變硬，然後再用黑色的鉛
將它染色。

availability〔ə͵velə'bɪlətɪ〕*n.* 可用；可得到

distribution〔͵dɪstrə'bjuʃən〕*n.* 分配；配給

production〔prə'dʌkʃən〕*n.* 生產；製造

multiply〔'mʌltə͵plaɪ〕*v.* 增加　　time〔taɪm〕*n.* 倍

railway〔'rel͵we〕*n.* 鐵路

interestingly〔'ɪntərɪstɪŋlɪ〕*adv.* 有趣地　　period〔'pɪrɪəd〕*n.* 期間

adulteration〔ə͵dʌltə'reʃən〕*n.* 降低品質的粗劣品；成分不純的低劣品

rapidly〔'ræpɪdlɪ〕*adv.* 迅速地

increasing〔ɪn'krisɪŋ〕*adj.* 逐漸增加的

industry〔'ɪndəstrɪ〕*n.* 工業；產業

have a difficult time V-ing 做～事感到困難

deal with 處理　　shortage〔'ʃɔrtɪdʒ〕*n.* 短缺；不足

material〔mə'tɪrɪəl〕*n.* 材料　　cost〔kɔst〕*n.* 成本；花費

bulk〔bʌlk〕*v.* 使（體積）漲大＜*up*＞

questionable〔'kwɛstʃənəbl̩〕*adj.* 可疑的；有問題的

additional〔ə'dɪʃənl̩〕*adj.* 添加的；額外的

particular〔pə'tɪkjələ〕*adj.* 特別的；特定的

target〔'tɑrgɪt〕*n.* 目標　　tax〔tæks〕*n.* 稅金

cleaner〔'klinə〕*n.* 清潔工　　used〔juzd〕*adj.* 用過的

leaves〔livz〕*n. pl.* 葉子　　bin〔bɪn〕*n.* 大箱

trash bin 垃圾桶　　stiffen〔'stɪfən〕*v.* 使變硬

gum〔gʌm〕*n.* 膠水；膠質　　solution〔sə'luʃən〕*n.* 溶液

dye〔daɪ〕*v.* 染色　　lead〔lɛd〕*n.* 鉛

These days we are hard pressed to imagine life without a variety of foods, preservatives, transportation, tools, and microwaves. In addition, we are now offered new sweeteners, new fat substitutes, juice boxes, aseptic meat packages, freeze dried items and "functional foods". Manufacturers and food technologists are scrambling to provide what consumers want most — taste, cost, and convenience. No doubt, the technological explosion will continue to affect why we eat what we eat.

　　現在我們很難去想像生活中缺少各式各樣的食品、防腐劑、交通工具、各種器具跟微波。此外，我們現在也有新的人工甘味料、新脂肪替代品、盒裝果汁、無菌肉類包裝、冷凍乾燥產品，以及「功能性保健食品」。製造商跟食品科技學家，爭相提供消費者最想要的東西——好味道、低價格，便利性。無疑地，科技突飛猛進，影響我們為什麼會吃我們所吃的東西。

hard〔hɑrd〕*adv.* 困難地　　press〔prɛs〕*v.* 強迫
be hard pressed to V. 很難去做～；做～陷於窘境
imagine〔ɪ'mædʒɪn〕*v.* 想像　　***a variety of*** 各式各樣的
preservative〔prɪ'zɝvətɪv〕*n.* 防腐劑
transportation〔ˌtrænspɚ'teʃən〕*n.* 運輸工具
microwave〔'maɪkrəˌwev〕*n.* 微波　　***in addition*** 此外
sweetener〔'switn̩ɚ〕*n.* 人工甘味料　　fat〔fæt〕*n.* 脂肪
substitute〔'sʌbstəˌtjut〕*n.* 替代品　　aseptic〔ə'sɛptɪk〕*adj.* 無菌的
package〔'pækɪdʒ〕*n.* 包裝　　freeze〔friz〕*n.* 冷凍；結冰
functional〔'fʌŋkʃən̩l〕*adj.* 功能性的
functional food 功能性保健食品
manufacturer〔ˌmænjə'fæktʃərɚ〕*n.* 製造商
technologist〔tɛk'nɑlədʒɪst〕*n.* 科學技術專家
scramble〔'skræmbl̩〕*v.* 爭搶　　provide〔prə'vaɪd〕*v.* 提供
consumer〔kən'sumɚ〕*n.* 消費者　　taste〔test〕*n.* 味道
no doubt 無疑地　　technological〔ˌtɛknə'lɑdʒɪkl̩〕*adj.* 科技的
explosion〔ɪk'sploʒən〕*n.* 爆炸性的增加
affect〔ə'fɛkt〕*v.* 影響

1.(**B**) 下列敘述何者「沒有」在工業革命的時候影響食品生產？

(A) 人口急遽增加。　　　　(B) 精緻的茶葉包裝。
(C) 對於低食品價格的渴望。　(D) 交通運輸系統的進步。

　* delicate〔'dɛləkət〕*adj.* 精緻的　　desire〔dɪ'zaɪr〕*n.* 渴望
　　packaging〔'pækɪdʒɪŋ〕*n.* 包裝
　　improvement〔ɪn'pruvmənt〕*n.* 進步

2. (**D**) 本文提到，食品科技專家跟製造商找尋方法提供 ＿＿＿＿＿＿＿＿＿＿
給消費者。

(A) 滿足、溫暖，和慷慨

(B) 人工甘味料、脂肪替代品，和盒裝果汁

(C) 防腐劑、微波，和罐裝食物

(D) 低價格、好口味，和便利性

* seek〔sik〕v. 找尋（方法）
satisfaction〔ˌsætɪsˈfækʃən〕n. 滿足
warmth〔wɔrmθ〕n. 溫暖
hospitality〔ˌhɑspɪˈtælətɪ〕n. 款待；慷慨
canned〔kænd〕adj. 罐裝的

3. (**B**) 本文主題是關於什麼？

(A) 航海時飲食扮演的重要角色。

(B) 文明跟食物之間的關係。 (C) 不同年代的主要工具。

(D) 製造商對消費習慣的影響。

* relationship〔rɪˈleʃənˌʃɪp〕n. 關係
civilization〔ˌsɪvḷəˈzeʃən〕n. 文明 era〔ˈɪrə〕n. 年代
consumption〔kənˈsʌmpʃən〕n. 消費

4. (**D**) 根據本文，水手們應該吃什麼來避免罹患壞血症？

(A) 水 (B) 馬芬

(C) 培根 (D) 橘子

* muffin〔ˈmʌfɪn〕n. 馬芬；鬆餅；杯狀甜蛋糕
bacon〔ˈbekən〕n. 培根

5. (**C**) 在第三段第七行中 "adulteration" 這個字的意思是 ＿＿＿＿＿＿＿＿＿＿。

(A) 提高產品價值 (B) 增加食物香氣

(C) 在食物中添加混雜物 (D) 避免高額稅金

*raise〔rez〕v. 提高 product〔ˈprɑdəkt〕n. 產品
improve〔ɪmˈpruv〕v. 增加 flavor〔ˈflevɚ〕n. 香氣；味道
impurity〔ɪmˈpjurətɪ〕n. 混雜物

TEST 19

Read the following passage and choose the best answer for each question.

Sports have always been ruled by the weather. Rain, sleet, snow, and cold called the plays. Baseball fans often sat in the rain without cover, waiting for the sun to come out and the game to begin. Football lovers sometimes took days to warm up after sitting through a freezing cold Sunday game. For both sports fans and players, the domed stadium was like something out of a dream. A huge **plastic bubble** kept out rain and snow. There was heat to keep things comfortable year round.

Domed stadiums have clearly changed the course of sports. Still, they did have their problems at first. Most of these problems were discovered and solved at the Houston Astrodome. This was the world's first stadium with a lid. For the fans, it was great. But there were some problems for the players. Baseball outfielders had the most difficult time. They had to learn to catch in a field with a roof. At first this was almost as difficult as playing in the dark. The panes of the roof were light colored to let sunlight in. Sunlight was needed to keep the grass on the field alive. But the light roof blended too well with the white baseball.

Fly balls seemed to drop out of nowhere. Even skilled fielders were making errors. Finally, the decision was made to paint the panes of the roof dark. The problem was solved. What about the grass? Well, the real grass was dug up and replaced with artificial turf! 【明倫高中】

1. Which of the following is TRUE?
   (A) Domed stadiums had all of their problems solved at Houston Astrodome.
   (B) The Houston Astrodome was the first stadium in the world.
   (C) Sunlight was necessary for the artificial turf on the stadium field to grow.
   (D) Even skilled fielders had to learn to catch in a field with a roof.

2. According to the passage, why did the outfielders have the most difficult time with the domed stadium? Because
   (A) they couldn't change the course of sports.
   (B) they couldn't see fly balls against the light roof.
   (C) they couldn't run on artificial turf.
   (D) they couldn't see in the dark.

3. What does "**plastic bubble**" in line 5 refer to?

   (A) a baseball or football

   (B) the fans and the players

   (C) the roof of a stadium

   (D) rain and snow

4. What does the article imply about football?

   (A) It is a snow sport.

   (B) It is always played on Sunday.

   (C) It is often played in the winter.

   (D) It cannot be played indoors.

5. What do rain, sleet, snow, and cold have in common?

   (A) They are all forms of precipitation.

   (B) They can all be found at domed stadiums.

   (C) They are necessary sports conditions.

   (D) They are all adverse weather conditions.

TEST 19 詳解

Sports have always been ruled by the weather. Rain, sleet, snow, and cold called the plays. Baseball fans often sat in the rain without cover, waiting for the sun to come out and the game to begin. Football lovers sometimes took days to warm up after sitting through a freezing cold Sunday game. For both sports fans and players, the domed stadium was like something out of a dream. A huge **plastic bubble** kept out rain and snow. There was heat to keep things comfortable year round.

運動比賽總是被天氣所左右。雨水、凍雨、下雪，跟寒冷會讓比賽中止，棒球迷常常毫無遮蔽地坐在雨中，等待太陽出現，等待比賽開始。美式足球愛好者在非常冷的天氣中，坐著看完週日比賽後，有時要花好幾天來讓身體回暖。對於球迷跟球員來說，圓頂巨蛋簡直像從夢中出現的事物。一個巨型塑膠製的圓頂將雨雪阻擋在外，還有整年供應暖氣，讓裡面一切都很舒服。

sports〔sports〕*n. pl.* 運動；競賽　　rule〔rul〕*v.* 支配；控制
sleet〔slit〕*n.* 凍雨【雨中夾帶著雪】
call〔kɔl〕*v.* (因下雨、天候等) 使比賽中止
fan〔fæn〕*n.* 迷；支持者
cover〔'kʌvɚ〕*n.* 遮蔽物　　football〔'fʊt,bɔl〕*n.* 美式足球
lover〔'lʌvɚ〕*n.* 愛好者　　***warm up*** 使身體溫暖
freezing〔'frizɪŋ〕*adj.* 嚴寒的；極冷的
player〔'pleɚ〕*n.* 運動員　　domed〔domd〕*adj.* 有圓形屋頂的
stadium〔'stedɪəm〕*n.* 體育場
domed stadium 圓頂體育場；巨蛋
plastic〔'plæstɪk〕*adj.* 塑膠 (製) 的　　bubble〔'bʌbḷ〕*n.* 透明圓頂
keep out 將…阻擋在外　　heat〔hit〕*n.* 暖氣

Domed stadiums have clearly changed the course of sports. Still, they did have their problems at first. Most of these problems were discovered and solved at the Houston Astrodome. This was the world's first stadium with a lid. For the fans, it was great. But there were some problems for the players.

圓頂巨蛋顯著地改變了運動的發展。但它們起初也有些問題。大部分問題都在休士頓圓頂棒球場被發現，也被解決。這是世界上第一個有蓋的體育場。對於球迷來說，這真是太棒了。但是對球員來說，卻有某些困難。

course〔kors〕*n.* 發展；過程　　***at first*** 起初；一開始
discover〔dɪˈskʌvɚ〕*v.* 發現　　solve〔sɑlv〕*v.* 解決
Houston〔ˈhjustən〕*n.* 休士頓【美國德州的城市名】
Astrodome〔ˈæstroˌdom〕*n.* 天文觀測窗
the Houston Astrodome 休士頓市的圓頂棒球場
lid〔lɪd〕*n.* 蓋子

Baseball outfielders had the most difficult time. They had to learn to catch in a field with a roof. At first this was almost as difficult as playing in the dark. The panes of the roof were light colored to let sunlight in. Sunlight was needed to keep the grass on the field alive. But the light roof blended too well with the white baseball. Fly balls seemed to drop out of nowhere. Even skilled fielders were making errors. Finally, the decision was made to paint the panes of the roof dark. The problem was solved. What about the grass? Well, the real grass was dug up and replaced with artificial turf!

棒球外野手所經歷的問題最大。他們必須要學習在有屋頂的場上接球。起初，這就像在黑暗中打球一樣困難。屋頂嵌版的顏色明亮，讓陽光能透進來，場上的綠草必須要有陽光才能生存。但明亮屋頂跟白色的球兩者融合得太好了，高飛球就像不知從哪個地方突然墜落一樣，即使是老練的野手也會失誤。最後決定把屋頂嵌版漆成深色，這樣問題就解決了。可是那綠草怎麼辦呢？嗯，真正的草被連根挖起，然後被人造草皮所取代！

outfielder (ˈaʊtˌfildɚ) *n.* 外野手

roof (ruf) *n.* 屋頂

pane (pen) *n.* 嵌版；窗玻璃

light (laɪt) *adv.* 明亮地　　color (ˈkʌlɚ) *v.* 著色；塗上顏色

sunlight (ˈsʌnˌlaɪt) *n.* 陽光

alive (əˈlaɪv) *adj.* 活的

blend (blɛnd) *v.* 調和；融入

fly ball 高飛球　　drop (drɑp) *v.* 突然下降

nowhere (ˈnoˌhwɛr) *n.* 無人知道的地方

skilled (skɪld) *adj.* 經驗老到的

fielder (ˈfildɚ) *n.* 野手

error (ˈɛrɚ) *n.* 錯誤

dig up 挖起　　replace (rɪˈples) *v.* 取代

artificial (ˌɑrtəˈfɪʃəl) *adj.* 人造的

turf (tɝf) *n.* 草皮　　*artificial turf* 人工草皮

1. (**D**) 下列何者為真？

(A) 休士頓圓頂棒球場把所有圓頂巨蛋的問題都解決了。

(B) 休士頓圓頂棒球場是世界上第一個體育場。

(C) 體育場上的人工草皮需要陽光才能生長。

(D) 即使經驗老到的野手也要學習如何在有屋頂的場上接球。

2. (**B**) 根據本文，為什麼外野手在圓頂巨蛋中經歷到最大的難題？

因為 ＿＿＿＿＿＿＿＿。

(A) 外野手無法改變運動的發展

(B) <u>外野手無法在明亮的屋頂下看見高飛球</u>

(C) 外野手無法在人造草皮上奔跑

(D) 外野手在黑暗中看不見

3. (**C**) 第八行的 "plastic bubble" 指的是什麼？

(A) 一顆棒球或足球　　　(B) 球迷跟球員

(C) <u>體育場的屋頂</u>　　　(D) 雨跟雪

　* ***refer to*** 是指

4. (**C**) 關於美式足球，本文中暗示什麼？

(A) 是一種雪上運動。

(B) 總是在週日比賽。

(C) <u>經常在冬天比賽。</u>

(D) 不能在室內比賽。

　* imply〔ɪm'plaɪ〕*v.* 暗示　　indoors〔'ɪn'dorz〕*adv.* 在室內

5. (**D**) 雨水、凍雨、雪、跟寒冷的共同點為何？

(A) 它們都是某種降水形式。

(B) 它們都能在圓頂巨蛋中被找到。

(C) 它們都是運動比賽中必要的情況。

(D) <u>它們都是不好的天氣狀況。</u>

　* ***in common*** 共同的

　　precipitation〔prɪ,sɪpə'teʃən〕*n.* 降雨（量）；下雪

　　condition〔kən'dɪʃən〕*n.* 情況

　　adverse〔əd'vɝs〕*adj.* 不利的

TEST 20

Read the following passage and choose the best answer for each question.

Studies point out that stress is a major obstacle to effective learning. Therefore, the ability to relax is just as important to success in school as the ability to read. Too much stress may cause students to forget chapters they have read, to "go blank" at quiz time, or to fail to meet deadlines and to complete assignments on schedule. However, any student can learn to rid himself of stress by resting the body, breathing slowly and deeply, and relaxing for three to four minutes before a test. Besides, attention to details such as outlining, note taking, and time scheduling can also help relieve stress and free mental energy to work on the tasks of learning. Finally, planning one day ahead on a pocket calendar can actually do more to improve the grades of some students than any memory or speed-reading course. 【恆毅高中】

1. In this passage, "to 'go blank' at quiz time" means
   _____.

   (A) to complete the quiz
   (B) to forget everything when taking the quiz
   (C) to take a rest at the quiz time
   (D) to give wrong answers to the quiz questions

2. Some suggestions are made to alleviate stress but they
   do NOT include _____.

   (A) breathing deeply
   (B) noticing details
   (C) taking speed-reading courses
   (D) planning beforehand

3. The author of this passage suggests that stress

   _____.

   (A) will affect our memory power
   (B) is something we can never get rid of
   (C) occurs when we fail to meet deadlines
   (D) makes us attentive to details

4. According to the passage, which of the following
   statements is true?

   (A) Improving reading ability can relieve stress.
   (B) The ability to read is the only decisive factor in
       academic success.
   (C) Stress can stimulate students to study hard.
   (D) The key to success is to cope with stress well.

5. What would the author most likely advise a student to
   do right before a test?

   (A) Take careful notes.
   (B) Forget about reading chapters and just outline them.
   (C) Take a break and relax.
   (D) Hold the breath for as long as possible.

TEST 20 詳解

Studies point out that stress is a major obstacle to effective learning. Therefore, the ability to relax is just as important to success in school as the ability to read. Too much stress may cause students to forget chapters they have read, to "go blank" at quiz time, or to fail to meet deadlines and to complete assignments on schedule.

研究指出，壓力是有效學習的主要阻礙。因此，要在學業上成功的話，放鬆的能力，就跟閱讀能力一樣重要。過多壓力可能導致學生忘記所讀過的章節，在小考時腦袋一片空白，或是無法趕上截止時間，以及無法準時地完成指定作業。

study (ˈstʌdɪ) *n.* 研究　　***point out*** 指出
stress (strɛs) *n.* 壓力
major (ˈmedʒɚ) *adj.* 主要的　　obstacle (ˈɑbstəkḷ) *n.* 障礙 < *to* >
effective (əˈfɛktɪv) *adj.* 有效的　　ability (əˈbɪlətɪ) *n.* 能力
relax (rɪˈlæks) *v.* 放鬆　　cause (kɔz) *v.* 引起；導致
chapter (ˈtʃæptɚ) *n.* 章節　　blank (blæŋk) *adj.* 空白的；茫然的
go blank （腦袋）變空白　　quiz (kwɪz) *n.* 小考
fail to V. 未能～　　deadline (ˈdɛd͵laɪn) *n.* 最後期限
meet the deadline 趕上截止日期　　complete (kəmˈplit) *v.* 完成
assignment (əˈsaɪnmənt) *n.* 作業
schedule (ˈskɛdʒul) *n.* 時間表　　***on schedule*** 按照時間表；準時

However, any student can learn to rid himself of stress by resting the body, breathing slowly and deeply, and relaxing for three to four minutes before a test. Besides, attention to details such as outlining, note taking, and time scheduling can also help relieve stress and free mental energy to work on the tasks of learning.

然而，每個學生都能藉由讓身體休養、緩慢地深呼吸、在考前三到四分鐘放鬆，來學會如何擺脫壓力。除此之外，對於注意細節，像是畫出要點、作筆記、跟安排時間，都能幫助減輕壓力，釋放心理能量，來繼續學習。

rid〔rɪd〕*v.* 除去　　***rid sb. of*** … 使某人擺脫…
rest〔rɛst〕*v.* 休息；靜養　　breathe〔brið〕*v.* 呼吸
deeply〔'diplɪ〕*adv.* 深深地　　attention〔ə'tɛnʃən〕*n.* 注意力
detail〔'ditel〕*n.* 細節　　outline〔'aʊt,laɪn〕*v.* 畫出要點
note〔not〕*n.* 筆記　　***note-taking*** 作筆記
time scheduling 安排時間　　relieve〔rɪ'liv〕*v.* 減輕；緩和
free〔fri〕*v.* 使自由；釋放　　mental〔'mɛntḷ〕*adj.* 心理的
energy〔'ɛnədʒɪ〕*n.* 能量；精力　　***work on*** 致力於；著手
task〔tæsk〕*n.* 工作；任務

Finally, planning one day ahead on a pocket calendar can actually do more to improve the grades of some students than any memory or speed-reading course.

最後，在小行事曆上提前一天做好計畫，比任何記憶或速讀課程，更能夠實際地改善某些學生的成績。

ahead〔ə'hɛd〕*adv.* 在…之前
pocket〔'pɑkɪt〕*adj.* 可放入口袋的；攜帶型的
calendar〔'kæləndə〕*n.* 行事曆　　***pocket calendar*** 小行事曆
actually〔'æktʃʊəlɪ〕*adv.* 實際上　　improve〔ɪm'pruv〕*v.* 改善
grade〔gred〕*n.* 成績　　speed-reading〔'spid,ridɪŋ〕*n.* 速讀
course〔kors〕*n.* 課程

1.（**B**）本文中，"to 'go blank' at quiz time" 的意思是 ＿＿＿＿＿＿。

(A) 完成小考　　　　　　　(B) 在小考時忘記所有事情

(C) 在小考時休息　　　　　(D) 在小考裡寫錯答案

2. (**C**) 有些建議可以減輕壓力，但「不」包括 ＿＿＿＿＿＿＿＿＿。

    (A) 深呼吸　　　　　　(B) 注意細節

    (C) <u>去上速讀課</u>　　　(D) 提前計畫

    ＊ suggestion〔səg'dʒɛstʃən〕 *n.* 建議
       include〔ɪn'klud〕 *v.* 包括　　notice〔'notɪs〕 *v.* 注意到
       beforehand〔bɪ'for,hænd〕 *adv.* 預先；事先

3. (**A**) 本文作者暗示壓力 ＿＿＿＿＿＿＿＿＿。

    (A) <u>會影響記憶力</u>　　(B) 是我們永遠無法擺脫的東西

    (C) 發生在當我們無法趕上截止日期的時候

    (D) 讓我們注意細節

    ＊ suggest〔səg'dʒɛst〕 *v.* 暗示；建議
       affect〔ə'fɛkt〕 *v.* 影響　　***memory power*** 記憶力
       get rid of 擺脫　　occur〔ə'kɝ〕 *v.* 發生
       attentive〔ə'tɛntɪv〕 *adj.* 注意的 < *to* >

4. (**D**) 根據本文，下列敘述何者為真？

    (A) 增進閱讀能力可以釋放壓力。

    (B) 閱讀能力是學業成功的唯一決定性因素。

    (C) 壓力能刺激學生努力學習。

    (D) <u>成功的關鍵就是好好地處理壓力。</u>

    ＊ decisive〔dɪ'saɪsɪv〕 *adj.* 決定性的　　factor〔'fæktɚ〕 *n.* 因素
       academic〔,ækə'dɛmɪk〕 *adj.* 學業的
       stimulate〔'stɪmjə,let〕 *v.* 刺激；激發　　***cope with*** 處理；應付

5. (**C**) 作者最有可能建議學生在考試前做什麼？

    (A) 作詳細的筆記。　　(B) 忘掉閱讀章節，只畫出章節重點。

    (C) <u>休息一下並放鬆。</u>　(D) 儘可能長時間地屏住呼吸。

    ＊ careful〔'kɛrfəl〕 *adj.* 仔細的　　***take a break*** 休息一下
       hold the breath 屏住呼吸　　***as…as possible*** 儘可能…

TEST 21

Read the following passage and choose the best answer for each question.

Blue jeans are America's favorite kind of pants. Today, their popularity has spread to every country in the world.

Blue jeans were invented by a German, Levi Strauss, who went to San Francisco during the California Gold Rush to sell tools and provisions to miners. He saw that they needed sturdy pants, so he tailored some using a durable type of cotton cloth from Nimes, France. "De Nimes" is French for "from Nimes," and that's how this cloth got the name "denim." For centuries, denim was a material used to make sails for ships. When Christopher Columbus sailed to America, his ship was rigged with denim sails. But Levi Strauss made pants out of it, and he dyed them blue with indigo, the world's oldest known dye.

The Levi Strauss Company still makes blue jeans today, and there are scores of other blue jeans companies from Hong Kong to Paris. Jeans were originally workers' clothing, made for men who dug for gold in dirty and dangerous mines. Now they are worn by both the rich and the poor, both men and women, from Russia, to America, to China. 【景美女中】

1. What is the article about?

   (A) The worldwide popularity of blue jeans.

   (B) The general origin of blue jeans.

   (C) The influence of blue jeans on cultures.

   (D) The history of the Levi Strauss Company.

2. Which of the following statements is <u>TRUE</u>?

   (A) Blue jeans were invented because there was no traditional American clothing.

   (B) Denim is a kind of provision used in the mining industry.

   (C) Indigo is used to make clothing sturdy and durable.

   (D) Jeans are popular with people from all walks of life.

3. Where did blue jeans first appear?

   (A) Nimes, France.   (B) Hong Kong.

   (C) San Francisco.   (D) Germany.

4. What were Strauss's pants made out of?

   (A) Cotton.   (B) Sails.

   (C) Indigo.   (D) Provisions.

5. When did denim first appear?

   (A) During the Gold Rush.

   (B) When Columbus discovered America.

   (C) Several centuries ago.

   (D) In the nineteenth century.

TEST 21 詳解

Blue jeans are America's favorite kind of pants. Today, their popularity has spread to every country in the world.

牛仔褲在美國是最受人喜愛一種褲子。現在，它們受歡迎的程度已經遍及了全世界每個國家。

jeans〔dʒinz〕*n. pl.* 牛仔褲　　***blue jeans*** （藍色斜紋布）牛仔褲
favorite〔'fevrɪt〕*adj.* 最喜愛的　　pants〔pænts〕*n. pl.* 褲子
popularity〔ˌpɑpjə'lærətɪ〕*n.* 流行；受歡迎
spread〔sprɛd〕*v.* 遍及；流傳

Blue jeans were invented by a German, Levi Strauss, who went to San Francisco during the California Gold Rush to sell tools and provisions to miners. He saw that they needed sturdy pants, so he tailored some using a durable type of cotton cloth from Nimes, France. "De Nimes" is French for "from Nimes," and that's how this cloth got the name "denim." For centuries, denim was a material used to make sails for ships. When Christopher Columbus sailed to America, his ship was rigged with denim sails. But Levi Strauss made pants out of it, and he dyed them blue with indigo, the world's oldest known dye.

牛仔褲是由德國人李維·史特勞斯所發明的，他在加州淘金熱潮時前往舊金山，販售工具跟糧食給礦工。他發現礦工們需要堅固的褲子，所以他用來自法國尼姆的一種耐久棉布衣料，縫製一些褲子。「De Nimes」是法文，意思是「來自尼姆」，這也是這種布料被取名為「丹寧布」的原因。好幾世紀以來，丹寧布一直是被用來作為製造船帆的材料。當克里斯多福·哥倫布航行到美洲的時候，他的船就裝配有丹寧船帆。但是李維·史特勞斯用單寧布來做褲子，而且他用世界上已知最古老的靛青染料，把褲子染成藍色。

invent（ ɪn'vɛnt ）v. 發明　　German（'dʒɝmən ）n. 德國人
Levi Strauss（'livaɪ'straʊs ）n. 李維・史特勞斯【牛仔褲的發明者】
San Francisco（ˌsænfrən'sɪsko ）n. 舊金山；三藩市【加州中部的大城】
California（ˌkælə'fɔrnjə ）n. 加州【美國西海岸的一州】
rush（ rʌʃ ）n. 熱潮
California Gold Rush 加州淘金熱【發生在 1848-1855 年，當時約有三
　十萬人湧入加州，使加州從原本的小村落，發展成大都會型態】
provisions（ prə'vɪʒənz ）n. pl. 糧食　　miner（'maɪnɚ ）n. 礦工
sturdy（'stɝdɪ ）adj. 堅固的；耐用的　　tailor（'telɚ ）v. 縫製（衣服）
durable（'djʊrəbḷ ）adj. 耐久的　　cotton（'kɑtn̩ ）n. 棉；棉布
cloth（ klɔθ ）n. 布；衣料　　Nimes（ nim ）n. 尼姆【法國城市名】
denim（'dɛnəm ）n. 丹寧布　　material（ mə'tɪrɪəl ）n. 材料
sail（ sel ）n. 船帆
Christopher Columbus（'krɪstəfɚˌkə'lʌmbəs ）n. 克里斯多福・哥倫布
　【1451-1506，義大利航海冒險家，1492 年發現美洲大陸】
sail（ sel ）v. 航行　　rig（ rɪg ）v. 裝索具於（船）；將…配備於～
be rigged with　（船）被裝上…　　*make* A *out of* B　用 B 做成 A
dye（ daɪ ）v. 染色　　n. 染料　　indigo（'ɪndɪˌgo ）n. 靛青

The Levi Strauss Company still makes blue jeans today, and
there are scores of other blue jeans companies from Hong Kong
to Paris. Jeans were originally workers' clothing, made for men
who dug for gold in dirty and dangerous mines. Now they are
worn by both the rich and the poor, both men and women, from
Russia, to America, to China.

　　李維・史特勞斯公司現在還在製造牛仔褲，而且從香港到巴黎，還有
很多其他牛仔褲公司。牛仔褲起初是工人的衣服，給那些在航髒、危險的
礦坑中挖掘黃金的男人穿。現在不管富人或窮人、男人或女人，從俄羅
斯、美洲、到中國，每個人都穿牛仔褲。

　　score（ skor ）n. 大量；許多
scores of　許多的　　Hong Kong（'haŋ'kaŋ ）n. 香港

originally〔ə'rɪdʒənlɪ〕*adv.* 原本；最初
clothing〔'kloðɪŋ〕*n.* 衣服【集合名詞】　　dig〔dɪg〕*v.* 挖
mine〔maɪn〕*n.* 礦坑　　Russia〔'rʌʃə〕*n.* 俄羅斯

1. (**B**) 本文主題是關於什麼？
   (A) 牛仔褲在全世界流行。　　(B) 牛仔褲的概略起源。
   (C) 牛仔褲對於文化的影響。
   (D) 李威‧史特勞斯公司的歷史。
   * worldwide〔'wɜld'waɪd〕*adj.* 遍及世界的；世界性的
     general〔'dʒɛnərəl〕*adj.* 一般的；概略的
     origin〔'ɔrədʒɪn〕*n.* 來源　　influence〔'ɪnfluəns〕*n.* 影響

2. (**D**) 下列敘述何者為真？
   (A) 藍色牛仔褲被發明，是因為美國沒有傳統服飾。
   (B) 丹寧布是一種被用於挖礦工業的糧食。
   (C) 靛青染料被用來使衣服堅固又耐久。
   (D) 牛仔褲受到各行各業的人歡迎。
   * mining〔'maɪnɪŋ〕*n.* 採礦；礦業
     industry〔'ɪndəstrɪ〕*n.* 產業；工業　　*all walks of life* 各行各業

3. (**C**) 牛仔褲最早出現在何地？
   (A) 法國尼姆。　　(B) 香港。　　(C) 舊金山。　　(D) 德國。
   * appear〔ə'pɪr〕*v.* 出現　　Germany〔'dʒɜmənɪ〕*n.* 德國

4. (**A**) 史特勞斯的牛仔褲是用什麼製成的？
   (A) 棉布。　　(B) 船帆。　　(C) 靛青染料。　　(D) 糧食。

5. (**C**) 丹寧布最早出現在何時？
   (A) 在淘金熱的時候。　　(B) 當哥倫布發現美洲的時候。
   (C) 好幾個世紀以前。　　(D) 十九世紀時。
   * discover〔dɪ'skʌvɚ〕*v.* 發現

TEST 22

Read the following passage and choose the best answer for each question.

If you wish to have a happy marriage or romantic relationship, try buying the "Love Tree" for your lover. The Love Tree is said to increase the chances of having a happy marriage. It is believed that the green heart-shaped leaves and white orchid-like flowers will help relieve conflict and promote love.

The Love Tree, also known as the White Orchid Tree, is a type of Bauhinia, which means small trees. The Love Tree is commonly found in Asia, especially in India, where the hot weather allows it to grow easily. In colder areas though, you can still grow the tree indoors. The flower buds and leaves are edible and are considered vegetables.

Growing the Love Tree definitely requires dedication. Before you sow the seeds, you must soak them in water for at least 24 hours. Also, when watering the plant, be careful. The soil should be moist but not over-watered. Finally, remember to use fertilizers on the plant once a month. With some tender loving care, your Love Tree will blossom and help you hang on to a good relationship with your lover!

【新店高中】

1. According to the passage, which of the following is **TRUE**?

   (A) The Love Tree can help you find your parents.
   (B) The Love Tree can help you find a lover.
   (C) The Love Tree can make you fall in love.
   (D) The Love Tree can help you maintain a good marriage.

2. In what way is the Love Tree symbolic of love?

   (A) It is a small tree.
   (B) Its leaves are shaped like hearts.
   (C) Its leaves and buds are edible.
   (D) It grows well in a warm climate.

3. What should be done with the seeds of the Love Tree?

   (A) They should be eaten on one's wedding night.
   (B) They should be soaked before planting.
   (C) They should be grown indoors only.
   (D) They should be used as fertilizer.

4. What can a Love Tree do?

   (A) Last as long as a couple's marriage.
   (B) Ensure that a couple have healthy children.
   (C) Blossom once a month.
   (D) Help people avoid arguments.

5. Which of the following descriptions best describes a Love Tree?

   (A) A short, beautiful tree.   (B) A healthful vegetable.
   (C) A small, loving tree.
   (D) A white, heart-shaped blossom.

TEST 22 詳解

If you wish to have a happy marriage or romantic relationship, try buying the "Love Tree" for your lover. The Love Tree is said to increase the chances of having a happy marriage. It is believed that the green heart-shaped leaves and white orchid-like flowers will help relieve conflict and promote love.

如果你想要有一段幸福的婚姻，或是浪漫的戀情，試著買「愛之樹」給你的情人。據說愛之樹可以增加擁有幸福婚姻的可能性。大家都相信它綠色心型的葉子，以及白色蘭花般的花朵，能幫助減輕衝突，並增進愛情。

marriage ('mærɪdʒ) *n.* 婚姻　　romantic (ro'mæntɪk) *adj.* 浪漫的
relationship (rɪ'leʃən,ʃɪp) *n.* 關係
Love Tree 愛之樹【此指南歐紫荊花，學名 Cercis siliquastrum，屬於羊蹄甲屬的植物，原產於歐洲東南部及亞洲西南部。葉片心形，綠偏藍色，花種有粉紫、玫瑰紅或白色花種】
lover ('lʌvɚ) *n.* 愛人；情人　　increase (ɪn'kris) *v.* 增加
heart-shaped ('hɑrt'ʃept) *adj.* 心型的
leaves (livz) *n. pl.* 葉子【單數為 leaf】　　orchid ('ɔrkɪd) *n.* 蘭花
orchid-like ('ɔrkɪd,laɪk) *adj.* 像蘭花般的
relieve (rɪ'liv) *v.* 緩和；減輕
conflict ('kɑnflɪkt) *n.* 衝突
promote (prə'mot) *v.* 提升；促進

The Love Tree, also known as the White Orchid Tree, is a type of Bauhinia, which means small trees. The Love Tree is commonly found in Asia, especially in India, where the hot weather allows it to grow easily. In colder areas though, you can still grow the tree indoors. The flower buds and leaves are edible and are considered vegetables.

　　愛之樹，又稱爲白色蘭花樹，是羊蹄甲屬的一種，羊蹄甲的意思是小樹。愛之樹在亞洲很常見，特別是印度，那裡炎熱的天氣讓它很容易茁壯。即使在較冷的地區，還是可以在室內種植它。它的花苞跟葉子都可以食用，而且被認爲是一種蔬菜。

be known as 以…聞名；被稱爲
Bauhinia〔͵bauˈhɪnɪə〕*n.* 羊蹄甲屬
commonly〔ˈkamənlɪ〕*adv.* 一般；通常　　allow〔əˈlau〕*v.* 允許
indoors〔ˈɪnˈdorz〕*adv.* 在室內　　bud〔bʌd〕*n.* 花苞；芽
edible〔ˈɛdəb!〕*adj.* 可食用的　　consider〔kənˈsɪdɚ〕*v.* 認爲

Growing the Love Tree definitely requires dedication. Before you sow the seeds, you must soak them in water for at least 24 hours. Also, when watering the plant, be careful. The soil should be moist but not over-watered. Finally, remember to use fertilizers on the plant once a month. With some tender loving care, your Love Tree will blossom and help you hang on to a good relationship with your lover!

　　種植愛之樹確實需要全心全力。在播種之前，你必須要先把種子浸泡在水中至少二十四個小時。還有，澆水的時候要小心，土壤必須微微濕潤，卻不能過度灌溉。最後，記得每個月對這種植物施肥一次。用溫柔且充滿愛意的照料，你的愛之樹就會開花，也能幫助你跟你的情人維持良好的關係！

definitely〔ˈdɛfənɪtlɪ〕*adv.* 確實地　　require〔rɪˈkwaɪr〕*v.* 需要
dedication〔͵dɛdəˈkeʃən〕*n.* 奉獻；獻身　　sow〔so〕*v.* 播種；撒
seed〔sid〕*n.* 種子　　soak〔sok〕*v.* 浸泡　　*at least* 至少
water〔ˈwɔtɚ〕*v.* 給…澆水　　soil〔sɔɪl〕*n.* 土壤
moist〔mɔɪst〕*adj.* 潮濕的；微濕的
over-watered〔ˈovɚˈwɔtɚd〕*adj.* 過度灌溉的
fertilizer〔ˈfɝt!͵aɪzɚ〕*n.* 肥料　　tender〔ˈtɛndɚ〕*adj.* 溫柔的
loving〔ˈlʌvɪŋ〕*adj.* 充滿愛的
blossom〔ˈblasəm〕*v.* 開花；繁榮　　*hang on to* 緊握住；保持

1.(**D**) 根據本文，下列何者爲眞？

    (A) 愛之樹能幫助你找到父母。

    (B) 愛之樹能幫你找到戀人。   (C) 愛之樹能讓你墜入愛河。

    (D) 愛之樹能幫助你維持一段美好的婚姻。

   * maintain (men'ten) v. 維持；保持

2.(**B**) 愛之樹在哪方面象徵愛情？

    (A) 它是小樹。   (B) 它葉子的形狀像愛心。

    (C) 它的葉子跟花苞可以食用。

    (D) 它在溫暖的氣候中長得很好。

   * symbolic (sɪm'balɪk) adj. 象徵性的；表示的

3.(**B**) 應該如何處理愛之樹的種子？

    (A) 應該在婚禮之夜吃下種子。

    (B) 應該在種植之前先將種子泡水。

    (C) 種子只能在室內種植。   (D) 種子應該被用來當肥料。

4.(**D**) 愛之樹能做什麼？

    (A) 存活時間跟夫妻的婚姻一樣長。

    (B) 保證夫妻有健康的小孩。

    (C) 每個月開花一次。   (D) 幫助人們避免爭執。

   * last (læst) v. 持續   couple ('kʌpḷ) n. 一對（情侶、夫妻）
    ensure (ɪn'ʃur) v. 保證   avoid (ə'vɔɪd) v. 避免
    argument ('argjəmənt) n. 爭執；爭論

5.(**A**) 下列何者是愛之樹的最佳描述？

    (A) 低矮、美麗的樹。   (B) 有益健康的蔬菜。

    (C) 很小、充滿愛意的樹。   (D) 一種開白色、心型的花。

   * description (dɪ'skrɪpʃən) n. 描述；敘述
    describe (dɪ'skraɪb) v. 描述；說明
    healthful ('hɛlθfəl) adj. 有益健康的   blossom ('blasəm) n. 花

TEST 23

Read the following passage and choose the best answer for each question.

Seattle, located in Washington, the state farthest north and west in the contiguous United States, is known for its picturesque scenery, history, and the prosperity of contemporary industries. Surrounded by beautiful landscapes and magnificent snow-covered mountains, Seattle is sited on hills overlooking two lakes and Puget Sound, a body of water that leads to the Pacific Ocean.

This city was named after a Native American Indian chief who was friendly and hospitable. Chief Seattle signed a peace treaty with the U.S. government in 1854, which allowed U.S. citizens to settle in the area, in a hope that the conflicts that had occurred in other parts of the country when settlers moved into Native American lands could be avoided. In a famous speech, Chief Seattle eloquently declared, "The earth does not belong to man; man belongs to the earth." Afterwards, Seattle was officially founded in 1869 and its population grew rapidly after the Alaskan gold rush, which started in 1897.

Although much younger than other major cities in America, Seattle has come to serve as an important trade center with major industries such as Boeing, which manufactures airplanes and spacecraft. It is also renowned as the center of such major corporations as Starbucks, a leading coffee company since 1971. Another significant industry founded in Seattle is the giant computer software company — Microsoft. What's more, the founder of the biggest online bookstore — Amazon.com — moved to Seattle to establish its headquarters there. Seattle has turned into a cosmopolitan city with a thriving economy.

【大同高中】

1. Chief Seattle signed a treaty with U.S. government because _____

   (A) he wanted to protect the beautiful landscapes and magnificent mountains of Seattle.
   (B) he wanted to avoid conflicts between settlers and Native Americans.
   (C) more and more U.S. citizens wanted to settle in Seattle.
   (D) the earth does not belong to human beings.

2. According to the passage, which of the following is **NOT** one of the industries in Seattle?

   (A) A software company.
   (B) A copy machine company.
   (C) An online bookstore company.
   (D) An airplane manufacturer.

3. Which of the following statements is **TRUE** according to this passage?

   (A) Seattle has transformed into an important center of many current industries.

   (B) Seattle derived its name from a body of water that leads to the Pacific Ocean.

   (C) The Alaskan gold rush took place before Chief Seattle signed a treaty.

   (D) Nowadays, Seattle plays an important role in gold mining.

4. How long has the city of Seattle been in existence?

   (A) Since ancient times.

   (B) Almost 40 years.

   (C) Since Chief Seattle was born.

   (D) More than a century.

5. What does the passage imply about Seattle?

   (A) It is much more prosperous than other American cities.

   (B) It is the best place in America to look for a job.

   (C) Its economy and industry grew rapidly.

   (D) It is well-developed despite its rural location.

TEST 23 詳解

Seattle, located in Washington, the state farthest north and west in the contiguous United States, is known for its picturesque scenery, history, and the prosperity of contemporary industries. Surrounded by beautiful landscapes and magnificent snow-covered mountains, Seattle is sited on hills overlooking two lakes and Puget Sound, a body of water that leads to the Pacific Ocean.

西雅圖位於美國本土最西北方華盛頓州,以它如圖畫般的風景、歷史,以及繁榮的現代工業而聞名。西雅圖被美麗的風景,以及靄靄的白雪、壯麗的山脈所圍繞,它座落於山丘上,俯瞰著兩座湖泊,還有流向太平洋的一塊水域——普吉灣。

Seattle〔si'ætḷ〕*n.* 西雅圖　　locate〔lo'ket〕*v.* 使位於
Washington〔'waʃɪŋtən〕*n.* 華盛頓州　　state〔stet〕*n.* 州
contiguous〔kən'tɪgjuəs〕*adj.* 相鄰的;連續的
be known for 以…而聞名
picturesque〔ˌpɪktʃə'rɛsk〕*adj.* 如畫的　　scenery〔'sinərɪ〕*n.* 風景
prosperity〔prɑs'pɛrətɪ〕*n.* 繁榮
contemporary〔kən'tɛmpəˌrɛrɪ〕*adj.* 現代的;當代的
industry〔'ɪndəstrɪ〕*n.* 工業;產業　　surround〔sə'raund〕*v.* 圍繞
landscape〔'lændskep〕*n.* 風景
magnificent〔mæg'nɪfəsṇt〕*adj.* 壯麗的;宏偉的
snow-covered〔'sno'kʌvəd〕*adj.* 被雪覆蓋的
be sited on 座落於　　overlook〔ˌovə'luk〕*v.* 俯瞰
sound〔saund〕*n. 海灣;海峽*
Puget Sound〔'pjudʒɪt'saund〕*n.* 普吉灣【華盛頓州西北部與太平洋接壤的狹長海灣】　　***a body of water*** 水域;海域
lead to 導致;通往　　***the Pacific Ocean*** 太平洋

This city was named after a Native American Indian chief who was friendly and hospitable. Chief Seattle signed a peace treaty with the U.S. government in 1854, which allowed U.S. citizens to settle in the area, in a hope that the conflicts that had occurred in other parts of the country when settlers moved into Native American lands could be avoided. In a famous speech, Chief Seattle eloquently declared, "The earth does not belong to man; man belongs to the earth." Afterwards, Seattle was officially founded in 1869 and its population grew rapidly after the Alaskan gold rush, which started in 1897.

這個城市的名字，是以一位友善又好客的美國印地安酋長的名字命名。西雅圖酋長希望能避免在美國的其他地方，因為開墾者遷入美國原住民土地而引起的衝突，所以在西元 1854 年，跟美國政府簽署和平協議，允許美國人民在西雅圖定居。在一場著名的演講中，西雅圖酋長令人動容地說：「地球並不屬於人類，而是人類屬於地球。」之後，西雅圖正式地在 1869 年被建立，在 1897 年開始的阿拉斯加淘金熱之後，它的人口急速成長。

be named after ⋯ 以⋯的名字命名
native ('netɪv) *adj.* 原產的；土著的
Native American 美國原住民；美國印地安人
Indian ('ɪndɪən) *adj.* 美國印地安人的　　*n.* 美國印地安人
chief (tʃif) *n.* 酋長　　hospitable ('hɑspɪtəbl̩) *adj.* 好客的
sign (saɪn) *v.* 簽署　　treaty ('tritɪ) *n.* 條約
peace treaty 和平協議　　citizen ('sɪtəzn̩) *n.* 公民
settle ('sɛtl̩) *v.* 定居　　***in a hope that*** 希望～
conflict ('kɑnflɪkt) *n.* 衝突　　settler ('sɛtlə) *n.* 開墾者；殖民者
eloquently ('ɛləkwəntlɪ) *adv.* (文章、演說等) 動人地
declare (dɪ'klɛr) *v.* 宣布　　earth (ɝθ) *n.* 地球
belong to 屬於　　afterwards ('æftəwədz) *adv.* 此後；後來

officially〔ə'fɪʃəlɪ〕*adv.* 正式地
population〔ˌpɑpjə'leʃən〕*n.* 人口
Alaska〔ə'læskə〕*n.* 阿拉斯加州
gold rush 淘金熱

found〔faʊnd〕*v.* 創立；建立
rapidly〔'ræpɪdlɪ〕*adv.* 快速地
rush〔rʌʃ〕*n.* 熱潮

Although much younger than other major cities in America, Seattle has come to serve as an important trade center with major industries such as Boeing, which manufactures airplanes and spacecraft. It is also renowned as the center of such major corporations as Starbucks, a leading coffee company since 1971. Another significant industry founded in Seattle is the giant computer software company — Microsoft. What's more, the founder of the biggest online bookstore —Amazon.com — moved to Seattle to establish its headquarters there. Seattle has turned into a cosmopolitan city with a thriving economy.

雖然西雅圖比美國其他許多大都市都還要年輕，但它已經成為許多產業——例如製造飛機跟太空船的波音公司——的重要貿易中心。它以身為許多大公司的總部而聞名，例如 1971 年時創立的咖啡公司的領導者星巴克。另一個設立在西雅圖的重要產業，就是大型電腦軟體公司——微軟。此外，線上購書公司的龍頭——亞馬遜購書網——也搬到西雅圖，把總部設在此處。西雅圖繁榮的經濟，已讓它成為國際性的都市。

trade center 貿易中心　　　***such as*** 例如
Boeing〔'boɪŋ〕*n.* 波音公司【全球最大的航空及太空飛行器製造商】
manufacture〔ˌmænjə'fæktʃə〕*v.* 製造
spacecraft〔'spesˌkræft〕*n.* 太空船
renowned〔rɪ'naʊnd〕*adj.* 有名的
be renowned as 以⋯聞名

corporation〔͵kɔrpə'reʃən〕 *n.* 股份有限公司

Starbucks〔'stɑr͵bʌks〕 *n.* 星巴克【全球最大的連鎖咖啡店，總部在
西雅圖】 leading〔'lidɪŋ〕 *adj.* 領導的；主要的

significant〔sɪg'nɪfəkənt〕 *adj.* 重要的

giant〔'dʒaɪənt〕 *adj.* 巨大的 software〔'sɔft͵wɛr〕 *n.* 軟體

Microsoft〔'maɪkro͵sɔft〕 *n.* 微軟公司【全球最大電腦軟體供應商】

founder〔'faʊndɚ〕 *n.* 創立者 online〔͵ɑn'laɪn〕 *adj.* 線上的

Amazon〔'æmə͵zɑn〕 *n.* 亞馬遜河

***Amazon*.com** 亞馬遜購書網【美國最大網路商務公司，總部設在
西雅圖】 establish〔ə'stæblɪʃ〕 *v.* 創立

headquarters〔'hɛd͵kwɔrtɚz〕 *n. pl.* 總部；總公司

turn into 轉變成

cosmopolitan〔͵kɑzmə'pɑlətn̩〕 *adj.* 國際性的

thriving〔'θraɪvɪŋ〕 *adj.* 繁榮的 economy〔ɪ'kɑnəmɪ〕 *n.* 經濟

1.(**B**) 西雅圖酋長跟美國政府簽署和平協議的原因是 ＿＿＿＿＿＿＿

(A) 他想要保護西雅圖美麗的風景跟壯麗的山脈。

(B) 他想要避免開墾者跟美國原住民之間的衝突。

(C) 越來越多美國人民想要在西雅圖定居。

(D) 地球不屬於人類。

　*　protect〔prə'tɛkt〕 *v.* 保護 ***human beings*** 人類

2.(**B**) 根據本文，下列何者「不是」西雅圖的產業之一？

(A) 電腦軟體公司。

(B) 影印機公司。

(C) 線上圖書公司。

(D) 飛機製造商。

　*　***copy machine*** 影印機

　　manufacturer〔͵mænjə'fæktʃərɚ〕 *n.* 製造商

3. (**A**) 根據本文，下列敘述何者爲眞？

(A) 西雅圖已成爲許多現代工業的重心。

(B) 西雅圖這個名字是來自於一塊流向太平洋的水域。

(C) 阿拉斯加淘金熱發生在西雅圖酋長簽署和平協議之前。

(D) 現在，西雅圖在金礦業中扮演重要的角色。

* statement〔'stetmənt〕 *n.* 敘述

   transform into 轉變爲

   derive〔dəˈraɪv〕 *v.* 得到；引出　　***derive from*** 來自於

   take place 發生　　nowadays〔'nauə,dez〕 *adv.* 現在

   play an important part 扮演重要的角色

   mining〔'maɪnɪŋ〕 *n.* 礦業

4. (**D**) 西雅圖這個城市存在多久了？

(A) 從古到今。　　　　(B) 將近四十年了。

(C) 從西雅圖酋長出生到現在。

(D) 超過一個世紀。

* ***in existence*** 存在的　　ancient〔'enʃənt〕 *adj.* 古代的

5. (**C**) 關於西雅圖，本文暗示什麼？

(A) 它比美國其他城市都還要更繁榮。

(B) 在美國，它是找工作的最佳地點。

(C) 它的經濟跟工業發展迅速。

(D) 雖然地處偏遠，但發展完善。

* imply〔ɪm'plaɪ〕 *v.* 暗示

   prosperous〔'prɑspərəs〕 *adj.* 繁榮的　　***look for*** 尋找

   well-developed〔'wɛl,dɪ'vɛləpt〕 *adj.* 發展良好的

   despite〔dɪ'spaɪt〕 *prep.* 儘管；雖然

   rural〔'rurəl〕 *adj.* 鄉下的

   location〔lo'keʃən〕 *n.* 地點；位置

TEST 24

Read the following passage and choose the best answer for each question.

Love moves mountains, but rarely does it provide work for the architect. Vanity and religious faith, throughout the centuries, have often been the qualities that have inspired men to build. The majestic Taj Mahal, however, is an obvious exception. The famous domed building is a memorial to the strong love of Shah Jahan, the fifth ruler of the Mogul empire, for a cherished wife, who died in childbirth.

According to legend, the queen's last wish was that the shah build a monument so beautiful that whoever saw it could not help but sense the perfection of their love. Indeed, since its construction in the mid-17th century, the shimmering monument of white marble, set among quiet gardens and pools, has attracted many tourists and pilgrims.

Magnificent as this structure is, strangely enough, the architect of the Taj Mahal is unknown. The Indian version of the history of the Taj Mahal credits Ustad Isa, a worker from Turkey or Persia, as being the designer.

One legend tells that Ustad Isa himself was an inconsolable widower in search of an opportunity to build a worthy monument to his own wife.

It is probable that the Taj Mahal was not the work of a single master at all but the cooperative efforts of many artists and craftsmen from all over Asia. Begun in 1631, the **mausoleum** took some 20,000 workmen 22 years to build at a cost of 40 million rupees.

Not only does the Taj Mahal reveal how deeply the shah loved his wife, but it also demonstrates a harmonious combination of the architecture of Persia, India, and central Asia. It blends the traditional design of Mogul gardens with the characteristically Indian use of minarets, or towers, and a dominant dome. However, all legends agree with one disgraceful detail. Shah Jahan was apparently so pleased with the elegant mausoleum that he beheaded his chief architect, cut off the hands of the architect's assistants, and blinded the draftsmen, so that they would never be able to create a building to rival it.

One more detail is worth mentioning. The shah's tomb was not part of the original plan. Shah Jahan had planned to build another vast mausoleum for himself across the river from that of his loved one. However, when he died, his son betrayed his father's last wish and buried him beside his beloved wife. 【板橋高中】

1. In which of the following sources are we most likely to find this article?

   (A) The journal *Applied Physics*.

   (B) The channel *Animal Planet*.

   (C) The magazine *National Geographic*.

   (D) The book *Greek Mythology*.

2. Which of the following information is **NOT** mentioned in this article?

   (A) The reason the Taj Mahal was built.

   (B) The name of the queen.

   (C) The duration of the construction work.

   (D) The architectural characteristics of the Taj Mahal.

3. Which of the following statements is **TRUE**?

   (A) The chief architect was later promoted.

   (B) Ustad Isa's wife asked him to design a monument in memory of her.

   (C) The Taj Mahal was built more for faith and vanity than for love.

   (D) The Taj Mahal was not completed until 1653.

4. Based on the context, what does the word **mausoleum** mean?

   (A) A building where a body is buried.

   (B) A temple where monks or nuns live.

   (C) A tower where people ring a large bell.

   (D) A dynasty which rules over a region.

5. According to Indian legend, what happened to Ustad Isa when the Taj Mahal was finished?

   (A) He was able to forget the sad memory of his wife.

   (B) He was buried next to his wife.

   (C) He was killed.

   (D) Ustad Isa did not really exist.

TEST 24 詳解

Love moves mountains, but rarely does it provide work for the architect.　Vanity and religious faith, throughout the centuries, have often been the qualities that have inspired men to build.　The majestic Taj Mahal, however, is an obvious exception.　The famous domed building is a memorial to the strong love of Shah Jahan, the fifth ruler of the Mogul empire, for a cherished wife, who died in childbirth.

　　愛情可以移動山脈，但愛情卻很少讓建築師有工作做。數百年以來，虛榮與宗教信仰，經常是能激勵人們建造的特質。但是雄偉的泰姬瑪哈陵，卻是個明顯的例外。這座著名的圓頂建築物，是蒙兀兒帝國的第五位統治者沙賈汗，強烈愛情的紀念物，獻給他因難產而死的珍愛妻子。

rarely (ˈrɛrlɪ) *adv.* 很少地；罕見地

provide (prəˈvaɪd) *v.* 提供

work (wɝk) *n.* 工作；作品

architect (ˈɑrkə͵tɛkt) *n.* 建築師

vanity (ˈvænətɪ) *n.* 虛榮心　　religious (rɪˈlɪdʒəs) *adj.* 宗教的

faith (feθ) *n.* 信仰　　quality (ˈkwɑlətɪ) *n.* 特質

inspire (ɪnˈspaɪr) *v.* 激勵

majestic (məˈdʒɛstɪk) *adj.* 雄偉的；富麗的

Taj Mahal 泰姬瑪哈陵【17 世紀時，蒙兀兒帝國的第五位皇帝沙賈汗，
　　為了紀念愛妻所建的雄偉陵墓，全白大理石的建築外觀，被譽為「完美
　　的建築」，1983 年被聯合國教科文組織列為世界遺產】

obvious (ˈɑbvɪəs) *adj.* 明顯的

exception (ɪkˈsɛpʃən) *n.* 例外

domed (domd) *adj.* 圓頂狀的　　building (ˈbɪldɪŋ) *n.* 建築物

memorial (məˈmorɪəl) *n.* 紀念物；紀念碑

Shah Jahan 沙賈汗【1592-1666，蒙兀兒帝國的第五位皇帝，死後與
愛妻合葬在泰姬瑪哈陵內】

ruler〔'rulə〕*n.* 統治者　　empire〔'ɛmpaɪr〕*n.* 帝國

the Mogul empire 蒙兀兒帝國【1526-1858，突厥人在西南亞所建立
的帝國】

cherished〔'tʃɛrɪʃt〕*adj.* 珍愛的　childbirth〔'tʃaɪld,bɝθ〕*n.* 生產；分娩

According to legend, the queen's last wish was that the shah
build a monument so beautiful that whoever saw it could not help
but sense the perfection of their love. Indeed, since its construction
in the mid-17th century, the shimmering monument of white marble,
set among quiet gardens and pools, has attracted many tourists and
pilgrims.

傳說指出，那位皇后的遺願，是希望沙賈汗建造一座非常美麗的紀念
建築物，無論誰看到它，都一定能感受到他們之間完美的愛情。的確，自
從十七世紀中期建造泰姬瑪哈陵以來，這座閃亮白色大理石的紀念建築，
座落於安靜的庭園跟水池之間，吸引了許多遊客與朝聖者。

legend〔'lɛdʒənd〕*n.* 傳說
queen〔kwin〕*n.* 皇后　　***last wish*** 遺願
monument〔'manjəmənt〕*n.* 紀念建築物
can not help but + *V.* 忍不住～；不得不～
perfection〔pə'fɛkʃən〕*n.* 完美　　indeed〔ɪn'did〕*adv.* 的確
construction〔kən'strʌkʃən〕*n.* 建造
mid-17th〔'mɪd,sɛvən'tinθ〕*adj.* 十七世紀中期的
shimmer〔'ʃɪmə〕*v.* 閃閃發亮　　marble〔'marbl̩〕*n.* 大理石
set〔sɛt〕*v.* 設立；安置　　attract〔ə'trækt〕*v.* 吸引
pilgrim〔'pɪlgrɪm〕*n.* 朝聖者；旅客

Magnificent as this structure is, strangely enough, the architect of the Taj Mahal is unknown. The Indian version of the history of the Taj Mahal credits Ustad Isa, a worker from Turkey or Persia, as being the designer. One legend tells that Ustad Isa himself was an inconsolable widower in search of an opportunity to build a worthy monument to his own wife.

雖然這座建築如此雄偉，奇怪的是，卻不知道泰姬瑪哈陵的建築師是誰。印度版本的泰姬瑪哈陵歷史中，相信從土耳其或波斯來的工人兀斯塔‧以薩，就是它的設計者。有個傳說提到，兀斯塔‧以薩本身是個非常悲傷的喪妻者，他一直找尋機會，想建造一座足以紀念亡妻的建築物。

magnificent〔mæg'nɪfəsn̩t〕*adj.* 壯麗的；雄偉的
structure〔'strʌktʃə〕*n.* 建築物
strangely enough 奇怪的是
unknown〔ʌn'non〕*adj.* 未知的；不詳的
Indian〔'ɪndɪən〕*adj.* 印度的
version〔'vɝʒən〕*n.* 版本
credit〔'krɛdɪt〕*v.* 相信；歸功於
Ustad Isa 兀斯塔‧以薩【波斯人，據傳是泰姬瑪哈陵的主要建築師】
Turkey〔'tɝkɪ〕*n.* 土耳其　　Persia〔'pɝʒə〕*n.* 波斯
designer〔dɪ'zaɪnə〕*n.* 設計師
inconsolable〔‚ɪnkən'soləbl̩〕*adj.* 無法安慰的；極悲傷的
widower〔'wɪdəwə〕*n.* 鰥夫；喪妻者　　***in search of*** 尋找
opportunity〔‚apə'tjunətɪ〕*n.* 機會
worthy〔'wɝðɪ〕*adj.* 值得⋯的；足以⋯的

It is probable that the Taj Mahal was not the work of a single master at all but the cooperative efforts of many artists and craftsmen from all over Asia. Begun in 1631, the **mausoleum** took some 20,000 workmen 22 years to build at a cost of 40 million rupees.

　　也有可能泰姬瑪哈陵不是出自一位大師的傑作，而是全亞洲許多藝術家跟工匠的共同努力。這座陵寢從 1631 年開始動工，有大約兩萬名工人，用二十二年的時間來建造，花費了共四千萬盧比。

probable〔'prɑbəbḷ〕*adj.* 可能的

master〔'mæstɚ〕*n.* 大師　　***not…at all*** 一點也不…

cooperative〔ko'ɑpə,retɪv〕*adj.* 合作的

artist〔'ɑrtɪst〕*n.* 藝術家

craftsman〔'kræftsmən〕*n.* 工匠　　***all over*** 遍及

mausoleum〔,mɔsə'liəm〕*n.*（尤指壯觀的）陵墓

take〔tek〕*v.* 耗費　　workman〔'wɝkmən〕*n.* 工人

at a cost of ~ 花費~　　rupee〔ru'pi〕*n.* 盧比【印度貨幣】

Not only does the Taj Mahal reveal how deeply the shah loved his wife, but it also demonstrates a harmonious combination of the architecture of Persia, India, and central Asia. It blends the traditional design of Mogul gardens with the characteristically Indian use of minarets, or towers, and a dominant dome. However, all legends agree with one disgraceful detail. Shah Jahan was apparently so pleased with the elegant mausoleum that he beheaded his chief architect, cut off the hands of the architect's assistants, and blinded the draftsmen, so that they would never be able to create a building to rival it.

　　泰姬瑪哈陵不只顯示沙賈汗多麼深愛他的妻子，也展現波斯、印度、跟中亞建築學的和諧融合。它混合蒙兀兒的傳統花園設計，跟印度式回教高塔的使用特色，還有個大圓頂。然而，所有傳言都同意它有個不光榮的小細節。沙賈汗顯然對於這座高雅的陵墓感到非常滿意，以致於將主建築師斬首，砍斷建築助手的雙手，並且把所有繪圖師的眼睛都弄瞎，讓他們再也無法建造出能夠比得上泰姬瑪哈陵的建築物。

not only…but also~　不僅…而且~

reveal〔rɪ'vil〕*v.* 顯示

deeply〔'diplɪ〕*adv.* 深深地；強烈地

demonstrate〔'dɛmən,stret〕*v.* 證明；表露

harmonious〔har'monɪəs〕*adj.* 和諧的

combination〔,kɑmbə'neʃən〕*n.* 結合

architecture〔'ɑrkə,tɛktʃə〕*n.* 建築學；建築物

central Asia 中亞　　blend〔blɛnd〕*v.* 混合

characteristically〔,kærɪktə'rɪstɪklɪ〕*adv.* 特徵地；特質上

minaret〔,mɪnə'rɛt〕*n.* (回教式的)尖塔

tower〔'tauə〕*n.* 塔；高樓

dominant〔'dɑmənənt〕*adj.* 支配的；高聳的

dome〔dom〕*n.* 圓頂　　*agree with* 同意

disgraceful〔dɪs'gresfəl〕*adj.* 不光榮的

detail〔'ditel〕*n.* 細節；小事

apparently〔ə'pærəntlɪ〕*adv.* 顯然；似乎

pleased〔plizd〕*adj.* 滿意的　　elegant〔'ɛləgənt〕*adj.* 高雅的

behead〔bɪ'hɛd〕*v.* 砍(人的)頭　　chief〔tʃif〕*adj.* 主要的

cut off 切斷　　assistant〔ə'sɪstənt〕*n.* 助手

blind〔blaɪnd〕*v.* 使眼盲　　draftsman〔'dræftsmən〕*n.* 繪圖者

so that 以便於　　rival〔'raɪvl̩〕*v.* 與…競爭

One more detail is worth mentioning. The shah's tomb was
not part of the original plan. Shah Jahan had planned to build
another vast mausoleum for himself across the river from that of his
loved one. However, when he died, his son betrayed his father's
last wish and buried him beside his beloved wife.

　　還有一個值得一提的細節。沙賈汗的墓穴，並不是原先設計中的一部
分。他原本計畫隔著河，在他所愛之人的陵墓的對岸，替自己建造另一座
大型陵寢。然而，他死的時候，他的兒子違背父親的遺願，將沙賈汗埋在
他摯愛的妻子身旁。

be worth* + *V-ing 值得～　　mention〔ˋmɛnʃən〕v. 提到
tomb〔tum〕n. 墳墓　　original〔əˋrɪdʒənḷ〕adj. 原本的
vast〔væst〕adj. 巨大的
betray〔bɪˋtre〕v. 辜負；背叛
bury〔ˋbɛrɪ〕v. 埋葬　　beside〔bɪˋsaɪd〕prep. 在…旁邊
beloved〔bɪˋlʌvɪd〕adj. 心愛的

1. (**C**)　下列何者最有可能是本文的出處？

　(A) 應用物理學期刊。

　(B) 動物星球頻道。

　(C) 國家地理雜誌。

　(D) 希臘神話故事這本書。

　* source〔sors〕n. 來源　　***be likely to* + *V*.** 可能～
　journal〔ˋdʒɝnḷ〕n. 期刊　　applied〔əˋplaɪd〕adj. 應用的
　physics〔ˋfɪzɪks〕n. 物理學　　planet〔ˋplænɪt〕n. 行星
　geographic〔͵dʒiəˋgræfɪk〕adj. 地理學的
　Greek〔grik〕adj. 希臘的
　mythology〔mɪˋθɑlədʒɪ〕n. 神話

2. (**B**)　文章中沒有提到下列何種資訊？

　(A) 建造泰姬瑪哈陵的原因。

　(B) 皇后的名字。

　(C) 建造工程耗費的時間。

　(D) 泰姬瑪哈陵的建築特色。

　* information〔͵ɪnfɚˋmeʃən〕n. 資訊
　duration〔duˋreʃən〕n. 持續期間
　architectural〔͵ɑrkəˋtɛktʃərəl〕adj. 建築上的
　characteristic〔͵kærɪktəˋrɪstɪk〕n. 特色

3. (**D**) 下列敘述何者為「眞」？

(A) 主要的建築師後來升官了。

(B) 兀斯塔・以薩的妻子，要求他設計一座陵墓來紀念她。

(C) 泰姬瑪哈陵是為了信仰與虛榮，而不是為了愛情所建造的。

(D) <u>泰姬瑪哈陵直到 1653 年才完工。</u>

* promote〔prə'mot〕*v.* 使升職　　***in memory of*** 紀念
complete〔kəm'plit〕*v.* 完成

4. (**A**) 根據上下文，"mausoleum" 的意思為何？

(A) <u>埋葬屍體的地方。</u>

(B) 和尚與尼姑居住的寺廟。

(C) 人民敲響大鐘的高塔。

(D) 一個統治某地區的朝代。

* ***based on*** 依據　　context〔'kɑntɛkst〕*n.* 上下文
body〔'bɑdɪ〕*n.* 屍體　　temple〔'tɛmpḷ〕*n.* 寺廟
monk〔mʌŋk〕*n.* 修道士；和尚　　nun〔nʌn〕*n.* 修女；尼姑
dynasty〔'daɪnəstɪ〕*n.* 朝代；豪門世家
rule〔rul〕*v.* 統治　　region〔'ridʒən〕*n.* 地區

5. (**C**) 根據印度傳說，當泰姬瑪哈陵完工時，兀斯塔・以薩怎麼了？

(A) 他可以忘記亡妻的悲傷回憶。

(B) 他被埋葬在妻子身旁。

(C) <u>他被殺了。</u>

(D) 這個人根本不存在。

* exist〔ɪg'zɪst〕*v.* 存在

TEST 25

Read the following passage and choose the best answer for each question.

Advertising is now a multi-billion-dollar global industry. Companies spend almost as much on advertising as they do actually manufacturing the products.

Some well-known advertising slogans, like Nike's "Just do it," are so simple and easy to remember that they have become part of our everyday language. Some of the commercials that we see on TV or in movie theaters have even become more exciting, funny or interesting than the programs and movies we watch.

It wasn't always like this. Advertising used to just be a way to make consumers more familiar with a company's products. Advertisements would simply mention a product's good qualities in order to persuade people to buy it. Sometimes a famous person would recommend a product. Manufacturers presumed that consumers who liked the star would also be attracted to the product.

Nowadays, advertising is much more complex. Companies are in the business of selling brand names instead of products. Nike, for example, doesn't try to sell its products by telling us how well made or comfortable they are. The advertisements are designed instead to make us relate the Nike brand with being independent and cool, and the company hopes that this will make us buy the shoes. 【中正高中】

1. How much money is spent on advertising each year?
   (A) Many millions of dollars.
   (B) One billion dollars.
   (C) None; the brands are already known.
   (D) Nearly as much as is spent on production.

2. What was the original intention of advertising?
   (A) To make people know a product's good qualities.
   (B) To make people know advertising was interesting.
   (C) To make people happy when TV was boring.
   (D) To make people feel confident and cool.

3. Why have some advertising slogans become part of our language?

(A) Because the stars are attractive.

(B) Because the products are well made.

(C) Because the slogans are very catchy.

(D) Because people like to watch TV.

4. Many companies nowadays try to _____.

(A) teach people cool language that they can often use

(B) sell people an image rather than an individual product

(C) recommend famous people and make consumers like them

(D) run advertisements telling us how well made the products are

5. Which of the following best describes advertising today when compared with advertising of fifty years ago?

(A) It uses more celebrities.

(B) It uses more slogans.

(C) It is more subtle.

(D) It is more informative.

TEST 25 詳解

Advertising is now a multi-billion-dollar global industry. Companies spend almost as much on advertising as they do actually manufacturing the products.

　　廣告業現在是數十億美金的全球性產業。很多公司在廣告上的花費，幾乎就跟實際製造產品的花費一樣多。

　　advertising〔'ædvɚ͵taɪzɪŋ〕*n.* 廣告；廣告業
　　multi-〔'mʌltɪ〕*adj.* 多的；幾倍的　　billion〔'bɪljən〕*n.* 十億
　　multi-billion-dollar〔'mʌltɪ'bɪljən'dɑlɚ〕*adj.* 數十億美金的
　　global〔'globl̩〕*adj.* 全球的　　industry〔'ɪndəstrɪ〕*n.* 產業；工業
　　actually〔'æktʃʊəlɪ〕*adv.* 實際上
　　manufacture〔͵mænjə'fæktʃɚ〕*v.* 製造　　product〔'prɑdəkt〕*n.* 產品

Some well-known advertising slogans, like Nike's "Just do it," are so simple and easy to remember that they have become part of our everyday language. Some of the commercials that we see on TV or in movie theaters have even become more exciting, funny or interesting than the programs and movies we watch.

　　某些著名的廣告口號，像是耐吉公司的「做就對了」，既簡單又好記，已經成為我們日常語言的一部分。有些在電視上或電影院看到的廣告，甚至比我們看的節目或電影本身，來得更刺激，更好笑，或更有趣。

　　well-known〔'wɛl'non〕*adj.* 有名的；眾所皆知的
　　slogan〔'slogən〕*n.* 口號；標語
　　Nike〔'naɪkɪ〕*n.* 耐吉【原意為希臘神話勝利女神，現指美國運動產品的品牌】　　commercial〔kə'mɝʃəl〕*n.* 商業廣告
　　exciting〔ɪk'saɪtɪŋ〕*adj.* 令人興奮的　　funny〔'fʌnɪ〕*adj.* 好笑的
　　interesting〔'ɪntərɪstɪŋ〕*adj.* 有趣的　　program〔'progræm〕*n.* 節目

It wasn't always like this. Advertising used to just be a way to make consumers more familiar with a company's products. Advertisements would simply mention a product's good qualities in order to persuade people to buy it. Sometimes a famous person would recommend a product. Manufacturers presumed that consumers who liked the star would also be attracted to the product.

但廣告並非一直如此。廣告曾經是一種讓消費者更熟悉公司產品的方法。廣告會簡單地提及產品的優點，以說服人們買下它。有時名人會推薦某項產品。製造商認為，喜歡這位明星的消費者，也會被產品所吸引。

> **used to V.** 以前～　　consumer〔kənˋsumɚ〕 *n.* 消費者
> familiar〔fəˋmɪljɚ〕 *adj.* 熟悉的
> **be familiar with** 對…感到熟悉
> advertisement〔͵ædvɚˋtaɪzmənt〕 *n.* 廣告；宣傳
> mention〔ˋmɛnʃən〕 *v.* 提到　　quality〔ˋkwɑlətɪ〕 *n.* 品質；特質
> **in order to + V.** 為了～　　persuade〔pɚˋswed〕 *v.* 說服
> recommend〔͵rɛkəˋmɛnd〕 *v.* 推薦；介紹
> manufacturer〔͵mænjəˋfæktʃərɚ〕 *n.* 製造商
> presume〔prɪˋzum〕 *v.* 假定；推測；認為　　star〔stɑr〕 *n.* 明星
> attract〔əˋtrækt〕 *v.* 吸引　　**be attracted to** 被…所吸引

Nowadays, advertising is much more complex. Companies are in the business of selling brand names instead of products. Nike, for example, doesn't try to sell its products by telling us how well made or comfortable they are. The advertisements are designed instead to make us relate the Nike brand with being independent and cool, and the company hopes that this will make us buy the shoes.

　　現在的廣告業複雜多了。許多公司從事銷售品牌的工作，而不是在銷售產品。舉例來說，耐吉公司並非試著透過告訴我們產品做得多麼精緻舒適，來銷售產品。廣告反而是設計成讓我們將耐吉這個品牌，跟獨立、有魅力相連結，公司希望這樣能讓我們購買這些鞋子。

complex〔kəm'plɛks〕*adj.* 複雜的
be in the business of 從事⋯的工作　　brand〔brænd〕*n.* 品牌
instead〔ɪn'stɛd〕*adv.* 作爲代替；反而　　design〔dɪ'zaɪn〕*v.* 設計
relate〔rɪ'let〕*v.* 使連結
relate A ***with*** B　將 A 與 B 連結
independent〔ˌɪndɪ'pɛndənt〕*adj.* 獨立的
cool〔kul〕*adj.* 酷的；有魅力的

1. (**D**)　每年在廣告上的花費有多少？

　　(A)　好幾百萬美金。

　　(B)　十億美金。

　　(C)　不花錢，這些品牌都是已知的。

　　(D)　幾乎跟製造產品的花費一樣。

　　* million〔'mɪljən〕*n.* 百萬
　　　production〔prə'dʌkʃən〕*n.* 生產；製造

2. (**A**)　廣告原本的意圖是什麼？

　　(A)　讓人們知道產品的優點。

　　(B)　讓人們知道廣告很有趣。

　　(C)　當電視節目很無聊時讓人們開心。

　　(D)　讓人們覺得有信心且有魅力。

　　* original〔ə'rɪdʒənl〕*adj.* 最初的；原本的
　　　intention〔ɪn'tɛnʃən〕*n.* 意圖
　　　confident〔'kɑnfədənt〕*adj.* 有自信的

3. (**C**) 爲什麼有些廣告口號變成我們語言的一部分？

　　(A) 因爲明星很有吸引力。

　　(B) 因爲產品做得很棒。

　　(C) <u>因爲口號很吸引人。</u>

　　(D) 因爲人們喜歡看電視。

　　* attractive〔ə'træktɪv〕*adj.* 有吸引力的；吸引人的
　　　catchy〔'kætʃɪ〕*adj.* 引人注意的

4. (**B**) 現在很多公司嘗試要 ＿＿＿＿＿＿＿。

　　(A) 教導人們可以經常使用酷炫的語言

　　(B) <u>賣給人們一種形象而不是個別的產品</u>

　　(C) 推薦有名的人並且讓消費者喜歡他們

　　(D) 刊登廣告來告訴我們產品做得很好

　　* image〔'ɪmɪdʒ〕*n.* 形象　　　***rather than*** 而不是
　　　individual〔,ɪndə'vɪdʒuəl〕*adj.* 個別的；個人的
　　　run〔rʌn〕*v.* 刊登

5. (**C**) 跟五十年前的廣告相比，下列何者最能描述現代的廣告業？

　　(A) 使用更多名人。

　　(B) 使用更多口號。

　　(C) <u>比較巧妙。</u>

　　(D) 比較有教育性。

　　* describe〔dɪ'skraɪb〕*v.* 描述
　　　celebrity〔sə'lɛbrətɪ〕*n.* 名人
　　　subtle〔'sʌtḷ〕*adj.* 巧妙的；細密的
　　　informative〔ɪn'fɔrmətɪv〕*adj.* 有教育性的；提供知識的

TEST 26

Read the following passage and choose the best answer for each question.

Loneliness

I was about to go, and said so;

And I had almost started for the door.

But he was all alone in the sugar-house,

And more lonely than he'd ever been before.

We'd talked for half an hour, almost,

About the price of sugar, and how I liked my school,

And he had made me drink some syrup hot,

Telling me it was better that way than when cool.

And I agreed, and thanked him for it,

And said good-bye, and was about to go.

Want to see where I was born?

He asked me quickly. How to say no?

The sugar-house looked over miles of valley.

He pointed with a sticky finger to a patch of snow

Where he was born. The house, he said, was gone.

I understand these people better, now I know.

— *Brooks Jenkins* 【中正高中】

1. Why is this poem called "Loneliness"?

   (A) The poet is lonely.

   (B) The poet knows the old man is lonely.

   (C) The poet has never seen a lonely person.

   (D) The old man was lonely as a boy.

2. What does the old man do in the sugar-house?

   (A) bake cookies   (B) write letters

   (C) run a school   (D) make syrup

3. The old man doesn't want his visitor to _____.

   (A) talk   (B) leave

   (C) eat   (D) laugh

4. What probably happened to the house the old man was born in?

   (A) It was covered with dust.

   (B) It was torn down.

   (C) It has been painted.

   (D) Other people bought it.

5. Who is the narrator?

   (A) A sugar maker.

   (B) A schoolboy.

   (C) A sugar buyer.

   (D) The man's brother.

TEST 26 詳解

Loneliness

I was about to go, and said so;
And I had almost started for the door.
But he was all alone in the sugar-house,
And more lonely than he'd ever been before.
We'd talked for half an hour, almost,
About the price of sugar, and how I liked my school,
And he had made me drink some syrup hot,
Telling me it was better that way than when cool.
And I agreed, and thanked him for it,
And said good-bye, and was about to go.
Want to see where I was born?
He asked me quickly. How to say no?
The sugar-house looked over miles of valley.
He pointed with a sticky finger to a patch of snow
Where he was born. The house, he said, was gone.
I understand these people better, now I know.

— Brooks Jenkins

寂　寞

我本來正要走，也已經這麼說；
我幾乎動身走到門口。
他如此孤寂，在這糖果屋中，
而且比以往任何時候，都更寂寞。
我們幾乎聊了半個鐘頭，

談到糖價，談到我如何愛我的學校，

他要我在糖漿還熱著的時候喝下，

告訴我這樣比冷的喝更好。

我同意，也向他表示感激，

說了再見，準備離去。

想不想看看我的出生地？

他很快地問我，我如何能轉身就走？

糖果屋看來遠在山谷外好幾英里。

他用黏黏的手指，指向一塊雪地，

那是我的出生地。那房子，他說，已經消失。

我更了解這些人了，現在我終於懂了。

——布魯克・詹金斯

loneliness〔'lonlınıs〕*n.* 孤獨；寂寞　　***start for*** 動身前往

all alone 獨自地　　sugar-house〔'ʃugɚ'haus〕*n.* 糖果屋

lonely〔'lonlı〕*adj.* 孤單的；寂寞的

half〔hæf〕*n.* 一半　　make〔mek〕*v.* 使

syrup〔'sırəp〕*n.* 糖漿；糖蜜

be about to V. 正要～　　mile〔maıl〕*n.* 英里【約 1.6 公里】

valley〔'vælı〕*n.* 山谷　　point〔pɔınt〕*v.* 指出

sticky〔'stıkı〕*adj.* 黏黏的　　gone〔gɔn〕*adj.* 消失的

patch〔pætʃ〕*n.* 一塊（地）

1.(**B**) 為什麼這首詩叫作「寂寞」？

(A) 詩人很寂寞。

(B) <u>詩人知道老人很寂寞。</u>

(C) 詩人從沒見過寂寞的人。

(D) 老人像個男孩一樣寂寞。

* poem〔'poım〕*n.* 詩　　poet〔'poıt〕*n.* 詩人

2.(**D**) 老人在糖果屋裡做了什麼事？

  (A) 烤餅乾。   (B) 寫信。

  (C) 經營學校。   (D) <u>煮糖漿。</u>

  * bake〔bek〕*v.* 烘烤
   cookie〔ˋkʊkɪ〕*n.* 餅乾
   run〔rʌn〕*v.* 經營

3.(**B**) 這個老人不希望拜訪他的人 ＿＿＿＿＿＿＿。

  (A) 說話   (B) <u>離開</u>

  (C) 吃東西   (D) 笑

4.(**B**) 老人出生時的房子可能出了什麼事？

  (A) 被灰塵掩蓋。 (B) <u>被拆除了。</u>

  (C) 被油漆上色。 (D) 被其他人買走。

  * cover〔ˋkʌvɚ〕*v.* 覆蓋 dust〔dʌst〕*n.* 灰塵
   tear〔tɛr〕*v.* 撕裂；破裂【三態：tear-tore-torn】
   tear down 拆除 paint〔pent〕*v.* 油漆

5.(**B**) 誰是敘述者？

  (A) 製糖者。   (B) <u>男學生。</u>

  (C) 買糖的人。 (D) 男人的兄弟。

  * narrator〔ˋnæretɚ〕*n.* 敘述者
   schoolboy〔ˋskul͵bɔɪ〕*n.* (小學、國高中的) 男學生
   buyer〔ˋbaɪɚ〕*n.* 購買者

TEST 27

Read the following passage, and choose the best answer for each question.

As cell phones grow more and more unwelcome in places like theaters, hotels and churches, people are being asked more often to turn off their phones in those places. This is ironic, given the fact that an increasing number of people own mobile phones.

A hotel in Germany offers a phone sitting service for guests who cannot bear to switch off, even while they eat. Staff will take care of their phones, answer calls, and if necessary, bring messages or the handsets to guests.

A German minister named Hans Otto caused protests when he instituted a mobile phone ban in his church. People were even going outside to use the phone during services. When a phone rang during a funeral service, it was **the last straw** for pastor Otto. Since May all church events have been mobile-free. Young churchgoers in particular found the ban hard to endure, but the effect has been positive.

Mobile phone manufacturers are responding to the need for mobile phone-free zones by offering cellular disablers that transmit on the same frequency as mobile phone radio signals, thereby blocking a cell phone's signal to the network. 【松山高中】

1. Why is the situation ironic?

   (A) More people are using phones which are more advanced.

   (B) Cell phones users are banned from using them against their will.

   (C) People in theaters, hotels, and churches are asked to turn off their cell phones.

   (D) More people are using mobile phones while bans become more and more widespread.

2. What is the function of the phone sitting service?

   (A) To switch off the guests' cell phones.

   (B) To institute a ban on the use of cell phones.

   (C) To look after the guests' phones and calls.

   (D) To increase the number of people using mobile phones.

3. What does the phrase "the last straw" in the third paragraph probably mean? It means _____.

(A) the worst harvest a farmer can have

(B) the best food for pastors to eat

(C) something good for the churchgoers

(D) an event that makes a situation unbearable

4. What positive effect did Otto's cell phone ban have?

(A) Church services were uninterrupted.

(B) Younger churchgoers stopped going to church.

(C) The church was able to buy a cellular disabler.

(D) People were able to eat in peace.

5. How might a mobile phone manufacturer view the increasing number of cell phone bans?

(A) As a threat to his personal freedom.

(B) As a threat to phone sales.

(C) As an opportunity to enjoy a quiet place.

(D) As an opportunity to sell a new product.

TEST 27 詳解

As cell phones grow more and more unwelcome in places like theaters, hotels and churches, people are being asked more often to turn off their phones in those places. This is ironic, given the fact that an increasing number of people own mobile phones.

當手機在戲院、飯店、跟教堂這些地方越來越不受歡迎的時候，人們更常被要求在這些地方關掉電話。這很諷刺，因爲事實上持有手機的人數已經越來越多。

cell〔sɛl〕*n.* 小房間；細胞
cell phone 手機 (= *cellular phone* = *mobile phone* = *hand phone*)
unwelcome〔ʌn'wɛlkəm〕*adj.* 不受歡迎的
turn off 關掉　　ironic〔aɪ'rɑnɪk〕*adj.* 諷刺的
increasing〔ɪn'krisɪŋ〕*adj.* 日益增加的
mobile〔'mobḷ〕*adj.* 可移動的　　***mobile phone*** 行動電話

A hotel in Germany offers a phone sitting service for guests who cannot bear to switch off, even while they eat. Staff will take care of their phones, answer calls, and if necessary, bring messages or the handsets to guests.

德國有家飯店，提供暫時保管手機服務，給那些甚至在吃飯時，都無法忍受關上手機的客人。員工會留意客人的手機，接聽電話，若有必要的話，會把留言或是電話拿給客人。

Germany〔'dʒɝmənɪ〕*n.* 德國　　offer〔'ɔfɚ〕*v.* 提供
sit〔sɪt〕*v.* 當臨時保姆　　***phone sitting service*** 暫時保管手機服務
bear〔bɛr〕*v.* 忍受　　switch〔swɪtʃ〕*v.* 開關；轉變
switch off 關掉　　staff〔stæf〕*n.* 員工
take care of 照顧；留意
if necessary 如有必要　　handset〔'hænd,sɛt〕*n.* 電話聽筒

A German minister named Hans Otto caused protests when he instituted a mobile phone ban in his church. People were even going outside to use the phone during services. When a phone rang during a funeral service, it was **the last straw** for pastor Otto. Since May all church events have been mobile-free. Young churchgoers in particular found the ban hard to endure, but the effect has been positive.

當一名叫做哈斯‧奧圖的德國牧師，在他的教堂制定行動電話禁令時，引發了抗議。人們甚至必須在禮拜儀式中，到外面去使用手機。當葬禮儀式中有手機鈴聲響起時，會使得奧圖牧師無法忍受。從五月開始，所有教會活動都不能使用手機。那些按時上教堂的年輕人，發現這種禁令特別地難以忍受，但效果卻正面的。

German〔ˋdʒɝmən〕*adj.* 德國（人）的
minister〔ˋmɪnɪstɚ〕*n.* 牧師　　cause〔kɔz〕*v.* 引起；導致
protest〔ˋprotɛst〕*n.* 抗議
institute〔ˋɪnstəˏtjut〕*v.* 設立；制定（制度）
ban〔bæn〕*n.* 禁令　　service〔ˋsɝvɪs〕*n.* 禮拜儀式
funeral〔ˋfjunərəl〕*n.* 葬禮　　straw〔strɔ〕*n.* 稻草
the last straw 使人再也無法忍受的微小事件
It is the last straw that breaks the camel's back. 【諺】壓垮駱駝的
　最後一根稻草。

pastor〔ˋpæstɚ〕*n.* 牧師　　event〔ɪˋvɛnt〕*n.* 事件；大型活動
mobile-free〔ˋmobḷˋfri〕*adj.* 沒有手機的；不能用手機的
churchgoer〔ˋtʃɝtʃˏgoɚ〕*n.* 按時上教堂的人
particular〔pəˋtɪkjələ〕*adj.* 特別的
in particular 特別地　　endure〔ɪnˋdjur〕*v.* 忍受
effect〔ɪˋfɛkt〕*n.* 效果
positive〔ˋpɑzətɪv〕*adj.* 正面的

Mobile phone manufacturers are responding to the need for mobile phone-free zones by offering cellular disablers that transmit on the same frequency as mobile phone radio signals, thereby blocking a cell phone's signal to the network.

手機製造商也正在回應這種對無手機區域的需求，藉由提供行動電話的干擾器，傳送跟手機無線電訊號相同的頻率，阻擋手機訊號傳送到網路上。

manufacturer〔͵mænjə'fæktʃərə〕*n.* 製造商
respond〔rɪ'spɑnd〕*v.* 回答；回應　　zone〔zon〕*n.* 區域
mobile phone-free zones 不能使用行動電話的區域
cellular〔'sɛljələ〕*adj.* 行動電話的
disabler〔dɪs'eblə〕*n.* 使人殘廢之物；失效器
transmit〔træns'mɪt〕*v.* 傳送　　frequency〔'frikwənsɪ〕*n.* 頻率
radio〔'redɪ͵o〕*n.* 無線電　　signal〔'sɪgnḷ〕*n.* 訊號；信號
block〔blɑk〕*v.* 阻塞；阻礙　　thereby〔͵ðɛr'baɪ〕*adv.* 藉以
network〔'nɛt͵wɜk〕*n.* 聯絡網；廣播網

1. (**D**) 為什麼情況變得很諷刺？
   (A) 越來越多人使用更先進的手機。
   (B) 手機使用者不情願地被禁止使用手機。
   (C) 在電影院、飯店跟教堂中，人們被要求把手機關機。
   (D) <u>現在有更多人使用手機，但是禁令卻變得越來越普遍。</u>

   * situation〔͵sɪtʃʊ'eʃən〕*n.* 情況
     advanced〔əd'vænst〕*adj.* 進步的
     ban〔bæn〕*v.* 禁止　*n.* 禁令
     ban** sb. **from V-ing 禁止某人做～　　will〔wɪl〕*n.* 意志
     against** one's **will 違背某人的本意；不情願地
     freedom〔'fridəm〕*n.* 自由　　***at will*** 隨心所欲地
     widespread〔'waɪd'sprɛd〕*adj.* 普遍的

2. (**C**) 暫時照顧手機服務的功能是？

    (A) 關掉客人的手機。   (B) 制定使用手機的禁令。

    (C) 留意客人的手機跟來電。   (D) 增加使用手機的人數。

    * function〔ˋfʌŋkʃən〕*n.* 功能；作用   ***look after*** 照顧；留意

3. (**D**) 第三段的片語 "the last straw" 可能是什麼意思？

    它代表 ＿＿＿＿＿＿。

    (A) 農夫最慘淡的收成

    (B) 給牧師吃的最佳食物

    (C) 對按時上教堂的人來說很好的東西

    (D) 讓情況變得無法忍受的事件

    * harvest〔ˋhɑrvɪst〕*n.* 收成；收穫
      unbearable〔ʌnˋbɛrəbḷ〕*adj.* 令人難以忍受的

4. (**A**) 奧圖的手機禁令所帶來的正面影響是什麼？

    (A) 讓教堂禮拜儀式不受干擾。

    (B) 讓按時上教堂的年輕人不再上教堂。

    (C) 讓教堂能買一個行動電話干擾器。

    (D) 讓人們能夠安靜地吃東西。

    * uninterrupted〔ˏʌnɪntəˋrʌptɪd〕*adj.* 不受干擾的；不間斷的
      peace〔pis〕*n.* 和平；安靜

5. (**D**) 手機製造商可能會如何看待日益增加的手機禁令？

    (A) 是自己人身自由的威脅。

    (B) 是銷售手機的威脅。

    (C) 是一個能享有安靜的機會。

    (D) 是銷售新產品的機會。

    * threat〔θrɛt〕*n.* 威脅   opportunity〔ˏɑpəˋtjunətɪ〕*n.* 機會
      product〔ˋprɑdəkt〕*n.* 產品

TEST 28

Read the following passage and choose the best answer for each question.

Kenya is the most popular destination in the world for safaris. About the size of Texas, it is famous for its "Out Of Africa" scenic beauty, diverse cultures and rich wildlife. The wildlife is the major attraction of Kenya safaris, which take place in some of Africa's best-known national parks, including the Nairobi National Park, Meru National Park, Lake Turkana, Sibiloi National Park and Lake Nakuru. Want to learn first-hand about the wildlife in Kenya? Then join African Safari Program (ASP).

The program offers a five-week course which is set on the beautiful 20-acre campus of United States International University in Nairobi. The course includes three or four safaris. During each safari, participants camp outdoors for up to six days. One of the most popular destinations is the Masai Mara <u>Game Reserve</u>. An amazing collection of wildlife lives on the reserve. Students study elephants, zebras, giraffes, rhinos and other exotic animals in their natural habitat.

【内湖高中】

1. What can you find in Kenya?

    (A) Hip-hop culture and fashion.

    (B) Diverse cultures and rich wildlife.

    (C) Reserved camping sites.

    (D) Some national car parks.

2. Which of the following is **NOT TRUE** about safaris in Kenya?

    (A) The students in ASP camp outdoors and study wildlife.

    (B) Amazing wildlife can be found in Masai Mara <u>Game Reserve</u>.

    (C) Some of the Kenya safaris take place in national parks.

    (D) Hunting is the major attraction of ASP safaris.

3. How many days in total do ASP participants spend camping outdoors?

    (A) Three or four.   (B) Five weeks.

    (C) Up to 24.   (D) Around six.

4. What is a safari in this passage?

    (A) A trip to view animals.   (B) An environmental study.

    (C) A hunting trip.   (D) A cultural exchange.

5. What is true about Kenya?

    (A) It is the same as Texas.

    (B) It is home to several national parks.

    (C) It is part of the United States University.

    (D) There are several world-famous zoos there.

TEST 28 詳解

Kenya is the most popular destination in the world for safaris. About the size of Texas, it is famous for its "Out Of Africa" scenic beauty, diverse cultures and rich wildlife. The wildlife is the major attraction of Kenya safaris, which take place in some of Africa's best-known national parks, including the Nairobi National Park, Meru National Park, Lake Turkana, Sibiloi National Park and Lake Nakuru. Want to learn first-hand about the wildlife in Kenya? Then join African Safari Program (ASP).

肯亞是全世界最受歡迎的狩獵旅行目的地。肯亞大約跟德州一樣大，因為電影「遠離非洲」裡秀麗的風景、多樣文化，及豐富的野生動物而聞名。野生動物是肯亞狩獵旅行的最大魅力，經常出現在非洲一些最有名的國家公園，包括奈洛比國家公園、梅魯國家公園、圖爾卡納湖泊、錫比洛伊國家公園，和納庫魯湖泊。想學到有關肯亞野生動物的第一手訊息嗎？那就參加非洲狩獵旅行計畫（ASP）吧。

Kenya〔'kɛnjɑ〕*n.* 肯亞【東非大國，首都奈洛比（Nairobi）】

destination〔,dɛstə'neʃən〕*n.* 目的地

safari〔sə'fɑrɪ〕*n.* 狩獵旅行 Texas〔'tɛksəs〕*n.* 德州【美國西南部一州】

be famous for 因…而聞名 Africa〔'æfrɪkə〕*n.* 非洲

Out of Africa 遠離非洲【電影名】

scenic〔'sinɪk〕*adj.* 風景優美的

scenic beauty 風景之美；美景 diverse〔də'vɝs〕*adj.* 多種的

wildlife〔'waɪld,laɪf〕*n.* 野生動物【集合名詞】

major〔'medʒɚ〕*adj.* 主要的

attraction〔ə'trækʃən〕*n.* 吸引力；魅力

take place 舉行（活動）；（事件）發生

best-known〔'bɛst'non〕*adj.* 最有名的　　　*National Park* 國家公園

Nairobi National Park 奈洛比國家公園【位於肯亞北部奈洛比省】

Meru National Park 梅盧國家公園【肯亞東部，屬東非大裂谷一部分】

Lake Turkana 圖爾卡納湖泊【肯亞北部因斷層作用而形成的內流湖，
屬於東非大裂谷一部分，大部分在肯亞境內，僅北端在衣索比亞境內】

Sibiloi National Park 錫比洛伊國家公園【位於肯亞北部圖爾卡納湖
東岸，現在跟圖爾卡納國家公園合併成為「圖爾卡納國家公園群」，
1997 年被聯合國教科文組織選為世界遺產之一】

Lake Nakuru 納庫魯湖泊【位於肯亞北部奈洛比省的內陸湖】

first-hand〔'fɜst'hænd〕*adj.* 第一手的；直接的

African〔'æfrɪkən〕*adj.* 非洲的

African Safari Program 非洲狩獵旅行計畫【一項為期五週的旅行計
畫，課程中一半時間在肯亞戶外露營探險，觀察野生動物，另一半時間
在美國國際大學中授課，主要目的是讓參與者了解野生動物保育管理的
重要性，以及學習多元種族文化】

The program offers a five-week course which is set on the beautiful 20-acre campus of United States International University in Nairobi. The course includes three or four safaris. During each safari, participants camp outdoors for up to six days. One of the most popular destinations is the Masai Mara Game Reserve. An amazing collection of wildlife lives on the reserve. Students study elephants, zebras, giraffes, rhinos and other exotic animals in their natural habitat.

　　這項計畫提供五週的課程，地點在奈洛比省內，二十英畝大的美國國際大學美麗校園中。課程包括三到四次狩獵旅行。每次旅行中，參與者在戶外露營最長達六天。其中最受歡迎的地點之一，就是馬賽馬拉野生動物保護區。保護區中的野生動物數量很驚人。學生們在動物的天然棲息地中，研究大象、斑馬、長頸鹿、犀牛，以及其他外來的動物。

offer〔'ɔfɚ〕*v.* 提供　　course〔kors〕*n.* 課程

acre〔'ekɚ〕*n.* 英畝

campus〔'kæmpəs〕*n.* 校園

international〔͵ɪntɚ'næʃənḷ〕*adj.* 國際的

university〔͵junə'vɝsətɪ〕*n.* 大學

United States International University 美國國際大學

participant〔pɚ'tɪsəpənt〕*n.* 參與者

outdoors〔'aut'dorz〕*adv.* 在戶外

game〔gem〕*n.* 獵物　　reserve〔rɪ'zɝv〕*n.* 保護區

game reserve 野生動物保護區

Masai Mara Game Reserve 馬賽馬拉野生動物保護區【位於非
　　洲肯亞的西南部，與坦桑尼亞接壤的廣大地區，兩國在此共同建立
　　了一個野生動物保護區，致力保護自然環境。保護區在坦桑尼亞的
　　部份被稱爲塞拉蓋提，而肯亞的這一部分則被稱爲馬塞馬拉】

amazing〔ə'mezɪŋ〕*adj.* 令人吃驚的

collection〔kə'lɛkʃən〕*n.* 蒐集　　zebra〔'zibrə〕*n.* 斑馬

giraffe〔dʒə'ræf〕*n.* 長頸鹿

rhino〔'raɪno〕*n.* 犀牛（= *rhinoceros*）

exotic〔ɪg'zɑtɪk〕*adj.* 外來的　　habitat〔'hæbə͵tæt〕*n.* 棲息地

1. (**B**) 你在肯亞能找到什麼？

　　(A) 嘻哈文化和流行時尚。

　　(B) 多樣文化和豐富的野生動物。

　　(C) 露營保留地。

　　(D) 一些國立停車場。

　　* hip-hop〔'hɪp'hɑp〕*n.* 嘻哈【一種源於美國布魯克林區的
　　　　黑人文化】
　　　reserved〔rɪ'zɝvd〕*adj.* 保留的；預訂的
　　　site〔saɪt〕*n.* 地點　　***car park*** 停車場

2. (**D**) 關於在肯亞的狩獵旅行，下列何者爲「非」？

    (A) 非洲狩獵旅行計畫的學生在戶外露營，並研究野生動物。

    (B) 在馬賽馬拉野生動物保護區中能找到令人驚奇的野生動物。

    (C) 有些肯亞狩獵旅行是在國家公園中舉辦。

    (D) 打獵是非洲狩獵旅行計畫的主要魅力。

3. (**C**) 非洲狩獵旅行計畫的參與者，總共會花多少天在戶外露營？

    (A) 三到四天。   (B) 五週。

    (C) 最長達二十四天。   (D) 大約六天。

4. (**A**) 本文中的 "safari" 指什麼？

    (A) 觀賞野生動物的旅行。

    (B) 一項環境研究。

    (C) 一趟打獵之旅。

    (D) 一種文化交流。

    * view〔vju〕v. 觀看　cultural〔'kʌltʃərəl〕adj. 文化的
    exchange〔ɪks'tʃendʒ〕n. 交流；交換
    environmental〔ɪn,vaɪrən'mɛntl̩〕adj. 環境的

5. (**B**) 關於肯亞，何者爲眞？

    (A) 它跟德州一模一樣。

    (B) 有很多國家公園。

    (C) 是美國大學的一部分。

    (D) 有很多世界著名的動物園。

    * **be home to** 是…的所在地
    world-famous〔'wɜld'feməs〕adj. 世界知名的

TEST 29

Read the following passage and choose the best answer for each question.

Frogs

The storm broke and it rained,
And water rose in the pool,
And frogs hopped into the gutter,

With their skins of yellow and green,
And just their eyes shining above the surface
Of the warm solution of slime.

At night, when fireflies trace
Light lines between the trees and flowers
Exhaling perfume,

The frogs speak to each other
In rhythm. The sound is monstrous,
But their voices are filled with satisfaction.

In the city I pine for the country;
In the country I long for conversation —
Our happy croaking. 【師大附中】

1. What things are shining above the surface of the warm solution of slime?

    (A) The skins of the frogs.

    (B) The eyes of the frogs.

    (C) The eyes of the fireflies.

    (D) The heads of the fireflies.

2. The poet can tell that the frogs are _____.

    (A) boastful   (B) desperate

    (C) lonely   (D) satisfied

3. When do the frogs speak to each other?

    (A) When a storm has occurred.

    (B) When the fireflies come out.

    (C) When they hop into a pool.

    (D) When the flowers wither away.

4. What can we infer about the author?

    (A) Frogs are his favorite pet.

    (B) He is a frog.

    (C) He dislikes city life.

    (D) He is a good conversationalist.

5. What do the fireflies do?

    (A) Exhale perfume.

    (B) Race one another.

    (C) Converse with the frogs.

    (D) Fly between flowers and trees.

TEST 29 詳解

Frogs

The storm broke and it rained,
And water rose in the pool,
And frogs hopped into the gutter,

青蛙

風雨突然降臨天空開始下雨，
池子裡水面升起，
青蛙跳進溝渠，

frog〔frɑg〕*n.* 青蛙　　storm〔stɔrm〕*n.* 暴雨；風暴
break〔brek〕*v.* (風雨) 突然來臨【三態：break-broke-broken】
rise〔raɪz〕*v.* 升起；上漲【三態：rise-rose-risen】
hop〔hɑp〕*v.* 跳；蹦跳　　gutter〔'gʌtɚ〕*n.* 溝

With their skins of yellow and green,
And just their eyes shining above the surface
Of the warm solution of slime.

　　牠們的皮膚黃又綠，
　　眼睛在水面上閃閃發亮，
　　還流著溫熱的黏液。

skin〔skɪn〕*n.* 皮膚　　shine〔ʃaɪn〕*v.* 發光；照耀；閃亮
surface〔'sɝfɪs〕*n.* 水面　　solution〔sə'luʃən〕*n.* 溶液
slime〔slaɪm〕*n.* 黏液

At night, when fireflies trace
Light lines between the trees and flowers
Exhaling perfume,

在夜裡，當螢火蟲彼此追尋蹤跡，
光線交織在樹與花叢裡，
吐著香氣。

firefly (ˈfaɪrˌflaɪ) n. 螢火蟲　　trace (tres) v. 追尋 (痕跡)
line (laɪn) v. 排列　　exhale (ɛksˈhel) v. 呼出 (氣息)
perfume (ˈpɝfjum) n. 香氣

The frogs speak to each other
In rhythm. The sound is monstrous,
But their voices are filled with satisfaction.

青蛙們彼此交談，
用聲韻。那聲音好像怪物，
但牠們的話語充滿滿足。

rhythm (ˈrɪðəm) n. 韻律；節奏
monstrous (ˈmɑnstrəs) adj. 恐怖的；像怪物的
be filled with 充滿了　　satisfaction (ˌsætɪsˈfækʃən) n. 滿足

In the city I pine for the country;
In the country I long for conversation —
Our happy croaking.

在城市裡，我思念鄉村；
在鄉村裡，我渴望話語──
用我們快樂的呱呱聲。

pine (paɪn) v. 思念 *< for >*　　*long for* 渴望
conversation (ˌkɑnvɚˈseʃən) n. 對話；談話
croaking (ˈkrokɪŋ) n. (青蛙的) 呱呱叫

1. (**B**) 什麼東西在水面上閃閃發亮，而且有溫熱的黏液？

    (A) 青蛙的皮膚。   (B) <u>青蛙的眼睛。</u>

    (C) 螢火蟲的眼睛。   (D) 螢火蟲的頭。

2. (**D**) 作者能分辨青蛙是 ＿＿＿＿＿＿＿＿。

    (A) 愛自誇的   (B) 自暴自棄的   (C) 孤單的   (D) <u>滿足的</u>

    * poet〔'poɪt〕*n.* 詩人　　tell〔tɛl〕*v.* 分辨
      boastful〔'bostfəl〕*adj.* 自誇的
      desperate〔'dɛspərɪt〕*adj.* 自暴自棄的；絕望的
      satisfied〔'sætɪs,faɪd〕*adj.* 滿足的

3. (**B**) 什麼時候青蛙會彼此對話？

    (A) 發生暴風雨的時候。   (B) <u>螢火蟲出現的時候。</u>

    (C) 牠們跳進池子裡的時候。   (D) 花朵凋謝的時候。

    * occur〔ə'kɝ〕*v.* 發生　　***come out*** 出現
      wither〔'wɪðɚ〕*v.* 凋謝；衰微

4. (**C**) 我們能夠推論作者是怎樣的人？

    (A) 青蛙是他最喜歡的寵物。   (B) 他是一隻青蛙。

    (C) <u>他不喜歡城市生活。</u>   (D) 他是個健談的人。

    * infer〔ɪn'fɝ〕*v.* 推論　　author〔'ɔθɚ〕*n.* 作者
      pet〔pɛt〕*n.* 寵物　　dislike〔dɪs'laɪk〕*v.* 不喜歡；厭惡
      conversationalist〔,kɑnvɚ'seʃənlɪst〕*n.* 健談者

5. (**D**) 螢火蟲做了什麼事？

    (A) 吐出香氣。   (B) 相互賽跑。

    (C) 跟青蛙交談。   (D) <u>在花叢跟樹之間飛舞。</u>

    * race〔res〕*v.* 賽跑
      converse〔kən'vɝs〕*v.* 交談

TEST 30

Read the following passage and choose the best answer for each question.

Human language is a living thing. Each language has its own biological system, which makes it different from all other languages. This system must constantly adjust to a new environment and new situations to survive and flourish.

When we think of human language this way, it is an easy step to see the words of a language as being like the cells of a living organism — they are constantly forming and dying and splitting into parts as time changes and the language adapts.

There are several specific processes by which new words are formed. Some words that come into the language sound like what they refer to. Words like buzz and ding-dong are good examples of this process.

Still another way in which new words are formed is to use the name of a person or a place closely associated with that word's meaning. The words sandwich and hamburger are examples of this word-formation process. The Earl of Sandwich, an English aristocrat, was so fond of gambling at cards that he hated to be interrupted by the necessity of eating. He thus invented a new way of eating while he continued his game at the gambling table. This quick and convenient dish is what we now call a sandwich — a piece of meat between two slices of bread. The hamburger became the best-known sandwich in the world after it was invented by a citizen of Hamburg in Germany.

As long as a language is alive, its cells will continue to change, forming new words and getting rid of the ones that no longer have any use. 【清水高中】

1. The passage is mainly about
   (A) the biological system of a living organism.
   (B) the inventors of the sandwich and hamburger.
   (C) the development of human cells.
   (D) the changes of a language.

2. A language is a living thing in all of the ways below EXCEPT
   (A) it is similar to the biological system of a living organism.
   (B) it actually has many living cells that split and form constantly.
   (C) it must adjust to new environments to survive.
   (D) its old words die out while new words are constantly added.

3. The word sandwich came from

   (A) card games.

   (B) a piece of meat.

   (C) a person's title.

   (D) a restaurant in England.

4. The statements about hamburger are correct EXCEPT

   (A) it came from a place name.

   (B) it came from a person's name.

   (C) it became the best-known sandwich in the world.

   (D) it was invented by a German.

5. How many ways of word-formation are mentioned in the article?

   (A) Two.

   (B) Three.

   (C) Four.

   (D) Five.

TEST 30 詳解

Human language is a living thing. Each language has its own biological system, which makes it different from all other languages. This system must constantly adjust to a new environment and new situations to survive and flourish.

人類的語言是有生命的。每種語言都有自己的生物系統，讓語言彼此不同。這個系統一定要不斷地去適應新環境跟新情況，才能生存並繁盛。

living (ˈlɪvɪŋ) *adj.* 活的；現存的
biological (ˌbaɪəˈlɑdʒɪkl̩) *adj.* 生物學的
system (ˈsɪstəm) *n.* 系統
biological system 生物系統【生物學中，一組共同運作的器官系統】
be different from 跟…不同   constantly (ˈkɑnstəntlɪ) *adv.* 不斷地
adjust (əˈdʒʌst) *v.* 適應；調整
environment (ɪnˈvaɪrənmənt) *n.* 環境
situation (ˌsɪtʃʊˈeʃən) *n.* 情況   survive (səˈvaɪv) *v.* 生存
flourish (ˈflɝɪʃ) *v.* 興盛；繁榮

When we think of human language this way, it is an easy step to see the words of a language as being like the cells of a living organism — they are constantly forming and dying and splitting into parts as time changes and the language adapts.

當我們這樣思考人類的語言，就是一個簡單的步驟，把語言中的字彙，看成生物的細胞——當時代改變時，它們會不斷形成、死去，並分裂成小分子，語言才得以適應。

step (stɛp) *n.* 步驟   cell (sɛl) *n.* 細胞
organism (ˈɔrgənˌɪzəm) *n.* 有機體；生物
form (fɔrm) *v.* 形成
split (splɪt) *v.* 分裂【三態：split-split-split】
adapt (əˈdæpt) *v.* 適應

There are several specific processes by which new words are formed. Some words that come into the language sound like what they refer to. Words like buzz and ding-dong are good examples of this process.

形成新字彙有幾個特定的過程。有些字聽起來像它們所表示的東西，而變成語言。像是「嗡嗡聲」還有「叮噹聲」就是這種過程很好的例子。

specific〔spɪˋsɪfɪk〕*adj.* 特定的　　process〔ˋprɑsɛs〕*n.* 過程
refer to 是指　　　　buzz〔bʌz〕*n.* 嗡嗡聲
ding-dong〔ˋdɪŋˏdɔŋ〕*n.* 叮噹聲

Still another way in which new words are formed is to use the name of a person or a place closely associated with that word's meaning. The words sandwich and hamburger are examples of this word-formation process. The Earl of Sandwich, an English aristocrat, was so fond of gambling at cards that he hated to be interrupted by the necessity of eating. He thus invented a new way of eating while he continued his game at the gambling table. This quick and convenient dish is what we now call a sandwich — a piece of meat between two slices of bread. The hamburger became the best-known sandwich in the world after it was invented by a citizen of Hamburg in Germany.

還有另一種形成新字彙的方式，就是使用跟字詞意義有緊密關係的人名或地名。「三明治」跟「漢堡」兩個字，是這種字彙形成過程的例子。英國三明治伯爵是個貴族，他非常喜歡賭紙牌，討厭因爲必須吃飯而被打斷，因此他發明一種，當他在賭桌上繼續玩牌的時候，可以吃東西的新方法。這種快速又方便的菜餚，就是現在我們稱爲三明治的東西——將一片肉夾在兩片麵包中間。漢堡被德國漢堡市的市民發明之後，現在已成爲全世界最知名的三明治。

closely〔'kloslɪ〕*adv.* 緊密地

be associated with 與～有關

meaning〔'minɪŋ〕*n.* 意義

sandwich〔'sændwɪtʃ〕*n.* 三明治【三明治據説是英國肯特郡，三明治村
　的約翰·孟塔古伯爵所發明，故以他爲名】

hamburger〔'hæmbɝɡɚ〕*n.* 漢堡

formation〔fɔr'meʃən〕*n.* 形成；構成

word-formation〔'wɝd,fɔr'meʃən〕*n.* 字彙形成

Earl〔ɝl〕*n.* 伯爵　　aristocrat〔ə'rɪstə,kræt〕*n.* 貴族

fond〔fɑnd〕*adj.* 喜愛…的　　gambling〔'gæmblɪŋ〕*n.* 賭博

cards〔kɑrds〕*n. pl.* 紙牌　interrupt〔,ɪntə'rʌpt〕*v.* 打斷

necessity〔nə'sɛsətɪ〕*n.* 必要；需要　　invent〔ɪn'vɛnt〕*v.* 發明

gambling table 賭桌　　dish〔dɪʃ〕*n.* 菜餚；食物

slice〔slaɪs〕*n.* 薄片　　best-known〔'bɛst'non〕*adj.* 最著名的

citizen〔'sɪtəzn̩〕*n.* 市民　　Hamburg〔'hæmbɝg〕*n.* 漢堡【德國城市】

Germany〔'dʒɝmənɪ〕*n.* 德國

As long as a language is alive, its cells will continue to
change, forming new words and getting rid of the ones that no
longer have any use.

　　只要語言還有生命，它的細胞就會持續改變，形成新字彙，擺脫
那些不再使用的字彙。

　　　　as long as 只要　　alive〔ə'laɪv〕*adj.* 活的
　　　　get rid of 擺脫　　form〔fɔrm〕*v.* 形成　　***no longer*** 不再

1. (**D**)　本文主要是關於 ＿＿＿＿＿＿ 。

　　　(A) 活著有機體的生物系統　　(B) 三明治跟漢堡的發明者

　　　(C) 人類細胞的發育　　　　　(D) 語言的改變

　　　* mainly〔'menlɪ〕*adv.* 主要地　　inventor〔ɪn'vɛntɚ〕*n.* 發明者
　　　　development〔dɪ'vɛləpmənt〕*n.* 發展；發育

2. (**B**) 下列除了 _____ 之外，都表示語言是個有生命之物。

(A) 語言和生物的生物系統很相似

(B) 語言中確實有很多活著的細胞能不斷地分裂跟形成

(C) 語言必須要適應新環境才能生存

(D) 老的字彙死去，新的字彙不斷被加進來

* except〔ɪk'sɛpt〕*prep.* 除了…之外
  be similar to… 跟…相似
  actually〔'æktʃuəlɪ〕*adv.* 實際上　　***die out*** 死去

3. (**C**) 「三明治」這個字來自於 _____ 。

(A) 紙牌遊戲　　　　　(B) 一片肉

(C) 一個人的頭銜　　　(D) 英國的一家餐廳

* title〔'taɪtḷ〕*n.* 頭銜

4. (**B**) 關於漢堡的敘述，除了 _____ 以外都是正確的。

(A) 來自於地名　　　　(B) 來自於人名

(C) 成爲世界上最有名的三明治

(D) 是德國人發明的

5. (**A**) 文章中提到幾種字彙形成的方法？

(A) 兩種。　　　　　　(B) 三種。

(C) 四種。　　　　　　(D) 五種。

* mention〔'mɛnʃən〕*v.* 提到

TEST 31

Read the following passage and choose the best answer for each question.

A Renaissance person is somebody who wants to learn about arts, politics, science, etc., all fields of human knowledge. One example of such people was Benjamin Franklin. He was a politician, a diplomat, a scientist and an inventor and, above all, a philanthropist dedicated to charities and, for his whole life, fighting for the abolition of slavery — helping the poor black slaves to get free from the mistreatment of their white masters. He was born in 1706 in Boston. Surprisingly, when he was little, he had little chance to go to school. However, he taught himself many subjects, and remained a passionate, active learner through all his life.

He contributed with his advanced thinking to the progress of the early North American colonies. He first put down on paper his wit and humor, mixed with acute observations and practical philosophy, in his most successful literary work — *Poor Richard's Almanac* — published in 1733. Its fame and popularity was second only to the Bible in the early colonies.

In 1736, Franklin began his journey in politics. He first worked as a representative of England, but later became a revolutionary. In 1776, as a member of the Continental Congress, Franklin helped draft the Declaration of Independence.

As a scientist, he was a pioneer in the study of electricity. His most well-known invention is the lightning rod, but he also gave us bifocals and the odometer (to keep track of the distance that a vehicle has covered), *just to name a few*. Among his most innovative ideas was his proposal to adopt daylight saving time to take advantage of the extra hours of light in summer. He also started the first fire department in all the world. Later in his life, he was elected the first president of the Pennsylvania Society for Promoting the Abolition of Slavery, whose principles he had promoted since 1730. 【師大附中】

1. The topic of this reading is _____.

   (A) Benjamin Franklin and his first book

   (B) the contributions Benjamin Franklin made

   (C) the definition of a Renaissance person

   (D) Benjamin Franklin's role in the independence of the USA

2. The phrase "just to name a few" in the last paragraph means _____.

   (A) Franklin had a few inventions that we do not know about
   (B) there are more examples of Franklin's inventions
   (C) to name all his inventions does not takes much time
   (D) those inventions are known to just a few people

3. Which of the following is **NOT** true about *Poor Richard's Almanac*?

   (A) It was published in Benjamin Franklin's twenties.
   (B) It expressed Benjamin's advanced thinking.
   (C) The whole book was written in a serious tone.
   (D) It had a deep impact on the early North American colonies.

4. What did Benjamin Franklin fight for his whole life?

   (A) To free blacks from slavery.
   (B) To make more scientific inventions.
   (C) To help draft the Declaration of Independence.
   (D) To propose daylight saving time.

5. We can infer from the passage that Benjamin Franklin _____.

   (A) was a very skillful person
   (B) was the best politician in American history
   (C) took a negative attitude toward his life
   (D) majored in electric engineering in school

TEST 31 詳解

A Renaissance person is somebody who wants to learn about arts, politics, science, etc., all fields of human knowledge. One example of such people was Benjamin Franklin. He was a politician, a diplomat, a scientist and an inventor and, above all, a philanthropist dedicated to charities and, for his whole life, fighting for the abolition of slavery — helping the poor black slaves to get free from the mistreatment of their white masters. He was born in 1706 in Boston. Surprisingly, when he was little, he had little chance to go to school. However, he taught himself many subjects, and remained a passionate, active learner through all his life.

文藝復興時期的人會學習藝術、政治、科學等,所有人類知識的領域。班傑明‧富蘭克林就是一個例子。他是政治家、外交官、科學家、發明家,最重要的是,他是個獻身於慈善事業的慈善家,而且終其一生都在為廢除奴隸制度而奮鬥——幫助可憐的黑奴,脫離白人雇主的虐待,獲得自由。富蘭克林 1706 年出生於波士頓,令人驚訝的是,他小時候沒有什麼機會上學。然而,他自學很多科目,而且一生都是充滿熱情、主動的學習者。

Renaissance〔ˏrɛnə'zɑns〕*adj.* 文藝復興(時期)的【西元 14-17 世紀間一股再度提倡古典藝術及學術的運動】

etc.〔ɛt'sɛtrə〕*adv.* 等等　　field〔fild〕*n.* 領域

Benjamin Franklin〔'bɛndʒəmən'fræŋklɪn〕*n.* 班傑明‧富蘭克林【1706-1790;美國政治家、作家、外交官、慈善家以及物理學家】

politician〔ˏpɑlə'tɪʃən〕*n.* 政治家

diplomat〔'dɪpləˏmæt〕*n.* 外交官

inventor〔ɪn'vɛntɚ〕*n.* 發明家

above all 最重要的是　　philanthropist〔fə'lænθrəpɪst〕*n.* 慈善家

dedicate ('dɛdə,ket) v. 奉獻;獻身於　　***be dedicated to*** 致力於
charity ('tʃærətɪ) n. 慈善　　***fight for*** 為了…而奮鬥
abolition (,æbə'lɪʃən) n. 廢除
slavery ('slevərɪ) n. 奴隸制度
slave (slev) n. 奴隸　　***get free*** 獲得自由
mistreatment (mɪs'tritmənt) n. 虐待
master ('mæstɚ) n. 主人;雇主
Boston ('bɔstn̩) n. 波士頓【美國麻薩諸塞州首府】
surprisingly (sə'praɪzɪŋlɪ) adv. 令人驚訝的是
subject ('sʌbdʒɪkt) n. 科目　　remain (rɪ'men) v. 依然是
passionate ('pæʃənɪt) adj. 熱情的　　active ('æktɪv) adj. 主動的

He contributed with his advanced thinking to the progress of
the early North American colonies. He first put down on paper
his wit and humor, mixed with acute observations and practical
philosophy, in his most successful literary work — *Poor Richard's
Almanac* — published in 1733. Its fame and popularity was second
only to the Bible in the early colonies.

　他有進步的思維,對早期北美殖民地的發展上很有貢獻。一開始他以
書面寫下自己的智慧及幽默,在他最成功的文學書籍－1733年出版的《窮查
理的日曆》中,融入了敏銳觀察跟實踐哲學。這本書在早期北美殖民地時的
名氣跟受歡迎程度,僅次於聖經。

contribute (kən'trɪbjut) v. 貢獻;促成 *< to >*
advanced (əd'vænst) adj. 進步的;高深的
progress ('prɑgrɛs) n. 進步　　colony ('kɑlənɪ) n. 殖民地
North American colonies 北美殖民地【1776年美國獨立前,由英國
　統治的北美十三個殖民地總稱】　　***on paper*** 在紙上;書面上
wit (wɪt) n. 智慧　　mix (mɪks) v. 混合
acute (ə'kjut) adj. 敏銳的
observation (,ɑbzɚ'veʃən) n. 觀察
practical ('præktɪk̩l) adj. 實踐的;實用的

philosophy〔fəˈlɑsəfɪ〕*n.* 哲學
practical philosophy 實踐哲學
literary〔ˈlɪtəˌrɛrɪ〕*adj.* 文學的　　work〔wɝk〕*n.* 作品
almanac〔ˈɔlməˌnæk〕*n.* 年曆
Poor Richard's Almanac　窮查理的日曆【班傑明・富蘭克林用「窮查
　理」作爲筆名，在 1732-1758 年之間每年出版年曆。內容包括占星術跟
　天文學資訊、日記、天氣、詩句，以及使他成名的格言佳句】
publish〔ˈpʌblɪʃ〕*v.* 出版　　fame〔fem〕*n.* 名聲
popularity〔ˌpɑpjəˈlærətɪ〕*n.* 受歡迎　　***be second only to*** 僅次於
Bible〔ˈbaɪbḷ〕*n.* 聖經

In 1736, Franklin began his journey in politics.　He first
worked as a representative of England, but later became a
revolutionary.　In 1776, as a member of the Continental Congress,
Franklin helped draft the Declaration of Independence.

在 1736 年，富蘭克林展開政治之旅。他先擔任英格蘭的民意代表，後
來卻成爲革命家。在 1776 年，他擔任大陸會議的一員，協助起草美國的獨
立宣言。

journey〔ˈdʒɝnɪ〕*n.* 旅行　　politics〔ˈpɑləˌtɪks〕*n.* 政治（學）
work as 擔任　　representative〔ˌrɛprɪˈzɛntətɪv〕*n.* 民意代表
England〔ˈɪŋglənd〕*n.* 英格蘭
revolutionary〔ˌrɛvəˈluʃənˌɛrɪ〕*n.* 革命家
continental〔ˌkɑntəˈnɛntḷ〕*adj.* 大陸的
congress〔ˈkɑŋgrɛs〕*n.* 國會；議會；代表大會
the Continental Congress 大陸會議【1774-1789 美國獨立戰爭期間，
　北美十三州的代表所召開的制憲會議】
draft〔dræft〕*v.* 起草
declaration〔ˌdɛkləˈreʃən〕*n.* 宣布；宣言
independence〔ˌɪndɪˈpɛndəns〕*n.* 獨立
the Declaration of Independence　（美國的）獨立宣言

As a scientist, he was a pioneer in the study of electricity. His most well-known invention is the lightning rod, but he also gave us bifocals and the odometer (to keep track of the distance that a vehicle has covered), ***just to name a few***. Among his most innovative ideas was his proposal to adopt daylight saving time to take advantage of the extra hours of light in summer. He also started the first fire department in all the world. Later in his life, he was elected the first president of the Pennsylvania Society for Promoting the Abolition of Slavery, whose principles he had promoted since 1730.

作為科學家，他是研究電的先驅。他最知名的發明，就是避雷針，其他還留給我們雙焦點眼鏡，跟里程表（可以記錄交通工具行走的距離），這只是其中的一些例子。他最創新的思想，就是提議採用日光節約時間，利用夏日額外的日照時間。他也設立全世界第一座消防局。在晚年，他當選「賓州促進廢止奴隸制度協會」的會長，這個協會的宗旨，是富蘭克林從 1730 年起就提倡的。

pioneer〔͵paɪə'nɪr〕*n.* 先鋒；先驅

electricity〔ɪ͵lɛk'trɪsətɪ〕*n.* 電；電流

well-known〔'wɛl'non〕*adj.* 著名的

invention〔ɪn'vɛnʃən〕*n.* 發明物　　lightning〔'laɪtnɪŋ〕*n.* 閃電

rod〔rɑd〕*n.* 細桿　　***lightning rod*** 避雷針

bifocals〔baɪ'foklz〕*n. pl.* 雙焦點眼鏡

odometer〔o'dɑmətɚ〕*n.* 里程表　　track〔træk〕*n.* 蹤跡

keep track of 追尋⋯的蹤跡；掌握⋯的行蹤

vehicle〔'viɪkl̩〕*n.* 汽車；交通工具

cover〔'kʌvɚ〕*v.* 行走（距離）　　name〔nem〕*v.* 提出例子

innovative〔'ɪnə͵vetɪv〕*adj.* 創新的

proposal〔prə'pozl̩〕*n.* 提議　　adopt〔ə'dɑpt〕*v.* 採用

saving〔'sevɪŋ〕*adj.* 節約的　　***to name just a few*** 僅舉數例

daylight saving time 日光節約時間【在美國，夏季時會把時鐘往前調快一個小時，以利用夏季較多的日照時間，秋季時再調整回來】

take advantage of 利用　　extra〔ˈɛkstrə〕*adj.* 額外的

department〔dɪˈpɑrtmənt〕*n.* 部門　　*fire department* 消防局

elect〔ɪˈlɛkt〕*v.* 選舉　　president〔ˈprɛzədənt〕*n.* 會長；主席

Pennsylvania〔ˌpɛnslˈvenjə〕*n.* 賓夕凡尼亞州【簡稱賓州】

society〔səˈsaɪətɪ〕*n.* 協會　　promote〔prəˈmot〕*v.* 促進

Pennsylvania Society for Promoting the Abolition of Slavery
賓州奴隸制度廢止促進協會

principle〔ˈprɪnsəpḷ〕*n.* 原則；宗旨

promote〔prəˈmot〕*v.* 提倡；使（法案）通過

1. (**B**) 本文的題目是 ＿＿＿＿＿＿。

    (A) 班傑明・富蘭克林跟他的第一本書

    (B) 班傑明・富蘭克林所做的貢獻

    (C) 文藝復興時期人物的定義

    (D) 班傑明在美國獨立中的角色

    * topic〔ˈtɑpɪk〕*n.* 題目

      contribution〔ˌkɑntrəˈbjuʃən〕*n.* 貢獻

      definition〔ˌdɛfəˈnɪʃən〕*n.* 定義　　role〔rol〕*n.* 角色

2. (**B**) 最後一段中，"just to name a few" 這個片語代表的意思

    是 ＿＿＿＿＿＿。

    (A) 富蘭克林有一些我們所不知道的發明

    (B) 還有更多富蘭克林發明的東西的例子

    (C) 舉出他所有的發明為例子不用花太多時間

    (D) 這些發明只被少數人知道

    * paragraph〔ˈpærəˌgræf〕*n.* 段落

      mean〔min〕*v.* 意指；意味　　*take time* 花費時間

      be known to… 被…所知

3. (**C**)　關於《窮查理的日曆》這本書,下列何者為非?

　　(A)　在班傑明・富蘭克林二十幾歲的時候發行。

　　(B)　表達班傑明進步的思想。

　　(C)　整本書以嚴肅的語調寫成。

　　(D)　對於早期北美洲殖民地有深遠的影響。

　　＊ express〔ɪk'sprɛs〕v. 表達　　serious〔'sɪrɪəs〕adj. 嚴肅的
　　　 tone〔ton〕n. 語調　　impact〔'ɪmpækt〕n. 影響

4. (**A**)　班傑明・富蘭克林一生都在為什麼而奮鬥?

　　(A)　讓黑人脫離奴役而自由。

　　(B)　創造更多科學發明。

　　(C)　幫助起草獨立宣言。

　　(D)　提議日光節約時間。

　　＊ free〔fri〕v. 釋放;使獲得自由

5. (**A**)　從本文中我們可以推論,班傑明・富蘭克林 ＿＿＿＿＿＿＿。

　　(A)　是個有很多技藝的人

　　(B)　是美國歷史上最好的政治人物

　　(C)　對自己的生活抱著負面態度

　　(D)　在學校主修電子工程學

　　＊ skillful〔'skɪlfəl〕adj. 靈巧的;技能熟練的
　　　 negative〔'nɛgətɪv〕adj. 負面的;消極的
　　　 attitude〔'ætə,tjud〕n. 態度
　　　 take a~attitude 採取~態度
　　　 major〔'medʒɚ〕v. 主修 < in >
　　　 electric〔ɪ'lɛktrɪk〕adj. 電的
　　　 engineering〔,ɛndʒə'nɪrɪŋ〕n. 工程(學)
　　　 electric engineering 電子工程學

TEST 32

Read the following passage and choose the best answer for each question.

In spite of the debate on the recognition of American Sign Language (ASL) as a foreign language, support for this movement has increased. However, certain concerns still remain, including whether ASL is a language or only a variation of English, whether it is really foreign, whether there is a body of literature linked with ASL and whether ASL learning includes a cultural aspect.

First of all, ASL has proved to be a completely developed language. Second, studies show that ASL is neither a type of English nor a simplified language, because it has structures that English lacks. Third, whether ASL is foreign or not depends on what "foreign" means. There are languages, like Navajo in the United States, considered foreign, yet only used in the States. ASL, on the other hand, plays an official role in international affairs such as conferences. Fourth, ASL possesses a rich body of literature, such as legends, naming practices, jokes, games and customs, by and about deaf people. Last, ASL students learn about the rich cultural life of deaf people such as the struggle of deaf people to gain control of individual and community identity.

Research shows that learning a foreign language, especially ASL, is an excellent intellectual exercise for students that helps them to appreciate their own language and culture. In addition, ASL graduates reported that taking ASL had made them better qualified or more employable in non-deafness related careers. With these favorable results, the acceptance of ASL as a foreign language is just a matter of time. 【師大附中】

1. What is the main topic of this passage?
   (A) Sign language and its history.
   (B) Advantages and disadvantages of American Sign Language.
   (C) Reasons against adding ASL to the curriculum.
   (D) The debate about ASL as a foreign language.

2. According to the passage, which of the following is NOT true?
   (A) ASL is a completely developed language.
   (B) Learning ASL is an excellent intellectual exercise for students.
   (C) Learning ASL helps prepare students for their future jobs.
   (D) The recognition of ASL as a foreign language is not a controversial issue any more.

3. Who might be most interested in this topic?

   (A) Blind people.

   (B) International issue observers.

   (C) Social linguists.

   (D) Economy experts.

4. Which of the following is a concern of people who have not accepted ASL as a foreign language?

   (A) It is not a Native American language.

   (B) It may simply be another form of English.

   (C) It is used internationally.

   (D) It has no educational value.

5. What DON'T ASL students learn?

   (A) How to communicate with deaf people.

   (B) How to speak at an international conference.

   (C) Legends about deaf people.

   (D) Jokes about deaf people.

TEST 32 詳解

In spite of the debate on the recognition of American Sign
Language (ASL) as a foreign language, support for this movement
has increased. However, certain concerns still remain, including
whether ASL is a language or only a variation of English, whether
it is really foreign, whether there is a body of literature linked
with ASL and whether ASL learning includes a cultural aspect.

儘管對於承認美國手語（ASL）是一種外國語言一事仍有爭論，對這個
行動的支持已經增加。然而，某些疑慮還是存在，包括美國手語是否能算
是一種語言，或只是英語的變化型態、美國手語眞的是外來的嗎、是否有
跟美國手語有關的文學作品，以及美國手語的學習是否包括文化觀點。

in spite of 雖然；儘管　　debate〔dɪ'bet〕*n.* 爭論；辯論
recognition〔͵rɛkəg'nɪʃən〕*n.* 承認
sign〔saɪn〕*n.* 手勢；符號　　*sign language* 手語
American Sign Language 美國手語【美國、加拿大英語區、墨西哥部
　　分地區所使用的手語，有其文法、結構、特徵，跟口說英語有所不同】
foreign〔'fɔrɪn〕*adj.* 外國的　　support〔sə'port〕*n.* 支持；贊成
movement〔'muvmənt〕*n.* 運動；行動
increase〔ɪn'kris〕*v.* 增加
concern〔kən'sɝn〕*n.* 關心的事　　remain〔rɪ'men〕*v.* 依然；維持
a body of 一群～；許多～
variation〔͵vɛrɪ'eʃən〕*n.* 變化；變種
literature〔'lɪtərətʃɚ〕*n.* 文學　　link〔lɪŋk〕*v.* 結合；連結
cultural〔'kʌltʃərəl〕*adj.* 文化的　　aspect〔'æspɛkt〕*n.* 方面；觀點

First of all, ASL has proved to be a completely developed
language. Second, studies show that ASL is neither a type of
English nor a simplified language, because it has structures that

English lacks. Third, whether ASL is foreign or not depends on what "foreign" means. There are languages, like Navajo in the United States, considered foreign, yet only used in the States. ASL, on the other hand, plays an official role in international affairs such as conferences.

　　首先，美國手語被證實是發展完全成熟的語言。其次，研究顯示，美國手語既不是英語的一種，也不是簡化的語言，因為它有英語所缺乏的結構。第三，美國手語屬於「外來」與否，端視「外來」的意義。例如美國的拿佛和語被認為是外來的，卻只在美國境內被使用。另一方面，美國手語在像是國際會議等事務上，扮演著正式的角色。

> **first of all** 首先　　prove〔pruv〕v. 證明
> completely〔kəm'plitlɪ〕adv. 完全地
> developed〔dɪ'vɛləpt〕adj. 已開發的；已發展的
> **neither…nor~** 既非…也不是~
> simplified〔'sɪmplə,faɪd〕adj. 簡化的
> structure〔'strʌktʃɚ〕n. 結構
> lack〔læk〕v. 缺乏　　**depend on** 依賴
> Navajo〔'nævə,ho〕n. 拿佛和語；拿佛和族【北美印地安人的一支】
> consider〔kən'sɪdɚ〕v. 考慮　　**on the other hand** 另一方面
> official〔ə'fɪʃəl〕n. 正式的；官方的
> **play a ~ role** 扮演~的角色
> international〔,ɪntɚ'næʃənl̩〕adj. 國際的
> affair〔ə'fɛr〕n. 事務　　conference〔'kɑnfərəns〕n. 會議

Fourth, ASL possesses a rich body of literature, such as legends, naming practices, jokes, games and customs, by and about deaf people. Last, ASL students learn about the rich cultural life of deaf people such as the struggle of deaf people to gain control of individual and community identity.

第四，美國手語擁有豐富文學作品，像是傳說、命名慣例、笑話、遊戲，和習俗，這些都是由聾人所創作或和他們有關。最後，美國手語的學生會學到聾人豐富的文化生活，像是聾人們為了掌握個人及社區認同，所付出的努力。

possess〔pəˈzɛs〕v. 擁有　　legend〔ˈlɛdʒənd〕n. 傳說
naming〔ˈnemɪŋ〕n. 命名　　practice〔ˈpræktɪs〕n. 習慣；慣例
naming practice 命名慣例　　custom〔ˈkʌstəm〕n. 風俗習慣
deaf〔dɛf〕*adj.* 聾的；聽不見的
struggle〔ˈstrʌgl̩〕n. 奮鬥；努力
gain〔gen〕v. 獲得　　control〔kənˈtrol〕n. 控制
individual〔ˌɪndəˈvɪdʒuəl〕n. 個人
community〔kəˈmjunətɪ〕n. 社區；社群
identity〔aɪˈdɛntətɪ〕n. 認同；身分

Research shows that learning a foreign language, especially ASL, is an excellent intellectual exercise for students that helps them to appreciate their own language and culture. In addition, ASL graduates reported that taking ASL had made them better qualified or more employable in non-deafness related careers. With these favorable results, the acceptance of ASL as a foreign language is just a matter of time.

研究顯示，學習外來語言，特別是美國手語，對學生來說是一種非常棒的腦力激盪，能幫助他們欣賞自己的語言和文化。此外，美國手語的畢業生指出，學習美國手語讓他們即使在跟聾人無關的職場上，更符合資格，也更適合被雇用。這麼多有利的結果，認為美國手語是外來語言，只不過是時間問題而已。

excellent〔ˈɛkslənt〕*adj.* 極好的
intellectual〔ˌɪntl̩ˈɛktʃuəl〕*adj.* 智力的

exercise (ˈɛksɚˌsaɪz) *n.* 運動　　appreciate (əˈpriʃɪˌet) *v.* 欣賞
in addition 此外　　　graduate (ˈgrædʒʊɪt) *n.* 畢業生
report (rɪˈport) *v.* 報告；說
qualified (ˈkwɑləˌfaɪd) *adj.* 符合資格的
employable (ɪmˈplɔɪəbḷ) *adj.* 適合被雇用的
deafness (ˈdɛfnɪs) *n.* 聾；聽力障礙
non-deafness (ˈnɑnˈdɛfnɪs) *adj.* 非耳聾的；非聽力障礙的
related (rɪˈletɪd) *adj.* 有關的　　career (kəˈrɪr) *n.* 事業；職業生涯
favorable (ˈfevrəbḷ) *adj.* 有利的　　acceptance (əkˈsɛptəns) *n.* 接受
matter (ˈmætɚ) *n.* 問題；事件　　***a matter of N.*** 只是～的問題

1. (**D**) 本文的主題是什麼？

   (A) 手語及其歷史。

   (B) 美國手語的優缺點。

   (C) 反對把手語加進課程中的理由。

   (D) 手語作為外來語的爭議。

   * main (men) *adj.* 主要的　　topic (ˈtɑpɪk) *n.* 主題
     advantage (ədˈvæntɪdʒ) *n.* 優點；好處
     disadvantage (ˌdɪsədˈvæntɪdʒ) *n.* 缺點
     curriculum (kəˈrɪkjələm) *n.* 學程；課程

2. (**D**) 根據本文，下列何者為「非」？

   (A) 美國手語是一種發展完成的語言。

   (B) 學習美國手語對學生來說是很棒的腦力激盪。

   (C) 學習美國手語能幫助學生替未來工作做準備。

   (D) 認為美國手語是外來語再也不是引發爭論的議題。

   * prepare (prɪˈpɛr) *v.* 使～做準備
     prepare *sb.* ***for*** *sth.* 使某人做好某事的準備
     controversial (ˌkɑntrəˈvɝʃəl) *adj.* 引起爭論的
     issue (ˈɪʃu) *n.* 議題

3. (**C**)　哪些人最有可能對這篇文章感興趣？

(A)　盲人。

(B)　國際議題觀察家。

(C)　社會語言學家。

(D)　經濟專家。

* blind〔blaɪnd〕*adj.* 盲的
observer〔əb'zɝvɚ〕*n.* 觀察家
linguist〔'lɪŋgwɪst〕*n.* 語言學家
economy〔ɪ'kɑnəmɪ〕*n.* 經濟　　expert〔'ɛkspɝt〕*n.* 專家

4. (**B**)　下列何者是不認為美國手語是外來語的那些人的顧慮？

(A)　它並不是美國本土的語言。

(B)　它可能只是英語的另一種形式。

(C)　它在國際上被使用。

(D)　它沒有教育價值。

* native〔'netɪv〕*adj.* 本國的　　form〔fɔrm〕*n.* 形式
internationally〔ˌɪntɚ'næʃənlɪ〕*adv.* 在國際上
educational〔ˌɛdʒə'keʃənl〕*adj.* 教育性的

5. (**B**)　學美國手語的學生「不會」學到什麼？

(A)　如何跟聾人溝通。

(B)　如何在國際會議上發言。

(C)　有關聾人的傳說。

(D)　有關聾人的笑話。

* communicate〔kə'mjunəˌket〕*v.* 溝通

TEST 33

Read the following passage and choose the best answer for each question.

I was walking around. It was cold and it started to rain. I was looking for a restaurant or a café where I could sit and have something to drink, when I saw one. I crossed the street and I was there. I sat at a round table and asked for a coffee.

While I was waiting for my beverage, I realized that there were other people in the place, but I felt their loneliness. I saw their bodies, but I couldn't feel their souls. That was because their souls didn't belong to them; instead, they belonged to the *Net*. I stood up and walked between the tables. When I came to the biggest computer, I saw a thin, small man sitting in front of it.

"I'm Steve," he answered after I asked him a couple of times what his name was. "I can't talk with you. I'm busy," he said. I thought he was working, and I apologized. He didn't say anything. Before going back to my seat, I wanted to see what he was doing. I stood behind him. He was not working. He was chatting online with somebody — probably someone he didn't know — and, at the same time, he was playing a computer game — a war game. I was surprised. Why didn't Steve want to talk with me?

I tried again to communicate with that computer geek, but not a word came out of his mouth. I touched his shoulder, but there was no reaction. I was getting upset. I put my hand in front of the monitor, and he shouted, "Leave me alone!" I took a few steps back. I was ashamed. I wanted to look and see if all those people in the café were looking at me, so I raised my head, but there was nobody interested in what was happening.

I walked back to my table, and I noticed everybody was using the computers. At this moment I realized the people in that place were having a cup of coffee and a nice conversation with their machines. All of them were more interested, particularly Steve, in having a relationship with the computer.

I didn't want to imagine the future of human beings if they preferred sharing their lives with machines instead of with people. I was worried and I sank in my thoughts. I didn't even realize that the coffee was bad, just as Steve didn't even realize that there was a person next to him. 【師大附中】

1. Why doesn't Steve want to talk to the narrator?

   (A) Because he is working.

   (B) Because he prefers being alone.

   (C) Because he does not know the narrator.

   (D) Because he is busy chatting online.

2. What is the main idea of this story?

(A) People are addicted to the Internet.

(B) People are crazy about coffee.

(C) The narrator in this story is a friendless person.

(D) It is natural to have an intimate relationship with a computer.

3. Which of the following sentences can best describe the narrator's feeling?

(A) The narrator may feel angry with the people in the café.

(B) The narrator may feel sad about this phenomenon.

(C) The narrator may have no feeling about this phenomenon.

(D) The narrator may feel happy to have companions.

4. Which of the following words best describes Steve's condition?

(A) Preoccupied.　　　(B) Aggressive.

(C) Unimaginable.　　(D) Embarrassed.

5. What did the narrator do when she returned to her table?

(A) She tried to contact Steve online.

(B) She started to converse with her computer.

(C) She forgot that she had ordered some coffee.

(D) She thought deeply about what had happened.

TEST 33 詳解

I was walking around. It was cold and it started to rain. I was looking for a restaurant or a café where I could sit and have something to drink, when I saw one. I crossed the street and I was there. I sat at a round table and asked for a coffee.

我到處走著。天氣寒冷而且開始下雨。正當我在尋找可以坐下來喝點東西的餐廳或咖啡店的時候，我看到一間店。我越過街道到那裡。我坐在圓桌旁，點了一杯咖啡。

around〔ə'raʊnd〕*adv.* 到處　　café〔kə'fe〕*n.* 咖啡店
cross〔krɔs〕*v.* 越過　　***ask for*** 要求

While I was waiting for my beverage, I realized that there were other people in the place, but I felt their loneliness. I saw their bodies, but I couldn't feel their souls. That was because their souls didn't belong to them; instead, they belonged to the *Net*. I stood up and walked between the tables. When I came to the biggest computer, I saw a thin, small man sitting in front of it.

當我在等飲料時，我知道這地方有其他人在，但我感覺得到他們的寂寞。我看得見他們的身體，但感覺不到他們的靈魂。那是因為他們的靈魂不屬於自己；而是屬於網路。我站起來，在桌子之間行走。當我來到最大的電腦前，我看見一個瘦小的男人坐在電腦前。

beverage〔'bɛvrɪdʒ〕*n.* 飲料
realize〔'rɪə,laɪz〕*v.* 了解；知道
loneliness〔'lonlɪnɪs〕*n.* 寂寞　　soul〔sol〕*n.* 靈魂
belong〔bə'lɔŋ〕*v.* 屬於 <*to*>　　instead〔ɪn'stɛd〕*adv.* 反而
net〔nɛt〕*n.* 網；網狀物　　***the Net*** 網際網路
thin〔θɪn〕*adj.* 瘦的　　***in front of*** 在…的前面

"I'm Steve," he answered after I asked him a couple of times what his name was. "I can't talk with you. I'm busy," he said. I thought he was working, and I apologized. He didn't say anything. Before going back to my seat, I wanted to see what he was doing. I stood behind him. He was not working. He was chatting online with somebody — probably someone he didn't know — and, at the same time, he was playing a computer game — a war game. I was surprised. Why didn't Steve want to talk with me?

「我是史蒂夫。」我問了幾次他叫什麼名字後，他回答。「我不能和你聊天。我很忙。」他說。我想他是在工作，所以我道了歉。他什麼都沒說。在回到我的座位之前，我想看他在做什麼。我站在他後面。他沒有在工作。他在線上和別人聊天——可能是他不認識的人——他同時也在玩電腦遊戲——戰爭遊戲。我很驚訝，為什麼史蒂夫不想和我說話？

a couple of 幾個的	time〔taɪm〕*n.* 次數
apologize〔ə'pɑlə,dʒaɪz〕*v.* 道歉	seat〔sit〕*n.* 座位
chat〔tʃæt〕*v.* 聊天	online〔,ɑn'laɪn〕*adv.* 在線上
war〔wɔr〕*n.* 戰爭	surprised〔sə'praɪzd〕*adj.* 驚訝的

I tried again to communicate with that computer geek, but not a word came out of his mouth. I touched his shoulder, but there was no reaction. I was getting upset. I put my hand in front of the monitor, and he shouted, "Leave me alone!" I took a few steps back. I was ashamed. I wanted to look and see if all those people in the café were looking at me, so I raised my head, but there was nobody interested in what was happening.

我再試著和那個電腦玩家溝通，但他一句話也沒說。我碰他的肩膀，他一點反應也沒有。我覺得不高興。我把手放在螢幕前面，然後他開始大吼：「不要打擾我！」我向後退了幾步。我感到很羞愧。我想看是否咖啡店裡所有的人都在看我，所以我抬起頭，但沒有人對發生的事情感興趣。

communicate ﹝ kə'mjunə,ket ﹞ *v.* 溝通

geek ﹝ gik ﹞ *n.* 電腦玩家；怪胎　　shoulder ﹝'ʃoldɚ ﹞ *n.* 肩膀

reaction ﹝ rɪ'ækʃən ﹞ *n.* 反應　　upset ﹝ ʌp'sɛt ﹞ *adj.* 不高興的

monitor ﹝'mɑnətɚ ﹞ *n.* 螢幕　　shout ﹝ ʃaʊt ﹞ *v.* 吼叫

leave sb. alone 不打擾某人　　step ﹝ stɛp ﹞ *n.* 一步

take a step back 向後退一步

ashamed ﹝ ə'ʃemd ﹞ *adj.* 羞愧的；感到羞恥的

raise ﹝ rez ﹞ *v.* 舉起；抬起

interested ﹝'ɪntrɪstɪd ﹞ *adj.* 感興趣的

be interested in 對…感興趣

I walked back to my table, and I noticed everybody was using the computers. At this moment I realized the people in that place were having a cup of coffee and a nice conversation with their machines. All of them were more interested, particularly Steve, in having a relationship with the computer.

我走回我的桌子，注意到每個人都在使用電腦。我這時才了解，那裡的人都在一邊喝咖啡，一邊和自己的機器愉快地對話。他們全部都對和電腦的關係比較有興趣，尤其是史帝夫。

notice ﹝'notɪs ﹞ *v.* 注意到　　moment ﹝'momənt ﹞ *n.* 時刻；片刻

nice ﹝ naɪs ﹞ *adj.* 愉快的　　machine ﹝ mə'ʃin ﹞ *n.* 機器

particularly ﹝ pɚ'tɪkjələ·lɪ ﹞ *adv.* 尤其；特別是

relationship ﹝ rɪ'leʃən,ʃɪp ﹞ *n.* 關係

I didn't want to imagine the future of human beings if they preferred sharing their lives with machines instead of with people. I was worried and I sank in my thoughts. I didn't even realize that the coffee was bad, just as Steve didn't even realize that there was a person next to him.

　　如果人們比較喜歡和機器分享自己的生活，而不是和別人分享，我就不願去想像人類的未來。我很擔心並陷入沉思。我甚至沒察覺咖啡很難喝，就像史蒂夫甚至不知道有個人在他旁邊一樣。

imagine〔ɪˋmædʒɪn〕v. 想像　　future〔ˋfjutʃɚ〕n. 未來
human beings 人類　　prefer〔prɪˋfɝ〕v. 比較喜歡
share〔ʃɛr〕v. 分享　　**instead of** 而不是
worried〔ˋwɝɪd〕adj. 擔心的
sink〔sɪŋk〕v. 陷入【三態變化：sink-sank-sunk】
thought〔θɔt〕n. 思考　　bad〔bæd〕adj. 壞掉的；不好的
next to 在…旁邊

1.(**D**) 為什麼史蒂夫不想跟這位敘述者說話？

(A) 因為他正在工作。

(B) 因為他比較喜歡獨處。

(C) 因為他不認識這位敘述者。

(D) 因為他忙著線上聊天。

　 * narrator〔ˋnæretɚ〕n. 敘述者　　alone〔əˋlon〕adj. 獨自的

2.(**A**) 本故事的主旨是什麼？

(A) 人們沉迷於網路。

(B) 人們很喜歡咖啡。

(C) 本故事的敘述者是一個沒有朋友的人。

(D) 和電腦有親密的關係是很自然的。

　 * main〔men〕adj. 主要的　　**main idea** 主旨
addicted〔əˋdɪktɪd〕adj. 沉迷的 < to >
crazy〔ˋkrezɪ〕adj. 很喜歡的 < about >
friendless〔ˋfrɛndlɪs〕adj. 沒有朋友的
intimate〔ˋɪntəmɪt〕adj. 親密的

3. (**B**) 下列哪一個句子最適合用來描述這位敘述者的感覺？

　　(A) 這位敘述者可能對咖啡店裡的人感到生氣。

　　(B) <u>這位敘述者可能對這個現象感到悲傷。</u>

　　(C) 這位敘述者可能對這個現象沒有感覺。

　　(D) 這位敘述者可能對擁有同伴感到高興。

　　* following〔ˋfaloɪŋ〕*adj.* 下列的
　　　describe〔dɪˋskraɪb〕*v.* 描述
　　　phenomenon〔fəˋnamə‚nan〕*n.* 現象
　　　companion〔kəmˋpænjən〕*n.* 同伴

4. (**A**) 下列哪一個字最適合用來描述史蒂夫的情況？

　　(A) <u>全神貫注的。</u>　　　　(B) 有攻擊性的。

　　(C) 無法想像的。　　　　(D) 尷尬的。

　　* preoccupied〔priˋakjə‚paɪd〕*adj.* 全神貫注的
　　　aggressive〔əˋgrɛsɪv〕*adj.* 有攻擊性的；積極進取的
　　　unimaginable〔‚ʌnɪˋmædʒɪnəbl̩〕*adj.* 無法想像的
　　　embarrassed〔ɪmˋbærəst〕*adj.* 尷尬的

5. (**D**) 這位敘述者回到自己的桌子時，她做了什麼？

　　(A) 她試著在線上和史蒂夫連絡。

　　(B) 她開始和自己的電腦交談。

　　(C) 她忘記自己已經點了一些咖啡。

　　(D) <u>她深思所發生的事。</u>

　　* return〔rɪˋtɝn〕*v.* 返回
　　　contact〔ˋkantækt‚kanˋtækt〕*v.* 與…連絡
　　　converse〔kənˋvɝs〕*v.* 交談　　order〔ˋɔrdə〕*v.* 點（菜）

TEST 34

Read the following passage and choose the best answer for each question.

We are a passing guest of the Earth. Despite our mental limitations, questions raised by physicists, from Newton to Kurt Gödel to Einstein to Stephen Hawking, are among the most profound we can ask. Today, we know that time travel is possible. For example, if you were to travel into outer space and return, moving close to light speed, you could travel thousands of years into the Earth's future.

Newton's most important contribution to science was his mathematical definition of how motion changes with time. He showed that the force that causes apples to fall is the same force that drives planetary motions and produces tides. However, Newton was puzzled by the fact that gravity seemed to operate right away at a distance. He admitted he could only describe it without understanding how it worked. For Newton, both space and time were absolute. Space was a fixed, *infinite*, unmoving measurement against which absolute motions could be measured. Newton also believed the universe was pervaded by a single absolute time that could be symbolized by an imaginary clock off somewhere in space. Einstein changed all this with his relativity theories, and once wrote, "Newton, forgive me."

Einstein's first major contribution to the study of time occurred when he revolutionized physics with his "special theory of relativity" by showing how time changes with motion. Today, scientists think that because time is relative to the speed one is traveling at, there can never be a clock at the center of the universe to which everyone can set his watch.

Is time real? Does it flow in one direction only? Does it have a beginning or an end? None of these questions can be answered to scientists' satisfaction. Yet the mere asking of these questions stretches our minds, and the continual search for answers provides useful insights along the way. 【西松高中】

1. Which field of study did Newton, Kurt Gödel, Einstein and Stephen Hawking contribute to?
   (A) Biology.　　　(B) Physics.
   (C) Therapy.　　　(D) Nutrition.

2. The word "*infinite*" means _____.
   (A) before history
   (B) not limited
   (C) between nations
   (D) against the fact

3. Why did Einstein articulate *"**Newton**, **forgive me**"*?

(A) Einstein owed Newton an apology because Einstein lost track of the time.

(B) Newton didn't like to be excelled.

(C) Einstein changed Newton's theory with his relativity theory.

(D) Their argument was so violent that it destroyed their friendship.

4. According to the passage, which of the following statements is true?

(A) Newton understood how gravity worked and described it.

(B) Newton discovered that the force that causes apples to fall differs from the force that drives planetary motions and produces tides.

(C) Einstein claimed that time changes with motion.

(D) Einstein believed that there is an imaginary clock off somewhere in space.

5. What does the phrase "we are a passing guest of the Earth" mean?

(A) We are not welcome on Earth.

(B) The Earth is passing through space at the speed of light.

(C) Man now has the ability to travel backwards in time.

(D) The Earth will continue to exist after man is gone.

TEST 34 詳解

We are a passing guest of the Earth. Despite our mental limitations, questions raised by physicists, from Newton to Kurt Gödel to Einstein to Stephen Hawking, are among the most profound we can ask. Today, we know that time travel is possible. For example, if you were to travel into outer space and return, moving close to light speed, you could travel thousands of years into the Earth's future.

我們都只是地球的過客。雖然我們的智力有限，但對於這些物理學家所提出的問題，從牛頓到科特·哥德爾、愛因斯坦、史蒂芬·霍金，是一些我們可以問的最深奧的問題。現在我們知道時光旅行是可能的。例如，假如你能到外太空旅行，再返回地球，用接近光速的速度行進，你就能前往地球幾千年後的未來。

passing ('pæsɪŋ) *adj.* 經過的；短暫的　　guest (gɛst) *n.* 客人
the Earth 地球
despite (dɪ'spaɪt) *prep.* 儘管
mental ('mɛntl̩) *adj.* 精神的；智力的
limitation (,lɪmə'teʃən) *n.* 限制　　raise (rez) *v.* 提出 (問題)
physicist ('fɪzəsɪst) *n.* 物理學家
Newton ('njutn̩) *n.* 牛頓【1642-1727，英國物理學家，發現萬有引力，
　　以及三大運動定律，並發明微積分】
Kurt Gödel ('kɝt'godl̩) *n.* 科特·哥德爾【1906-1978，數理邏輯學家，
　　以「不完備定律」和證明相對論與循環時間並不矛盾而著名】
Einstein ('aɪnstaɪn) *n.* 愛因斯坦【1879-1955，德裔美籍物理學家，是
　　相對論的提出者】
Stephen Hawkin ('stivən'hɔkɪn) *n.* 史蒂芬·霍金【1942-，被譽爲是
　　愛因斯坦之後最偉大的物理學家】
profound (prə'faʊnd) *adj.* 深奧的　　***time travel*** 時光旅行
travel ('trævl̩) *v.* 移動；行進；旅行
space (spes) *n.* 太空　　***outer space*** 外太空
return (rɪ'tɝn) *v.* 返回　　***close to*** 接近　　***light speed*** 光速

Newton's most important contribution to science was his mathematical definition of how motion changes with time. He showed that the force that causes apples to fall is the same force that drives planetary motions and produces tides. However, Newton was puzzled by the fact that gravity seemed to operate right away at a distance. He admitted he could only describe it without understanding how it worked.

牛頓對於科學最大的貢獻，在於他用數學定義運動如何隨著時間改變。他指出，讓蘋果掉下來的力量，跟驅動行星運行，以及產生潮汐的力量是相同的。然而，牛頓對於地心引力似乎在一段距離之外，也能夠立刻運作，感到很困惑。他承認他只能描述地心引力的現象，但卻不了解它如何運作。

contribution〔͵kɑntrə'bjuʃən〕*n.* 貢獻
mathematical〔͵mæθə'mætɪkl̩〕*adj.* 數學的；數理的
definition〔͵dɛfə'nɪʃən〕*n.* 定義　　motion〔'moʃən〕*n.* 運動
show〔ʃo〕*v.* 指出　　force〔fors〕*n.* (物理上的) 力
cause〔kɔz〕*v.* 引起　　drive〔draɪv〕*v.* 驅動
planetary〔'plænə͵tɛrɪ〕*adj.* 行星的
produce〔prə'djus〕*v.* 引起；產生　　tide〔taɪd〕*n.* 潮汐
puzzle〔'pʌzl̩〕*v.* 使困惑　　gravity〔'ɡrævətɪ〕*n.* 重力；地心引力
operate〔'ɑpə͵ret〕*v.* 運轉　　*right away* 立刻
at a distance 在一段距離之外　　admit〔əd'mɪt〕*v.* 承認
describe〔dɪ'skraɪb〕*v.* 描述　　work〔wɜk〕*v.* 運作

For Newton, both space and time were absolute. Space was a fixed, *infinite*, unmoving measurement against which absolute motions could be measured. Newton also believed the universe was pervaded by a single absolute time that could be symbolized by an imaginary clock off somewhere in space. Einstein changed all this with his relativity theories, and once wrote, "Newton, forgive me."

對牛頓而言，空間跟時間都是絕對的。空間是固定的、無限的、靜止的測量標準，可以用來衡量純粹的運動。牛頓也相信，宇宙中遍布著單一的絕對時間，而絕對時間可以用位於空間中某處的虛擬時鐘來代表。愛因斯坦用他的相對論改變了這一切，而且曾經寫下「牛頓，原諒我。」這句話。

absolute (ˈæbsəˌlut) *adj.* 絕對的；純粹的
fixed (fɪkst) *adj.* 固定的　　infinite (ˈɪnfənɪt) *adj.* 無限的；無窮的
unmoving (ʌnˈmuvɪŋ) *adj.* 靜止的；固定的
measurement (ˈmɛʒəmənt) *n.* 測量法；衡量標準
measure (ˈmɛʒə) *v.* 測量
measure A *against* B　將 A 與 B 相比；用 B 來衡量 A
universe (ˈjunəˌvɝs) *n.* 宇宙　　pervade (pəˈved) *v.* 遍布
single (ˈsɪŋgl̩) *adj.* 單一的　　symbolize (ˈsɪmbl̩ˌaɪz) *v.* 象徵；代表
imaginary (ɪˈmædʒəˌnɛrɪ) *adj.* 想像的；虛構的
off (ɔf) *prep.* 在…外面
relativity (ˌrɛləˈtɪvətɪ) *n.* 相關性；相對論
theory (ˈθiərɪ) *n.* 理論　　*the relativity theory* 相對論
forgive (fəˈgɪv) *v.* 原諒

Einstein's first major contribution to the study of time occurred when he revolutionized physics with his "special theory of relativity" by showing how time changes with motion. Today, scientists think that because time is relative to the speed one is traveling at, there can never be a clock at the center of the universe to which everyone can set his watch.

　　愛因斯坦對於研究時間的第一個重大貢獻，就是他用「相對性的特殊理論」，說明時間如何隨著運動而改變，因而徹底改革物理學。現在，科學家認為，因為時間與物體移動的速度有關，所以在宇宙的中心，不會有單一的時鐘，讓每個人可以校準其手錶的時間。

major (ˈmedʒə) *adj.* 主要的；重大的　　occur (əˈkɝ) *v.* 發生；存在於
revolutionize (ˌrɛvəˈluʃənˌaɪz) *v.* 徹底改革
physics (ˈfɪzɪks) *n.* 物理學　　relative (ˈrɛlətɪv) *adj.* 相關的
be relative to 與…有關　　center (ˈsɛntə) *n.* 中心
set (sɛt) *v.* 對準（鐘錶的時間）

Is time real? Does it flow in one direction only? Does it have a beginning or an end? None of these questions can be answered to scientists' satisfaction. Yet the mere asking of these questions stretches our minds, and the continual search for answers provides useful insights along the way.

所以時間是眞實的嗎？它只會往單一的方向流動嗎？它有起點跟終點嗎？對於這些問題，沒有任何答案能讓科學家們滿意。但是，即使僅僅詢問這些問題，就能讓我們的心智延伸，而且在不斷地尋求答案的過程中，也能提供實用的洞察力。

flow〔flo〕v. 流動　　direction〔dəˋrɛkʃən〕n. 方向
satisfaction〔͵sætɪsˋfækʃən〕n. 滿足；滿意
to one's satisfaction 令某人滿意
mere〔mɪr〕adj. 僅僅；只　　stretch〔strɛtʃ〕v. 延伸；伸長
continual〔kənˋtɪnjuəl〕adj. 不斷的　　search〔sɝtʃ〕n. 尋找
provide〔prəˋvaɪd〕v. 提供　　useful〔ˋjusfəl〕adj. 有用的
insight〔ˋɪn͵saɪt〕n. 洞察力　　*along the way* 在途中

1.(**B**) 牛頓、科特·哥德爾、愛因斯坦和史蒂芬·霍金，他們對哪個研究領域有貢獻？

    (A) 生物學。　　　　　　(B) 物理學。

    (C) 治療法。　　　　　　(D) 營養學。

    * biology〔baɪˋɑlədʒɪ〕n. 生物學　　therapy〔ˋθɛrəpɪ〕n. 治療法
    　 nutrition〔nuˋtrɪʃən〕n. 營養學

2.(**B**) "infinite" 這個字的意思是 ＿＿＿＿＿＿。

    (A) 史前的　　　　　　　(B) 不受限制的

    (C) 兩國之間的　　　　　(D) 違背事實的

    * limit〔ˋlɪmɪt〕v. 限制

3. (**C**) 為什麼愛因斯坦會說「牛頓，原諒我」？

(A) 因為愛因斯坦忘了時間，因此他欠牛頓一個道歉。

(B) 牛頓不想要被超越。

(C) 愛因斯坦用他的相對論改變了牛頓的理論。

(D) 他們的爭論太激烈，以致於破壞他們的友誼。

* articulate〔ɑr'tɪkjə͵let〕v. 明確地表述；清楚地表達
owe〔o〕v. 欠　　track〔træk〕n. 蹤跡
lose track of 忘記　　excel〔ɪk'sɛl〕v. 勝過
argument〔'ɑrgjəmənt〕n. 爭論
violent〔'vaɪələnt〕adj. 激烈的
destroy〔dɪ'strɔɪ〕v. 摧毀；破壞

4. (**C**) 依據本文，下列敘述何者為真？

(A) 牛頓了解萬有引力如何運作，並且能描述這種現象。

(B) 牛頓發現讓蘋果掉落的力量，跟驅動星球運行，以及產生潮汐的力量不同。

(C) 愛因斯坦宣稱，時間會隨運動而改變。

(D) 愛因斯坦相信，在空間中的某處有個虛擬時鐘。

* state〔stet〕v. 敘述；說明　　statement〔'stetmənt〕n. 敘述
differ〔'dɪfɚ〕v. 不同　　*differ from* 和～不同
claim〔klem〕v. 宣稱

5. (**D**) "we are a passing guest of the Earth" 這個片語的意思是什麼？

(A) 我們在地球上不受歡迎。

(B) 地球以光速通過太空。

(C) 人類現在有能力可以在時光中逆向旅行。

(D) 在人類消失之後，地球還是會繼續存在。

* ability〔ə'bɪlətɪ〕n. 能力
backward〔'bækwɚd〕adv. 逆著；顛倒地
exist〔ɪg'zɪst〕v. 存在

TEST 35

Read the following passage and choose the best answer for each question.

The world-famous film director, Steven Spielberg, who worked his magic with *ET*, is now looking to do the same with games giant Electronic Arts (EA). He has agreed to develop three original games with EA. Work has already started on the first of the three projects, which EA says will be a next generation game which appeals to a broad audience. The deal is a further sign of how Hollywood and the games industry are moving closer together.

Spielberg, 58, has made blockbuster movies such as *ET*, *Close Encounters of the Third Kind* and *Raiders of the Lost Ark*. The Oscar-winning director is said to be a passionate gamer. For his work with EA, Spielberg will have an office at the company's LA studios to work side-by-side with the game developers. Spielberg's role will be similar to that of an executive producer on a film. The aim of the deal is to create three original games, rather than a title based on a movie. "Having watched the game industry grow from a *niche* into a major creative force in entertainment, I have a great deal of respect for EA's understanding of the interactive format," said Spielberg.

The games under development will take advantage of new technology in upcoming gaming consoles, which offer powerful processing power and more realistic graphics. "No one is more at the center of understanding gameplay and great storytelling than Steven Spielberg," the head of EA's LA studios, Neil Young, told the BBC News website. "Being able to draw from Steven Spielberg's experience in crafting incredible stories and combine that with our view of interactivity means you will have richer fiction, deeper characters and better sense of immersion."

Work has already started on the first of the three games. Electronic Arts has not released details of the project, but Young suggested it would take a couple of years to finish the game. "You can expect it to be something that appeals to a broad audience," he said. EA will own the intellectual properties on the games and will develop, publish and distribute them worldwide. 【大同高中】

1. From the context, what would be a possible meaning of "*niche*" in line 18?
   - (A) A special area of demand for a product.
   - (B) A tiny little part in a machine that breaks very often.
   - (C) A faint hope that few people stick with.
   - (D) A dirty trick that deceives many game players.

2. What would be an appropriate title for this passage?

(A) Steven Spielberg Has Gameplay Under His Belt

(B) Steven Spielberg Feels at Home at EA

(C) Steven Spielberg Looks out for EA's View of Interactivity

(D) Steven Spielberg Takes Film Magic to EA

3. According to Neil Young, the head of EA's LA studios, why was Steven Spielberg invited to work with Electronic Arts?

(A) Because of the popularity of his blockbuster movies.

(B) Because of his childhood dream of being an executive producer.

(C) Because of his skills in entertaining people with stories.

(D) Because of the fantastic special effects used in his films.

4. How many games is Spielberg currently working on?

(A) He has not started working yet.

(B) One.   (C) Two.

(D) Three.

5. What kind of game will Spielberg design?

(A) A family game.   (B) A traditional game.

(C) A movie game.   (D) A progressive game.

TEST 35 詳解

The world-famous film director, Steven Spielberg, who worked his magic with *ET*, is now looking to do the same with games giant Electronic Arts (EA). He has agreed to develop three original games with EA. Work has already started on the first of the three projects, which EA says will be a next generation game which appeals to a broad audience. The deal is a further sign of how Hollywood and the games industry are moving closer together.

曾經在電影「ET」中施展魔力的世界知名電影導演，史蒂芬・史匹柏，現在希望與電玩遊戲龍頭，美商藝電公司（EA）一起再次施展魔力。他已同意要和美商藝電，共同開發三款原創性的電玩遊戲。三項計畫中，第一項的工作已經展開，美商藝電說，這將會是新一代的電玩遊戲，會吸引許多支持者。本次交易更進一步表示，好萊塢跟電玩產業，兩者越走越近。

world-famous〔'wɝld'feməs〕*adj.* 世界知名的
film〔fɪlm〕*n.* 電影　　director〔də'rɛktɚ〕*n.* 導演
Steven Spielberg〔'stivən'spilbɝg〕*n.* 史蒂芬・史匹柏【1946-，
　　曾兩度獲得奧斯卡金像獎的美國知名導演】
ET〔'ɪ'ti〕*n.* 外星人（= *Extraterrestrial*〔'ɛkstrəˌtə'rɛstrɪəl〕）
game〔gem〕*n.* 電玩遊戲　　giant〔'dʒaɪənt〕*n.* 巨人；傑出人物
electronic〔ɪˌlɛk'trɑnɪk〕*adj.* 電子的
Electronic Arts 美商藝電【全球著名的互動娛樂軟體公司，創立於1982
　　年，主要進行電玩遊戲、線上遊戲的軟體開發、銷售、出版等業務】
look to + *V.* 希望；想要（= *want to* + *V.*）
develop〔dɪ'vɛləp〕*v.* 發展；開發
original〔ə'rɪdʒənl〕*adj.* 原本的；獨創性的
project〔'prɑdʒɛkt〕*n.* 計畫　　generation〔ˌdʒɛnə'reʃən〕*n.* 世代

appeal to 吸引|　　audience〔ˋɔdɪəns〕*n.* 觀眾；支持者
deal〔dil〕*n.* 交易　　further〔ˋfɝðɚ〕*adj.* 更進一步的
sign〔saɪn〕*n.* 符號；象徵
Hollywood〔ˋhɑlɪˏwud〕*n.* 好萊塢；美國電影業
industry〔ˋɪndəstrɪ〕*n.* 產業　　***game industry*** 電玩產業

Spielberg, 58, has made blockbuster movies such as *ET*, *Close Encounters of the Third Kind* and *Raiders of the Lost Ark*. The Oscar-winning director is said to be a passionate gamer. For his work with EA, Spielberg will have an office at the company's LA studios to work side-by-side with the game developers. Spielberg's role will be similar to that of an executive producer on a film.

　　五十八歲的史匹柏，拍過像是「ET」、「第三類接觸」、「法櫃奇兵」等賣座強片。這位拿過奧斯卡金像獎的導演，據說也是個電玩遊戲的愛好者。為了他在美國藝電的工作，史匹柏將在該公司的洛杉磯攝影棚擁有一間辦公室，讓他能夠與遊戲開發者一起工作。史匹柏的角色就像是電影的執行製作。

blockbuster〔ˋblɑkˏbʌstɚ〕*n.* (大成本的) 電影巨片；賣座強片
close〔klos〕*adj.* 接近的；親密的
encounter〔ɪnˋkauntɚ〕*n.* 遇見；邂逅
Close Encounters of the Third Kind 第三類接觸【由史帝芬・史匹柏
　　執導，1977 年上映的科幻巨片】　　raider〔ˋredɚ〕*n.* 侵略者
ark〔ɑrk〕*n.* 約櫃；神龕【聖經中裝有十戒碑文的聖箱】
Raiders of the Lost Ark 法櫃奇兵【史帝芬・史匹柏在 1980 年執導的
　　冒險動作巨片，是「印第安那瓊斯」系列電影的首部曲】
Oscar〔ˋɔskɚ〕*n.* 奧斯卡金像獎
Oscar-winning〔ˋɔskɚˏwɪnɪŋ〕*adj.* 贏得奧斯卡的
be said to* + *V. 據說
passionate〔ˋpæʃənɪt〕*adj.* 熱情的；很感興趣的

gamer〔ˈgemɚ〕*n.* 電玩玩家

LA 洛杉磯 (= *Los Angeles*〔lɔsˈændʒələs〕)

studio〔ˈstjudɪˏo〕*n.* 攝影棚

side-by-side〔ˈsaɪdˈbaɪˈsaɪd〕*adv.* 並肩；共同

developer〔dɪˈvɛləpɚ〕*n.* 開發者　　role〔rol〕*n.* 角色

executive〔ɪkˈzɛkjʊtɪv〕*adj.* 執行的

producer〔prəˈdjusɚ〕*n.* 製作人　　***executive producer*** 執行製作

The aim of the deal is to create three original games, rather than a title based on a movie. "Having watched the game industry grow from a *niche* into a major creative force in entertainment, I have a great deal of respect for EA's understanding of the interactive format," said Spielberg.

此次交易的目標是要創造三款原創性的電玩遊戲，而不是以電影的片名為基礎。「看著電玩產業從很小的市場，成長為娛樂產業的主要創意力量，我對於美商藝電能理解互動形式，充滿敬意，」史匹柏說。

aim〔em〕*n.* 目標　　create〔krɪˈet〕*v.* 創造

rather than 而不是　　title〔ˈtaɪtl̩〕*n.* (電影) 片名

be based on 以…為基礎　　niche〔nɪtʃ〕*n.* (產品的) 商機；市場定位

creative〔krɪˈetɪv〕*adj.* 有創造性的　　force〔fors〕*n.* 力量

entertainment〔ˏɛntɚˈtenmənt〕*n.* 娛樂

a great deal of 大量的　　respect〔rɪˈspɛkt〕*n.* 敬意

understanding〔ˏʌndɚˈstændɪŋ〕*n.* 理解

interactive〔ˏɪntɚˈæktɪv〕*adj.* 互動的

format〔ˈfɔrmæt〕*n.* 形式；格式

The games under development will take advantage of new technology in upcoming gaming consoles, which offer powerful processing power and more realistic graphics. "No one is more at the center of understanding gameplay and great storytelling than Steven Spielberg," the head of EA's LA studios, Neil Young, told the BBC News website. "Being able to draw from Steven Spielberg's experience in crafting incredible stories and combine that with our view of interactivity means you will have richer fiction, deeper characters and better sense of immersion."

這款開發中的遊戲，將使用即將上市的遊戲操控器的新科技，這將提供更強大的處理能力，以及更真實的圖片。「沒有人比史蒂芬・史匹柏更了解玩電玩，以及更會說故事，」美商藝電位於洛杉磯影棚的主管尼爾・楊，在英國廣播公司的網站上說。「能夠汲取史蒂芬・史匹柏精心製作驚奇故事的經驗，並將其與我們對於互動的看法相結合，這就代表會有更豐富的想像力、更深入的角色，以及更身歷其境的感受。」

under development 發展中的　　**take advantage of** 利用

technology（tɛkˈnɑlədʒɪ）*n.* 科技

upcoming（ˈʌpˌkʌmɪŋ）*adj.* 即將到來的

gaming（ˈgemɪŋ）*adj.* 電玩的

console（ˈkɑnsol）*n.*（電腦的）操控器　　offer（ˈɔfɚ）*v.* 提供

powerful（ˈpaʊɚfəl）*adj.* 強力的

process（ˈprɑsɛs）*v.* 處理　　realistic（ˌriəˈlɪstɪk）*adj.* 寫實的

graphics（ˈgræfɪks）*n.* 製圖　　**the center of** 在…的核心

gameplay（ˈgemˌple）*n.* 遊戲方式；電玩遊戲的劇情

storytelling（ˈstorɪˌtɛlɪŋ）*n.* 說故事　　head（hɛd）*n.* 主管

BBC 英國廣播公司（= *British Broadcasting Corporation*）

news（njuz）*n.* 新聞　　website（ˈwɛbˌsaɪt）*n.* 網站

draw from 從…獲得　　craft（kræft）*v.* 精心製作

incredible（ɪnˈkrɛdəbḷ）*adj.* 令人難以置信的

combine（kəmˈbaɪn）*v.* 結合

interactivity（ˌɪntɚˌækˈtɪvətɪ）*n.* 交互作用；互動

rich（rɪtʃ）*adj.* 豐富的

fiction（ˈfɪkʃən）*n.* 小說；虛構的事；想像

character（ˈkærɪktɚ）*n.* 角色　　sense（sɛns）*n.* 感覺

immersion（ɪˈmɜʃən）*n.* 沈浸；專心；陷入

Work has already started on the first of the three games.
Electronic Arts has not released details of the project, but Young
suggested it would take a couple of years to finish the game. "You
can expect it to be something that appeals to a broad audience,"
he said. EA will own the intellectual properties on the games
and will develop, publish and distribute them worldwide.

三款遊戲中，第一款遊戲的工作已經展開。美商藝電沒有發表該項計
畫的細節，但是尼爾・楊指出，可能要數年的時間才能完成遊戲。「你可
以預期它能成為吸引廣大支持者的商品，」他說。美商藝電將擁有遊戲的
智慧財產權，而將開發、發行，並在全球各地出售這些電玩遊戲。

release〔rɪ'lis〕*v.* 發表；公開　　detail〔'ditel〕*n.* 細節
suggest〔səg'dʒɛst〕*v.* 指出　　***a couple of*** 幾個
intellectual〔ˌɪntḷ'ɛktʃuəl〕*adj.* 智力的
property〔'prɑpətɪ〕*n.* 財產　　***intellectual property*** 智慧財產權
publish〔'pʌblɪʃ〕*v.* 出版；發行
distribute〔dɪ'strɪbjut〕*v.* 經銷；出售（= *sell*）
worldwide〔'wɝld'waɪd〕*adv.* 在全世界

1. (**A**) 從上下文看來，第十一行的 "niche" 這個字有可能是什麼意思？

　(A) 對某產品有需求的特殊領域。

　(B) 機器中經常故障的小零件。

　(C) 少部分人依舊堅持的微渺希望。

　(D) 欺騙許多遊戲玩家的一種卑劣技倆。

　* context〔'kɑntɛkst〕*n.* 上下文
　　area〔'ɛrɪə〕*n.* 領域
　　demand〔dɪ'mænd〕*n.* 需求
　　tiny〔'taɪnɪ〕*adj.* 極小的
　　break〔brek〕*v.* 損壞　　faint〔fent〕*adj.* 微弱的
　　stick with 堅持　　dirty〔'dɝtɪ〕*adj.* 卑劣的
　　trick〔trɪk〕*n.* 詭計　　deceive〔dɪ'siv〕*v.* 欺騙

2.(**D**) 下列何者是本文最適當的標題？

    (A) 史蒂芬・史匹柏玩電玩的經歷值得誇耀。

    (B) 史蒂芬・史匹柏在美商藝電公司裡如魚得水。

    (C) 史蒂芬・史匹柏尋求美商藝電關於產業互動的觀點。

    (D) <u>史蒂芬・史匹柏將電影的魔法帶到美國藝電。</u>

    * ***under*** *one's* ***belt*** 擁有（值得誇耀的）經歷
       feel at home 感到輕鬆自在   ***look out for*** 注意；尋找

3.(**C**) 根據美商藝電，洛杉磯攝影棚主管尼爾・楊的說法，為什麼史蒂芬・史匹柏被邀請與美商藝電共事？

    (A) 因為他所拍賣座強片電影很受歡迎。

    (B) 因為他小時候的夢想是當執行製作人。

    (C) <u>因為他用故事來娛樂大眾的技巧。</u>

    (D) 因為他電影中所使用的超棒特效。

    * popularity〔͵pɑpjəˈlærətɪ〕*n.* 受歡迎
      entertain〔͵ɛntɚˈten〕*v.* 娛樂
      fantastic〔fænˈtæstɪk〕*adj.* 很棒的   ***special effects*** 特效

4.(**B**) 史蒂芬・史匹柏現在正在進行幾種遊戲的工作？

    (A) 工作尚未開始進行。   (B) <u>一種。</u>

    (C) 兩種。   (D) 三種。

    * currently〔ˈkɝəntlɪ〕*adv.* 目前   ***work on*** 從事

5.(**D**) 史蒂芬・史匹柏會設計出哪種電玩遊戲？

    (A) 適合家庭的遊戲。   (B) 傳統的遊戲。

    (C) 電影的遊戲。   (D) <u>先進的遊戲。</u>

    * family〔ˈfæməlɪ〕*adj.* 適合家庭的
      progressive〔prəˈgrɛsɪv〕*adj.* 進步的

TEST 36

Read the following passage and choose the best answer for each question.

The Fourth of July is the most important day of the year for the United States of America. It is the day that is known as Independence Day. Every year on the Fourth of July, people gather in parts of a town or city to watch fireworks displays and celebrate with their family and friends. It is a day for all Americans because it celebrates the birthday of the U.S.A.

North America was settled by Europeans more than four hundred years ago. In the early years, life was difficult and the settlers had to work hard just to survive. At that time, North America was considered part of the British Empire, meaning the British monarch was also the monarch of America. But as the years passed, the settlers began to live a more comfortable life and, after a few generations, many became rich through farming.

In 1774, the American War of Independence broke out between the Americans and the British. The war was fought for the political control of North America. In 1776, Thomas Jefferson wrote down the opinions of the American Congress. It was a document that expressed America's desire to rule itself and be rid of the British. This document was the Declaration of Independence and it was approved by the American Congress on July 4, 1776.

Over the next ten years, the War of Independence was fought across the colony. The Americans were led by George Washington and fought in many battles against the British Army, who became known as the "Red Coats." Battles took place along the East Coast of America, in the countryside and in major cities like New York. Eventually, the Americans were victorious because they gained the loyalty of the settlers.

Ever since the victory, Americans have enjoyed marching bands, fireworks and family feasts on the Fourth of July. Today, there are many ways to celebrate Independence Day, and it doesn't really matter how it is done so long as the spirit of freedom is felt. 【木柵高工】

1. The Fourth of July is a day for all Americans because _____.
    (A) it was the birthday of the first president
    (B) it celebrates the birthday of the United States of America
    (C) it is a traditional festival
    (D) people can gather and eat turkey together

2. Who led the Americans to fight against the British Army in the War of Independence?

(A) George Washington.

(B) Thomas Jefferson.

(C) The mayor of New York.

(D) George Bush.

3. According to the passage, which of the following statements is NOT true?

(A) The American Army was called the "Red Coats."

(B) The battles took place along the East Coast of America.

(C) The British Army was called the "Red Coats."

(D) The Americans won the war eventually.

4. What do Americans do on the Fourth of July?

(A) Enjoy marching bands.

(B) Watch fireworks.

(C) Have family feasts.

(D) All of the above.

5. In 1776, Thomas Jefferson wrote a document about
_____.

(A) how to celebrate the Fourth of July

(B) the difficult life in America

(C) America's desire to rule itself and get rid of the British

(D) the war between the Americans and the British

TEST 36 詳解

The Fourth of July is the most important day of the year for the United States of America. It is the day that is known as Independence Day. Every year on the Fourth of July, people gather in parts of a town or city to watch fireworks displays and celebrate with their family and friends. It is a day for all Americans because it celebrates the birthday of the U.S.A.

七月四日對美國而言,是一年中最重要的一天。這一天被稱爲美國獨立紀念日。每年的七月四日,人們會聚集在鎮上或是城市中觀看煙火施放,跟家人以及朋友一起慶祝。這一天是屬於所有美國人的,因爲是要慶祝美國誕生。

be known as 被稱爲　　independence〔͵ɪndɪ'pɛndəns〕*n.* 獨立
the Independence Day 美國獨立紀念日
gather〔'gæðɚ〕*v.* 聚集　　firework〔'faɪr͵wɝk〕*n.* 煙火
display〔dɪ'sple〕*v.* 陳列;展示　　**fireworks display** 放煙火
celebrate〔'sɛlə͵bret〕*v.* 慶祝

North America was settled by Europeans more than four hundred years ago. In the early years, life was difficult and the settlers had to work hard just to survive. At that time, North America was considered part of the British Empire, meaning the British monarch was also the monarch of America. But as the years passed, the settlers began to live a more comfortable life and, after a few generations, many became rich through farming.

四百多年前,歐洲人到北美洲殖民。在早期,殖民者的生活很困苦,必須努力工作以求生存。當時北美洲被認爲是大英帝國的一部份,這意味著英國的君主也是美國的君主。但是經過許多年,殖民者開始過著比較舒適的生活,過了幾個世代之後,很多人因農業而致富。

North America 北美洲　　settle〔'sɛtl̩〕*v.* 殖民；定居
European〔ˌjʊrə'piən〕*n.* 歐洲人　　settler〔'sɛtlɚ〕*n.* 殖民者
survive〔sə'vaɪv〕*v.* 生存　　*at that time* 在當時
consider〔kən'sɪdɚ〕*v.* 認爲　　British〔'brɪtɪʃ〕*adj.* 英國（人）的
empire〔'ɛmpaɪr〕*n.* 帝國　　*the British Empire* 大英帝國
monarch〔'manɚk〕*n.* 君主　　pass〔pæs〕*v.* （時間）過去
generation〔ˌdʒɛnə'reʃən〕*n.* 世代　　farming〔'farmɪŋ〕*n.* 農業

In 1774, the American War of Independence broke out between the Americans and the British. The war was fought for the political control of North America. In 1776, Thomas Jefferson wrote down the opinions of the American Congress. It was a document that expressed America's desire to rule itself and be rid of the British. This document was the Declaration of Independence and it was approved by the American Congress on July 4, 1776.

在 1774 年，美國跟英國之間爆發了美國獨立戰爭。這是爲了爭取北美洲政權而打的戰役。1776 年，湯瑪斯・傑佛遜寫下關於美國國會的主張，這份文件表達出美國希望能自治，並擺脫英國的渴望。這份文件就是 1776 年七月四日，由美國國會所通過的美國獨立宣言。

the American War of Independence 美國獨立戰爭
break out 爆發　　political〔pə'lɪtɪkl̩〕*adj.* 政治的
control〔kən'trol〕*n.* 管理；支配
Thomas Jefferson〔'taməs'dʒɛfɚsn̩〕*n.* 湯瑪斯・傑佛遜【1743-1826，
　　美國獨立宣言起草人，也是美國第三任總統】
opinion〔ə'pɪnjən〕*n.* 看法；主張
Congress〔'kaŋgrəs〕*n.* 國會　　*the American Congress* 美國國會
document〔'dakjəmənt〕*n.* 文件
express〔ɪk'sprɛs〕*v.* 表達　　desire〔dɪ'zaɪr〕*n.* 渴望
rule〔rul〕*n.* 統治；管理　　*be rid of* 擺脫
declaration〔ˌdɛklə'reʃən〕*n.* 宣言
the Declaration of Independence 美國獨立宣言
approve〔ə'pruv〕*v.* 核准；認可

Over the next ten years, the War of Independence was fought across the colony. The Americans were led by George Washington and fought in many battles against the British Army, who became known as the "Red Coats." Battles took place along the East Coast of America, in the countryside and in major cities like New York. Eventually, the Americans were victorious because they gained the loyalty of the settlers.

接下來的十年內，殖民地都在進行獨立戰爭。喬治・華盛頓帶領美國人，在許多戰役中，跟以名為「紅衣軍」的英國軍隊作戰。戰爭發生在美國東部沿岸、在鄉間，以及像紐約這樣的大城市。最後，美國人因為得到殖民者的忠誠而勝利。

colony ('kɑlənɪ) *n.* 殖民地　　lead (lid) *v.* 領導
George Washington ('dʒɔrdʒ'wɑʃɪŋtən) *n.* 喬治・華盛頓
【1732-1799；美國第一任總統，被稱為美國國父】
fight against 跟…作戰　　battle ('bætḷ) *n.* 戰役
army ('ɑrmɪ) *n.* 陸軍　　***the British Army*** 英國陸軍
become known as 後來被稱為
Red Coat 紅衣軍【英國軍服外套顏色為鮮紅色，故英軍又叫作紅衣軍】
take place 發生　　coast (kost) *n.* 海岸
the East Coast 東海岸　　countryside ('kʌntrɪ,saɪd) *n.* 鄉間
major ('medʒɚ) *adj.* 主要的　　New York (nju'jɔrk) *n.* 紐約
eventually (ɪ'vɛntuəlɪ) *adv.* 最後
victorious (vɪk'torɪəs) *adj.* 戰勝的；勝利的
gain (gen) *v.* 獲得　　loyalty ('lɔɪəltɪ) *n.* 忠誠；忠心

Ever since the victory, Americans have enjoyed marching bands, fireworks and family feasts on the Fourth of July. Today, there are many ways to celebrate Independence Day, and it doesn't really matter how it is done so long as the spirit of freedom is felt.

從那次勝利之後，美國人會在七月四日享受軍樂隊、煙火表演，還有家族盛宴。現在，有很多方式來慶祝美國獨立紀念日，只要能感受到自由的精神，慶祝活動如何進行，其實並不重要。

ever since 自從　　victory〔ˋvɪktrɪ〕*n.* 勝利
march〔mɑrtʃ〕*v.* 行軍　　***marching band*** 軍樂隊
feast〔fist〕*n.* 盛宴；大餐　　***it doesn't matter*** 不重要；沒有關係
spirit〔ˋspɪrɪt〕*n.* 精神　　freedom〔ˋfridəm〕*n.* 自由

1. (**B**) 七月四日是屬於美國全體人民的日子，因為 ＿＿＿＿＿＿＿。
　　(A) 是美國第一任總統的生日
　　(B) 是要慶祝美國誕生　　　　(C) 是傳統的節慶
　　(D) 人們可以聚在一起吃火雞
　　＊ traditional〔trəˋdɪʃənḷ〕*adj.* 傳統的
　　　festival〔ˋfɛstəvḷ〕*n.* 慶典；節日　　turkey〔ˋtɝkɪ〕*n.* 火雞

2. (**A**) 美國獨立戰爭時，誰帶領美國人對抗英軍？
　　(A) 喬治·華盛頓。　　　　　　(B) 湯瑪斯·傑佛遜。
　　(C) 紐約市市長。　　　　　　　(D) 喬治·布希。
　　＊ mayor〔ˋmeɚ〕*n.* 市長
　　　George Bush〔ˋdʒɔrdʒˋbuʃ〕*n.* 喬治·布希【1924-，美國
　　　第 41 任總統】

3. (**A**) 根據本文，下列敘述何者為「非」？
　　(A) 美國陸軍又叫作「紅衣軍」。
　　(B) 戰役發生在美國東部沿岸。
　　(C) 英國陸軍又叫作「紅衣軍」。
　　(D) 美國人最後贏得這場戰爭。

4. (**D**) 美國人在七月四日會做什麼？
　　(A) 享受軍樂隊表演。　　　　　(B) 看煙火。
　　(C) 吃家族大餐。　　　　　　　(D) 以上皆是。

5. (**C**) 在 1776 年時，湯瑪斯·傑佛遜寫了一份關於 ＿＿＿＿＿＿
　　的文件。
　　(A) 如何慶祝七月四日　　　　　(B) 艱苦的美國生活
　　(C) 美國希望能自治並擺脫英國　(D) 美國與英國之間的戰爭

TEST 37

Read the following passage, and choose the best answer for each question.

Libraries have traditionally been the public's access to the important sources of information that are necessary to function in today's highly technical world. That function has been <u>called into question</u> by the fast-paced development of digital media over the past several decades. In order to continue to fulfill the public interest, libraries everywhere are forced to develop means of granting access to these expensive new services to average citizens.

In the past, the publishing industry maintained the rights of libraries to freely distribute published materials because libraries bought so many of their books. Since the new electronic publications can easily be copied in their entirety by the patrons of the library, the publishing industry is reconsidering its former support of the library system. There have even been attempts to stop libraries from distributing digital media.

In addition to the waning cooperation of the publishing industry, there is the problem that the newer forms of information are much more specialized than those which they replace. Deciding how to reallocate already limited resources is increasingly difficult as there are more options. Whereas a single reference index may have covered an entire field in the past, now there are frequently several specialized indexes available in electronic form. In order to continue to make use of the newer technology, libraries must decide which materials are most useful to the majority of their patrons. There are many different solutions being applied, but only the process of trial and error will determine the most effective strategy. 【建國中學】

1. What is the best title for this passage?
   (A) The Challenge for Today's Libraries
   (B) Information Technology and the Consumer
   (C) The Benefits of the Digital Revolution
   (D) Changes in Information Technology

2. In the first paragraph, the phrase "called into question" refers to
   (A) the importance of libraries in aiding the technical world.
   (B) the ability of the library to serve its historical function.
   (C) the significance of information technology.
   (D) the value of the new forms of media.

3. Why did publishers cooperate with libraries in the past?

(A) Libraries were under contract to the publishers.

(B) Libraries pay for their support.

(C) Libraries bought books.

(D) Libraries offered a tax reduction.

4. It can be inferred that the major problem for libraries is

(A) the legal problems with the publishing industry.

(B) the management of larger amounts of information.

(C) the changing nature of information.

(D) lack of public interest.

5. How will the most effective decision be made?

(A) A special committee will study the task.

(B) The government will examine the situation.

(C) The public will decide.

(D) It will be decided through experimentation.

TEST　37　詳解

Libraries have traditionally been the public's access to the important sources of information that are necessary to function in today's highly technical world.　That function has been <u>called into question</u> by the fast-paced development of digital media over the past several decades.　In order to continue to fulfill the public interest, libraries everywhere are forced to develop means of granting access to these expensive new services to average citizens.

　　傳統上，圖書館一直是大眾接觸重要資訊來源的管道，並且在現今高度科技化的世界中，它們有必要的作用。但在過去數十年間，數位媒體迅速發展，引發對圖書館功能的質疑。為了持續滿足公衆利益，各處的圖書館被迫開發一套，讓一般市民能使用這些昂貴的新公共設備的工具。

　　library (ˈlaɪˌbrɛrɪ) *n.* 圖書館
　　traditionally (trəˈdɪʃənl̩ɪ) *adv.* 傳統上
　　access (ˈæksɛs) *n.* 取得 (資料)；接近 (管道) 的方法
　　function (ˈfʌŋkʃən) *v.* 產生作用　　*n.* 功能
　　technical (ˈtɛknɪkl̩) *adj.* 技術的；科技的
　　question (ˈkwɛstʃən) *n.* 質疑
　　call…into question　對…產生質疑；對…提出異議
　　pace (pes) *n.* 步調
　　fast-paced (ˈfæstˈpest) *adj.* (步調) 迅速的
　　development (dɪˈvɛləpmənt) *n.* 發展
　　digital (ˈdɪdʒɪtl̩) *adj.* 數位的
　　media (ˈmidɪə) *n. pl.* 媒體【單數為 medium】
　　decade (ˈdɛked) *n.* 十年　　　***in order to V.*** 為了～
　　fulfill (fʊlˈfɪl) *v.* 滿足；達成　　interest (ˈɪntərɪst) *n.* 利益
　　force (fors) *v.* 強迫　　develop (dɪˈvɛləp) *v.* 發展；開發

means〔minz〕*n. pl.* 方法；手段　　grant〔grænt〕*v.* 給予
service〔'sɜvɪs〕*n.* 公共設施；公共服務
average〔'ævərɪdʒ〕*adj.* 一般的
citizen〔'sɪtəzn̩〕*n.* 市民；公民

In the past, the publishing industry maintained the rights
of libraries to freely distribute published materials because
libraries bought so many of their books. Since the new
electronic publications can easily be copied in their entirety
by the patrons of the library, the publishing industry is
reconsidering its former support of the library system. There
have even been attempts to stop libraries from distributing
digital media.

在過去，出版業讓圖書館保有自由流通已出版資料的權利，因
為圖書館買下了很多他們的書。自從新式電子出版品能夠輕易地，被
常去圖書館的人從館內全版拷貝之後，出版業正重新考慮先前對圖書
館系統的支持。出版業甚至想要讓圖書館停止流通數位媒體。

publishing〔'pʌblɪʃɪŋ〕*adj.* 出版的
industry〔'ɪndəstrɪ〕*n.* 工業；產業　　***publishing industry*** 出版業
maintain〔men'ten〕*v.* 維持；保持
right〔raɪt〕*n.* 權利
distribute〔dɪ'strɪbjut〕*v.* 分配；使（商品）流通
material〔mə'tɪrɪəl〕*n.* 材料；資料
electronic〔ɪ,lɛk'trɑnɪk〕*adj.* 電子的
publication〔,pʌblɪ'keʃən〕*n.* 出版；發表；出版品
copy〔'kɑpɪ〕*v.* 複製
entirety〔ɪn'taɪrtɪ〕*n.* 全體；原封不動
patron〔'petrən〕*n.* 支持者；老主顧
reconsider〔,rikən'sɪdə〕*v.* 再考慮　　former〔'fɔrmə〕*adj.* 之前的
support〔sə'port〕*n.* 支持　　attempt〔ə'tɛmpt〕*n.* 企圖；嘗試
stop~from··· 阻止～做···

In addition to the waning cooperation of the publishing industry, there is the problem that the newer forms of information are much more specialized than those which they replace. Deciding how to reallocate already limited resources is increasingly difficult as there are more options. Whereas a single reference index may have covered an entire field in the past, now there are frequently several specialized indexes available in electronic form. In order to continue to make use of the newer technology, libraries must decide which materials are most useful to the majority of their patrons. There are many different solutions being applied, but only the process of trial and error will determine the most effective strategy.

除了跟出版業的合作衰退之外，問題更在於，新的資訊形式，比它們所取代的那些還要更專門化。決定如何重新分配有限的資源，將變得日益困難，因為現在有更多選擇。雖然過去單一參照索引，就已經包含所有領域，現在卻常常可以從電子形式的索引中，取得很多專門化的索引。為了能持續使用這種更新穎的科技，圖書館必須決定哪些資料，對大多數使用者而言，是最有用的。已經使用過很多不同的解決之道，但只有反覆試驗的過程，才能決定最有效的策略。

in addition to 除了…之外　　wane〔wen〕*v.* 衰退
cooperation〔ko͵ɑpəˈreʃən〕*n.* 合作
specialize〔ˈspɛʃəl͵aɪz〕*v.* 使特殊化；使專門化
replace〔rɪˈples〕*v.* 取代　　reallocate〔riˈæləˌket〕*v.* 重新分配
limit〔ˈlɪmɪt〕*v.* 限制　　resource〔rɪˈsors〕*n.* 資源
increasingly〔ɪnˈkrisɪŋlɪ〕*adv.* 日益增加地
option〔ˈɑpʃən〕*n.* 選擇　　whereas〔hwɛrˈæz〕*conj.* 雖然；然而
reference〔ˈrɛfrəns〕*n.* 參考
index〔ˈɪndɛks〕*n.* 索引　　cover〔ˈkʌvɚ〕*v.* 涵蓋
entire〔ɪnˈtaɪr〕*adj.* 全體的　　field〔fild〕*n.* 範圍；領域
frequently〔ˈfrikwəntlɪ〕*adv.* 時常

available〔ə'veləbḷ〕*adj.* 可獲得的
make use of 利用　　technology〔tɛk'nɑlədʒɪ〕*n.* 科技
useful〔'jusfəl〕*adj.* 有用的　　majority〔mə'dʒɔrətɪ〕*n.* 大多數
solution〔sə'luʃən〕*n.* 解決之道
apply〔ə'plaɪ〕*v.* 運用　　process〔'prɑsɛs〕*n.* 過程
trial〔'traɪəl〕*n.* 嘗試　　error〔'ɛrə〕*n.* 錯誤
trial and error 反覆試驗；摸索中學習
determine〔dɪ'tɜmɪn〕*v.* 決定
effective〔ə'fɛktɪv〕*adj.* 有效的
strategy〔'strætədʒɪ〕*n.* 策略

1. (**A**) 本文的最佳標題是什麼？

　　(A) 現代圖書館的挑戰　　　(B) 資訊科技與消費者

　　(C) 數位革命的優點　　　　(D) 資訊革命的變革

　　* challenge〔'tʃælɪndʒ〕*n.* 挑戰
　　 consumer〔kən'sumə〕*n.* 消費者
　　 benefit〔'bɛnəfɪt〕*n.* 利益；好處
　　 revolution〔ˌrɛvə'luʃən〕*n.* 革命

2. (**B**) 第一段中的片語 "called into question" 是指

　　(A) 圖書館幫助科技界的重要性。

　　(B) 圖書館提供歷史性功能的能力。

　　(C) 資訊科技的重要性。

　　(D) 新式媒體的價值。

　　* phrase〔frez〕*n.* 片語　　***refer to*** 是指
　　 aid〔ed〕*v.* 幫助　　ability〔ə'bɪlətɪ〕*n.* 能力
　　 serve〔sɜv〕*v.* 提供服務；滿足（需求）
　　 historical〔hɪs'tɔrɪkḷ〕*adj.* 歷史的
　　 significance〔sɪg'nɪfəkəns〕*n.* 意義；重要性

3. (**C**) 爲何過去出版商會跟圖書館合作？

(A) 圖書館跟出版商有簽合約。

(B) 圖書館付費請出版商支持。

(C) 圖書館買書。

(D) 圖書館提供減稅。

* publisher〔'pʌblɪʃɚ〕*n.* 出版者；出版社

cooperate〔ko'ɑpə,ret〕*v.* 合作

contract〔'kɑntrækt〕*n.* 合約　　　 tax〔tæks〕*n.* 稅金

reduction〔rɪ'dʌkʃən〕*n.* 減少

4. (**C**) 本文指出，圖書館的主要問題在於 ＿＿＿＿＿＿＿＿

(A) 與出版業之間的法律問題。

(B) 管理較大量的資訊。

(C) 資訊本質的改變。

(D) 缺乏公衆利益。

* legal〔'ligl̩〕*adj.* 法律的

management〔'mænɪdʒmənt〕*n.* 管理　　 lack〔læk〕*v.* 缺乏

interest〔'ɪntərɪst〕*v.* 利益　　 *public interest* 公衆利益

5. (**D**) 如何才能做出最有效的決定？

(A) 一個特別委員會將研究這項工作。

(B) 政府會檢視情況。

(C) 由公衆決定。

(D) 由實驗來決定。

* committee〔kə'mɪtɪ〕*n.* 委員會　　 task〔tæsk〕*n.* 任務；工作

examine〔ɪg'zæmɪn〕*v.* 檢查；調查

situation〔,sɪtʃu'eʃən〕*n.* 情況

experimentation〔ɪk,spɛrəmɛn'teʃən〕*n.* 實驗

TEST 38

Read the following passage and choose the best answer for each question.

Rosa Parks — Mother of the Civil Rights Movement

On December 1, 1955, forty-three-year-old Rosa Parks boarded a Montgomery, Alabama city bus after finishing work at the Montgomery Fair department store. As all black patrons were required to do, she paid her fare at the front of the bus and then re-boarded in the rear. She sat in a vacant seat in the back next to a man and across the aisle from two women. After a few stops, the seats in the front of the bus became full and a white man who had boarded, stood in the aisle. The bus driver asked Parks, the man next to her, and the two women to let the white man have their seats. As the others moved, Parks remained in her seat. The bus driver again asked her to move, but she refused. The driver called the police and she was arrested. The arrest of Parks sparked a bus *boycott* in Montgomery.

As the bus boycott continued, the bus company began to lose money because 75 percent of its riders were black and all had joined the boycott. Finally, almost one year after Rosa Parks's refusal to give up her seat, the Supreme Court ruled — on November 13, 1956 — that Montgomery's segregation laws were illegal.

Rosa Parks won the Spingarn Medal for her civil rights work in 1979. She died in 2005 at the age of 92. After her death, her body was placed in the United States Capitol for two days, so the nation could pay its respects to the woman whose courage had changed the lives of so many. She was the first woman in American history to lie in state at the Capitol, an honor usually reserved for Presidents of the United States. 【大直高中】

1. Rosa Parks refused to give her seat to the white man because _____.
   (A) there were still empty seats in the front of the bus
   (B) she was waiting to be asked to by the driver
   (C) she thought she had the right to sit there
   (D) she was a senior citizen

2. The word "boycott" in the first paragraph means an act of _____.
   (A) attacking or destroying with bombs
   (B) refusing to buy, sell, or use
   (C) causing pain to others
   (D) selling goods in large quantities and at low prices

3. Which of the following is **TRUE**?

(A) Rosa Parks did not pay for the ticket when she got on the bus.

(B) The bus company began to lose money because 75 percent of its riders could not afford the ticket.

(C) Montgomery's segregation laws were declared to be illegal almost a year after Rosa Parks was arrested.

(D) Rosa Parks won a medal in 1979 for her hard work at the Montgomery Fair department store.

4. According to the article, what started the boycott?

(A) The segregation laws of Montgomery.

(B) A white passenger on the bus.

(C) 75 percent of bus passengers.

(D) The arrest of Rosa Parks.

5. Why was Rosa Parks's body placed in the United States Capitol for two days after her death?

(A) Because her contributions were as great as American presidents'.

(B) Because she was the first black president in American history.

(C) Because she had remarkably changed the American transportation system.

(D) Because she was the first woman in American history to live in the Capitol.

TEST 38 詳解

Rosa Parks — Mother of the Civil Rights Movement

On December 1, 1955, forty-three-year-old Rosa Parks boarded a Montgomery, Alabama city bus after finishing work at the Montgomery Fair department store. As all black patrons were required to do, she paid her fare at the front of the bus and then re-boarded in the rear. She sat in a vacant seat in the back next to a man and across the aisle from two women. After a few stops, the seats in the front of the bus became full and a white man who had boarded, stood in the aisle. The bus driver asked Parks, the man next to her, and the two women to let the white man have their seats. As the others moved, Parks remained in her seat. The bus driver again asked her to move, but she refused. The driver called the police and she was arrested. The arrest of Parks sparked a bus *boycott* in Montgomery.

羅莎・帕克斯——民權運動之母

　　1955 年十二月一日，四十三歲的羅莎・帕克斯在蒙哥馬利平價百貨公司結束工作之後，從阿拉巴馬州，蒙哥馬利市，搭上市公車。如同所有黑人乘客被要求的那樣，她在公車前門付費，然後再從公車後面上車。她坐在後方的空位上，旁邊是一位男性，走道另一端是兩位女性。經過幾站之後，公車前方的座位客滿了，此時一位白人男性上車，站在走道上。公車司機要求帕克斯、她旁邊的男性乘客、以及那兩位女性，讓白人坐在他們的位子上。當其他人都起身，帕克斯依然坐在位子上。公車司機再次要求帕克斯走開，但她拒絕了。公車司機報警，所以羅莎就被逮捕了。逮捕帕克斯這件事，在蒙哥馬利引發了公車的聯合抵制活動。

　　Rosa Parks〔'rosə'pɑrks〕*n.* 羅莎・帕克斯【1913-2005，美國黑人民權行動主義者，被美國國會稱爲「民權運動之母」。1955 年的公車事件，引發黑人集體大規模反抗種族隔離政策的運動。羅莎・帕克斯被時代雜誌選爲二十世紀最具影響力的百大人物之一】

civil〔ˋsɪvḷ〕*adj.* 市民的；公民的　　right〔raɪt〕*n.* 權利
civil rights 民權　　movement〔ˋmuvmənt〕*n.* 運動
board〔bord〕*v.* 登上（車、船等交通工具）
Montgomery〔mɑntˋgʌmərɪ〕*n.* 蒙哥馬利【美國阿拉巴馬州首府】
Alabama〔͵æləˋbæmə〕*n.* 阿拉巴馬【美國東南部的一個州】
fair〔fɛr〕*adj.*（價格）公道的
Montgomery Fair department store 蒙哥馬利平價百貨公司
patron〔ˋpetrən〕*n.* 顧客；支持者
require〔rɪˋkwaɪr〕*v.* 要求　　fare〔fɛr〕*n.* 車資
re-board〔rɪˋbord〕*v.* 再度登上（車、船）
rear〔rɪr〕*n.* 後面　　vacant〔ˋvekənt〕*adj.* 空著的
aisle〔aɪl〕*n.* 走道　　stop〔stɑp〕*n.* 停車站
remain〔rɪˋmen〕*v.* 依舊；停留　　refuse〔rɪˋfjuz〕*v.* 拒絕
arrest〔əˋrɛst〕*v.* 逮捕　　spark〔spɑrk〕*v.* 引起
boycott〔ˋbɔɪ͵kɑt〕*n.* 聯合抵制；拒絕購買

As the bus boycott continued, the bus company began to lose
money because 75 percent of its riders were black and all had
joined the boycott.　Finally, almost one year after Rosa Parks's
refusal to give up her seat, the Supreme Court ruled — on
November 13, 1956 — that Montgomery's segregation laws were
illegal.

抵制公車的活動持續進行，公車公司開始虧損，因為百分之七十五的
乘客是黑人，而且都參加了抵制活動。最後，羅莎・帕克斯拒絕讓座事件
發生將近一年後，最高法院在 1956 年十一月十三日裁定，蒙哥馬利市的種
族隔離法律是違法的。

percent〔pəˋsɛnt〕*n.* 百分之…　　rider〔ˋraɪdə〕*n.* 乘客
refusal〔rɪˋfjuzḷ〕*n.* 拒絕　　***give up*** 讓（座）；放棄
supreme〔səˋprim〕*adj.* 最高權力的　　court〔kort〕*n.* 法庭；法院
the Supreme Court（美國或州的）最高法院
rule〔rul〕*v.*（法院）裁決
segregation〔͵sɛgrɪˋgeʃən〕*n.* 種族隔離
illegal〔ɪˋligḷ〕*adj.* 違法的

Rosa Parks won the Spingarn Medal for her civil rights work in 1979. She died in 2005 at the age of 92. After her death, her body was placed in the United States Capitol for two days, so the nation could pay its respects to the woman whose courage had changed the lives of so many. She was the first woman in American history to lie in state at the Capitol, an honor usually reserved for Presidents of the United States.

在 1979 年，羅莎・帕克斯因爲在民權上的努力，贏得史賓剛獎。她在 2005 年去世，高齡 92 歲。在她死後，她的遺體被放置在美國國會大廈兩天，讓全國國民能對她致敬，她的勇氣改變了許多人的生命。她是美國歷史上第一位停靈在國會大廈的女人，這種榮耀通常都只保留給美國總統。

medal〔'mɛdl〕 *n.* 獎牌；勳章
Spingarn Medal 史賓剛獎【由 Joel Elias Spingarn 設立的獎項，
　目的在獎勵那些替非裔美國人作出重大貢獻的優秀黑人】
place〔ples〕 *v.* 放置
Capitol〔'kæpətl〕 *n.* 國會大廈【美國國會大廈位於華盛頓特區】
respect〔rɪ'spɛkt〕 *n.* 敬意；尊敬
pay one's respect to sb. 向某人表達敬意
courage〔'kɝɪdʒ〕 *n.* 勇氣
state〔stet〕 *n.* 莊嚴；正式；氣派
lie in state （遺體）殯殮後任人瞻仰；停靈
honor〔'ɑnɚ〕 *n.* 榮譽　　reserve〔rɪ'zɝv〕 *v.* 保留（權利）

1. (**C**) 羅莎・帕克斯拒絕將座位讓給白人是因爲 _____。
　　(A) 在公車前半部還有空位
　　(B) 她正在等司機要求她讓座
　　(C) 她認爲自己有權利坐在位子上
　　(D) 她是老人
　　* senior〔'sinjɚ〕 *adj.* 年長的
　　　citizen〔'sɪtəzn̩〕 *n.* 市民；公民　　***senior citizen*** 老人

2.(**B**) 第一段中的 "boycott" 這個字代表 ＿＿＿＿＿ 的行為。

    (A) 用炸彈攻擊或是破壞　　　(B) <u>拒絕買、賣或使用</u>

    (C) 帶給其他人痛苦　　　　　(D) 大量並低價銷售商品

    * attack〔əˋtæk〕*v.* 攻擊
    destroy〔dɪˋstrɔɪ〕*v.* 毀滅；破壞
    bomb〔bɑm〕*n.* 炸彈　　cause〔kɔz〕*v.* 造成
    goods〔gʊdz〕*n. pl.* 商品　quantity〔ˋkwɑntətɪ〕*n.* 數量

3.(**C**) 下列何者為「真」？

    (A) 羅莎‧帕克斯上公車的時候沒有付車資。

    (B) 公車公司開始虧損，因為百分之七十五的乘客無法負擔車資。

    (C) <u>蒙哥馬利的種族隔離法律在羅莎‧帕克斯被逮捕約一年後，被宣告是違法的。</u>

    (D) 羅莎‧帕克斯在 1979 年，因為她在蒙哥馬利平價百貨公司努力工作而贏得獎牌。

    * afford〔əˋford〕*v.* 負擔得起　declare〔dɪˋklɛr〕*v.* 宣布
    medal〔ˋmɛdḷ〕*n.* 獎牌

4.(**D**) 根據本文，抵制行動的起因為何？

    (A) 蒙哥馬利州的種族隔離法。　(B) 車上的一位白人乘客。

    (C) 百分之七十五的公車乘客。　(D) <u>羅莎‧帕克斯被逮捕。</u>

5.(**A**) 為什麼羅莎‧帕克斯死後，遺體被放置在美國國會大廈兩天？

    (A) <u>因為她的貢獻就跟美國總統一樣偉大。</u>

    (B) 因為她是美國史上第一位黑人總統。

    (C) 因為她大大地改變了美國的交通運輸系統。

    (D) 因為她是美國史上第一個住在國會大廈的女性。

    * contribution〔͵kɑntrəˋbjuʃən〕*n.* 貢獻
    remarkably〔rɪˋmɑrkəblɪ〕*adv.* 顯著地
    transportation〔͵trænspɚˋteʃən〕*n.* 運送；運輸工具
    transportation system 交通運輸系統

TEST 39

Read the following passage and choose the best answer for each question.

Is Dolly an exact reproduction of her only
"parent" — who supplied her with genes? I'd say she's
not. There are several reasons why she isn't exactly,
completely like her parent.

First, even though all her chromosomes came from
the adult sheep, Dolly's mitochondrial DNA still came
from the egg contributor. Mitochondrial DNA comes
only from the mother and, since <u>it</u> never combines with
the father's DNA, it can be used to trace the development
of animals.

Next, the immune system genes are not fully
developed at the very beginning stage. The genes
continue recombining after fertilization. Thus a clone
would have a slightly different immune system from
that of its parent.

Moreover, environment also has its effects. Even
twins, who share many characteristics, are not
completely identical, particularly when they're raised
separately. Experiments with rats have confirmed that

upbringing affects brain biochemistry, says Frank Farley, a psychologist at Temple University. In other words, you can create a person with the same genetic makeup of someone else, but who the person will become is affected by his or her environment, too. A clone is not going to be a perfect copy of the adult, since changes in environment, starting in the womb, affect which genes get expressed, and how the body and mind develop. Even if we cloned Einstein, due to the upbringing, the clone might not be identical to Einstein. 【新店高中】

1. What does the passage discuss?
   (A) The difference between human beings and rats.
   (B) Why a clone is not a perfect reproduction.
   (C) What the development of animal cells is.
   (D) How to clone Einstein successfully.

2. According to the passage, where does a clone's mitochondrial DNA come from?
   (A) The egg donor.
   (B) The father.
   (C) Both of the parents.
   (D) None of the above.

3. According to the passage, which of the following statements is NOT correct?

 (A) A clone would not have the same immune system as its parent.

 (B) The environment will have an effect on who you are.

 (C) Even if twins are raised separately, they are going to be fully identical.

 (D) A psychologist used rats to discover how the environment affects development.

4. What does "it" in the 4th line of the 2nd paragraph refer to?

 (A) Dolly the sheep.

 (B) The course of development.

 (C) Mitochondrial DNA.

 (D) The immune system.

5. How many reasons are provided in the article to explain why a clone can't be a perfect copy of the adult?

 (A) Two.

 (B) Three.

 (C) Four.

 (D) Five.

TEST 39 詳解

Is Dolly an exact reproduction of her only "parent" — who
supplied her with genes? I'd say she's not. There are several
reasons why she isn't exactly, completely like her parent.

桃莉羊是供給她基因的單一「父（母）」的完全複製品嗎？我得說她不
是。有很多理由說明她並非完全跟她的父母一樣。

> Dolly〔'dɑlɪ〕*n.* 桃莉羊【1996-2003，由蘇格蘭羅斯林研究所在1996
>   年成功培育出，第一隻由複製而成的哺乳動物】
> exact〔ɪg'zækt〕*adj.* 恰好的；精確的
> reproduction〔,riprə'dʌkʃən〕*n.* 複製品；繁殖
> supply〔sə'plaɪ〕*v.* 供應   gene〔dʒin〕*n.* 基因
> exactly〔ɪg'zæktlɪ〕*adv.* 精確地；恰好
> completely〔kəm'plitlɪ〕*adv.* 完全地

First, even though all her chromosomes came from the adult
sheep, Dolly's mitochondrial DNA still came from the egg
contributor. Mitochondrial DNA comes only from the mother, and
since <u>it</u> never combines with the father's DNA, it can be used to
trace the development of animals.

首先，即使她所有的染色體都來自同一隻成羊，桃莉的腺粒體去氧
核醣核酸，仍然來自卵子捐贈者。腺粒體去氧核醣核酸只取自母親，既
然它從來沒有跟父親的去氧核醣核酸結合，它就能夠被用來追溯動物的
演化。

> ***even though*** 即使   chromosome〔'kromə,som〕*n.* 染色體
> adult〔ə'dʌlt〕*adj.* 成年的   sheep〔ʃip〕*n.* 綿羊【單複數同型】
> mitochondrial〔,maɪtə'kɑndrɪəl〕*n. pl.* 腺粒體【單數為
>   mitochondrion〔,maɪtə'kɑndrɪən〕】

DNA〔ˈdiɛnˈe〕*n.* 去氧核醣核酸【生物學染色體和基因的組成分子，
全名為 Deoxyribonucleic acid〔diˌɑksiraɪbonuˈkliɪkˈæsɪd〕】
egg〔ɛg〕*n.* 卵子　　contributor〔kənˈtrɪbjətɚ〕*n.* 捐贈者
combine〔kəmˈbaɪn〕*v.* 結合　　trace〔tres〕*v.* 追尋；追溯
development〔dɪˈvɛləpmənt〕*n.* 發展；發育

Next, the immune system genes are not fully developed at the
very beginning stage. The genes continue recombining after
fertilization. Thus a clone would have a slightly different immune
system from that of its parent.

其次，免疫系統的基因在最初階段，並沒有完全發育。受精後基因繼
續再次結合。因此，複製的生物跟母體的免疫系統，會有些微不同。

immune〔ɪˈmjun〕*adj.* 免疫的　　***immune system*** 免疫系統
fully〔ˈfʊlɪ〕*adv.* 完全地　　develop〔dɪˈvɛləp〕*v.* 生長；發育
very〔ˈvɛrɪ〕*adj.* 最⋯的【加強語氣】
beginning〔bɪˈɡɪnɪŋ〕*adj.* 初期的
the very beginning 最初的；一開始的
stage〔stedʒ〕*n.* 階段　　recombine〔ˌrikəmˈbaɪn〕*v.* 再結合
fertilization〔ˌfɝtḷəˈzeʃən〕*n.* 受精
clone〔klon〕*n.* 複製的生物　　slightly〔ˈslaɪtlɪ〕*adv.* 稍微地

Moreover, environment also has its effects. Even twins,
who share many characteristics, are not completely identical,
particularly when they're raised separately. Experiments with rats
have confirmed that upbringing affects brain biochemistry, says
Frank Farley, a psychologist at Temple University. In other words,
you can create a person with the same genetic makeup of someone
else, but who the person will become is affected by his or her
environment, too. A clone is not going to be a perfect copy of the

adult, since changes in environment, starting in the womb, affect which genes get expressed, and how the body and mind develop. Even if we cloned Einstein, due to the upbringing, the clone might not be identical to Einstein.

此外，環境也有影響。即使是有許多共同特徵的雙胞胎，也不會完全相同，特別是當他們被分開養育的時候。坦普大學的心理學家法蘭克·法立表示，用老鼠做實驗已經證實，養育會影響腦部的生物化學物質。換句話說，你能創造出，跟另一個人有相同基因的人，但那個人會成為什麼樣的人，也會被環境所影響。複製的生物並不是成熟體的完美複製品，因為環境的改變，從子宮裡就開始了，這影響基因特徵如何被顯現出來，以及身體跟心靈如何發育。即使我們複製愛因斯坦，因為教養不同，複製體也可能不會跟愛因斯坦完全一樣。

environment〔ɪn'vaɪrənmənt〕*n.* 環境
effect〔ɪ'fɛkt〕*n.* 影響　　twins〔twɪnz〕*n. pl.* 雙胞胎
share〔ʃɛr〕*v.* 共享；共有　　characteristic〔ˌkærɪktə'rɪstɪk〕*n.* 特質
identical〔aɪ'dɛntɪkḷ〕*adj.* 完全相同的
particularly〔pə'tɪkjələlɪ〕*adv.* 尤其；特別是
raise〔rez〕*v.* 撫養　　separately〔'sɛprɪtlɪ〕*adv.* 分別地；各自地
experiment〔ɪk'spɛrəmənt〕*n.* 實驗　　rat〔ræt〕*n.* 老鼠
confirm〔kən'fɝm〕*v.* 證實　　upbringing〔'ʌpˌbrɪŋɪŋ〕*n.* 養育
affect〔ə'fɛkt〕*v.* 影響
biochemistry〔ˌbaɪo'kɛmɪstrɪ〕*n.* 生物化學
Frank Farley〔'fræŋk'farlɪ〕*n.* 法蘭克·法立
psychologist〔saɪ'kɑlədʒɪst〕*n.* 心理學家
university〔ˌjunə'vɝsətɪ〕*n.* 大學　　***Temple University*** 坦普大學
in other words 換句話說　　create〔krɪ'et〕*v.* 創造
genetic〔dʒə'nɛtɪk〕*adj.* 基因的；遺傳的
makeup〔'mekˌʌp〕*n.* 組成　　else〔ɛls〕*adj.* 其他的
copy〔'kɑpɪ〕*n.* 複製品　　womb〔wum〕*n.* 子宮
express〔ɪk'sprɛs〕*v.* 表達；顯示　　***even if*** 即使
Einstein〔'aɪnstaɪn〕*n.* 愛因斯坦【1879-1955，德裔美籍物理學家，
相對論的提出者】　　***due to*** 由於

1. (**B**)　本文在討論什麼？

(A) 人類跟老鼠的不同。

(B) 為什麼複製的生物不是完美的複製品。

(C) 動物細胞的發展為何。

(D) 如何成功地複製愛因斯坦。

* ***human beings*** 人類　　cell〔sɛl〕*n.* 細胞

clone〔klon〕*v.* 複製

2. (**A**)　根據本文，複製體的腺粒體去氧核醣核酸從何而來？

(A) 卵子捐贈者。　　　　(B) 父親。

(C) 父母雙方。　　　　(D) 以上皆非。

* donor〔'donɚ〕*n.* 捐贈者

3. (**C**)　根據本文，下列敘述何者錯誤？

(A) 複製的生物跟母體不會有相同的免疫系統。

(B) 環境也會影響你的性格。

(C) 即使雙胞胎被分開來養育，也會變得完全相同。

(D) 心理學家利用老鼠發現環境是如何影響發育。

* ***have an effect on*** 對～有影響

4. (**C**)　在第二段第四行的 "it" 指的是什麼？

(A) 桃莉羊。　　　　　(B) 發育過程。

(C) 腺粒體去氧核醣核酸。　(D) 免疫系統。

* course〔kors〕*n.* 進程　　immune〔ɪ'mjun〕*adj.* 免疫的

5. (**B**)　本文中提供幾個理由，解釋為什麼複製的生物並不會是成熟
體的完美複製品？

(A) 兩種。　　(B) 三種。　　(C) 四種。　　(D) 五種。

* provide〔prə'vaɪd〕*v.* 提供　　explain〔ɪk'splen〕*v.* 解釋；說明

TEST 40

Read the following passage and choose the best answer for each question.

The heat was intense as we moved down the long corridor. Not only was it a difficult blaze, but the July heat made things even worse as we struggled to get the best of the flames.

As we finally made the turn into the apartment where the fire had started, the words of the young mother outside screamed in my brain: "Please help! My baby is in there!"

We moved into the bedroom under cover of hoses from the engine company. I started looking in the usual spots where a child might seek refuge: under the bed, in the corners. As I groped my way through the thick smoke, I suddenly fell forward, tripping over something on the floor. It was the child.

Ripping off my mask to give mouth-to-mouth resuscitation, I grabbed the child and raced for the stairs. When we reached the waiting Rescue Squad members, my legs felt weak, and I collapsed in a heap in the gutter. The ambulance sped off into the night, its siren wailing.

Later that evening, we received word that the child had died in the hospital's emergency room. Another small life lost in the city.

Why do little children such as that one have to pay the price for the neglect of others? During my career as a fire fighter, I have seen this happen many times. You would think that we would become hard and callous, but we don't.

We mourn each person who dies. What bothers me is that many senseless tragedies could have been prevented. An overwhelming number of deaths in fires can be prevented by just one thing — a smoke detector.

It is estimated that fewer than 50 percent of all dwellings in the United States are protected by smoke detectors. Why are so many people ignorant about the need for smoke detectors? Smoke detectors save lives. They are easy to install. Their cost is reasonable, and they offer immediate protection. People must persuade their communities to provide fire education for everyone.

The money spent on fire education reaps a reward that cannot be measured. If you do not think so, then consider your reaction if the child I carried out of that flaming apartment had been a member of your own family. You would probably then be willing to do anything at all to undo that tragedy. 【延平高中】

1. In the section about carrying the child from the building, the author is describing
   - (A) an article in a newspaper.
   - (B) a personal experience.
   - (C) a tragedy in his family.
   - (D) a report from city police department.

2. The author's main purpose in the passage is to
   - (A) reveal some fire-fighting techniques.
   - (B) advertise a brand of smoke detector.
   - (C) encourage fire safety measures.
   - (D) plead for new fire-fighting equipment.

3. Which of these opinions would the author agree with?
   - (A) The death of the child could have been prevented.
   - (B) The fire in the apartment was caused by smoking.
   - (C) The Rescue Squad could have saved the child.
   - (D) Fires always result in tragedy.

4. The author blames the lack of smoke detectors in households on
   - (A) high cost.
   - (B) failure to work.
   - (C) difficult installation.
   - (D) ignorance.

5. The author used the story of the apartment fire to
   - (A) prove that fire fighting is dangerous.
   - (B) persuade readers to become firemen.
   - (C) support the case for smoke detectors.
   - (D) argue against smoking in apartments.

TEST 40 詳解

The heat was intense as we moved down the long corridor. Not only was it a difficult blaze, but the July heat made things even worse as we struggled to get the best of the flames.

當我們沿著長廊走的時候,溫度非常熱。不只是這猛烈的火焰,還有七月的熱度,在我們奮力要打火時,讓事情變得更糟糕。

heat〔hit〕*n.* 熱
intense〔ɪn'tɛns〕*adj.* 強烈的   move〔muv〕*v.* 移動
along〔əlɔŋ〕*prep.* 沿著   corridor〔'kɔrədə〕*n.* 走廊
blaze〔blez〕*n.* 火焰
struggle〔'strʌgl̩〕*v.* 掙扎;奮鬥   ***to get the best of*** 打敗
flames〔flemz〕*n. pl.* 火焰

As we finally made the turn into the apartment where the fire had started, the words of the young mother outside screamed in my brain: "Please help! My baby is in there!"

當我們終於成功越過轉角,進入起火的公寓時,火場外一位年輕母親的尖叫聲直入我腦海:「請幫幫忙!我的小孩在裡面!」

make a turn 轉彎   apartment〔ə'pɑrtmənt〕*n.* 公寓
scream〔skrim〕*v.* 大聲尖叫

We moved into the bedroom under cover of hoses from the engine company. I started looking in the usual spots where a child might seek refuge: under the bed, in the corners. As I groped my way through the thick smoke, I suddenly fell forward, tripping over something on the floor. It was the child.

在消防車的水管掩護下，我們走進臥室。我開始查看像是床底下、角落裡，這幾個孩子們通常會躲避的地方。當我在濃霧中摸索著前進時，我突然往前跌倒，被地板上的某個東西絆倒。是那個孩子。

cover〔ˈkʌvɚ〕 n. 掩護；遮蔽　　***under cover of*** … 在…的掩護下
hose〔hoz〕 n. 軟水管　　engine〔ˈɛndʒən〕 n. 消防車（= *fire engine*）
company〔ˈkʌmpənɪ〕 n. 全體成員
usual〔ˈjuʒʊəl〕 adj. 一般的；通常的　　spot〔spat〕 n. 地點
refuge〔ˈrɛfjudʒ〕 n. 避難所；藏匿處　　***seek refuge*** 避難；藏匿
corner〔ˈkɔrnɚ〕 n. 角落　　grope〔grop〕 v.（暗中）摸索
grope one's way 摸索而行　　thick〔θɪk〕 adj. 濃厚的
smoke〔smok〕 n. 煙霧　　trip〔trɪp〕 v. 絆倒　　***trip over*** 被…絆倒

Ripping off my mask to give mouth-to-mouth resuscitation, I grabbed the child and raced for the stairs. When we reached the waiting Rescue Squad members, my legs felt weak, and I collapsed in a heap in the gutter. The ambulance sped off into the night, its siren wailing.

我扯下面罩開始做口對口人工呼吸，我抓著那個孩子，快速跑向樓梯。當我們抵達正在等待的救援小組人員時，我的雙腿虛弱，癱倒在水溝上。救護車呼嘯著警鈴，在夜色中加速前進。

rip〔rɪp〕 v. 扯掉；撕下　　***rip off*** 扯下
mask〔mæsk〕 n. 面具
mouth-to-mouth〔ˈmaʊθtəˈmaʊθ〕 adj. 口對口的
resuscitation〔rɪˌsʌsəˈteʃən〕 n. 復甦；甦醒
mouth-to-mouth resuscitation 口對口人工呼吸法
grab〔græb〕 v. 抓住　　race〔res〕 v. 快跑
stair〔stɛr〕 n. 樓梯　　reach〔ritʃ〕 v. 抵達
rescue〔ˈrɛskju〕 n. 救援　　squad〔skwad〕 n. 小隊
the Rescue Squad 救援隊　　collapse〔kəˈlæps〕 v. 倒下；倒塌
heap〔hip〕 n. 一堆；許多　　***in a heap*** 成堆；一動也不動

collapse in a heap 癱倒

gutter〔'gʌtɚ〕*n.* 排水溝　　ambulance〔'æmbjələns〕*n.* 救護車

speed〔spid〕*v.* 疾行【三態：speed-sped-speeded】

speed off 加速離開　　siren〔'saɪrən〕*n.* 警報器

wail〔wel〕*v.*（警報器）發出尖嘯聲；哭號

Later that evening, we received word that the child had died in the hospital's emergency room. Another small life lost in the city.

當天稍晚我們收到消息，那個孩子在醫院急診室裡死去。又一個小生命在城市中殞落。

receive〔rɪ'siv〕*v.* 收到　　word〔wɝd〕*n.* 消息

emergency〔ɪ'mɝdʒənsɪ〕*adj.* 緊急的　　*emergency room* 急診室

Why do little children such as that one have to pay the price for the neglect of others? During my career as a fire fighter, I have seen this happen many times. You would think that we would become hard and callous, but we don't.

為什麼像這樣的小孩，必須要為其他人的疏忽付出代價？在我做消防員的生涯中，已經看過太多這樣的事。你可能覺得我們應該變得冷酷且無情，但是我們沒有。

pay the price 付出代價　　neglect〔nɪ'glɛkt〕*n.* 疏忽

career〔kə'rɪr〕*n.* 職業生涯　　*fire fighter* 消防隊員

hard〔hɑrd〕*adj.* 冷酷的　　callous〔'kæləs〕*adj.* 無情的；麻木的

We mourn each person who dies. What bothers me is that many senseless tragedies could have been prevented. An overwhelming number of deaths in fires can be prevented by just one thing — a smoke detector.

我們為每個死去的人哀悼。但讓我困擾的是，很多愚蠢的悲劇，原本是可以被預防的。只要有煙霧偵測器，就能避免火災中許多人死亡。

mourn〔morn〕*v.* 哀悼　　bother〔'baðə〕*v.* 困擾
senseless〔'sɛnslɪs〕*adj.* 愚蠢的；無常識的
tragedy〔'trædʒədɪ〕*n.* 悲劇　　prevent〔prɪ'vɛnt〕*v.* 預防；阻止
overwhelming〔,ovə'hwɛlmɪŋ〕*adj.* 壓倒性（多數）的
death〔dɛθ〕*n.* 死亡人數　　detector〔dɪ'tɛktə〕*n.* 偵測器

It is estimated that fewer than 50 percent of all dwellings in the United States are protected by smoke detectors. Why are so many people ignorant about the need for smoke detectors? Smoke detectors save lives. They are easy to install. Their cost is reasonable, and they offer immediate protection. People must persuade their communities to provide fire education for everyone.

　　據估計，只有不到百分之五十的美國住宅，有煙霧偵測器保護。為什麼如此多民眾不知道煙霧偵測器的必要性？煙霧偵測器能拯救生命，而且容易安裝，價格合理，能夠提供立即的保護。人們必須說服自己的社區，提供每個人火災教育。

estimate〔'ɛstə,met〕*v.* 估計　　dwelling〔'dwɛlɪŋ〕*n.* 住所
protect〔prə'tɛkt〕*v.* 保護
ignorant〔'ɪgnərənt〕*adj.* 無知的；不知道的
need〔nid〕*n.* 需要　　install〔ɪn'stɔl〕*v.* 安裝 cost〔kɔst〕*n.* 花費
reasonable〔'riznəbḷ〕*adj.* 合理的
offer〔'ɔfə〕*v.* 提供　　immediate〔ɪ'midɪɪt〕*adj.* 立即的
protection〔prə'tɛkʃən〕*n.* 保護　　persuade〔pə'swed〕*v.* 說服
community〔kə'mjunətɪ〕*n.* 社區
provide〔prə'vaɪd〕*v.* 提供

The money spent on fire education reaps a reward that cannot be measured. If you do not think so, then consider your reaction if the child I carried out of that flaming apartment had been a

member of your own family. You would probably then be willing
to do anything at all to undo that tragedy.

火災教育的費用所得到的回報是無法衡量的。如果你不這樣認為，那
麼請想一下，假如我從那幢著火的公寓所帶出來的孩子，是你家族成員之
一，你的反應會如何。那你可能會願意去做任何能來挽回這場悲劇的事。

reap〔 rip 〕v. 獲得（回報）　　reward〔 rɪ'wɔrd 〕n. 獎勵；報酬
measure〔'mɛʒɚ 〕v. 衡量；測量
consider〔 kən'sɪdɚ 〕v. 考慮　　reaction〔 rɪ'ækʃən 〕n. 反應
flaming〔'flemɪŋ 〕adj. 著火的；燃燒的
at all 絲毫；眞的…【用於強調】
undo〔 ʌn'du 〕v. 使復原；恢復

1. (**B**)　將孩子帶出建築物的那一段，作者描述的是

　　(A) 報紙上的文章。　　　　(B) 個人的經驗。

　　(C) 他的家庭悲劇。　　　　(D) 市警局的報告。

　　* section〔'sɛkʃən 〕n. 部分；片段
　　　describe〔 dɪ'skraɪb 〕v. 描述　　report〔 rɪ'port 〕n. 報告
　　　department〔 dɪ'pɑrtmənt 〕n. 部門

2. (**C**)　本文作者主要的目的是

　　(A) 透露一些滅火技巧。

　　(B) 爲某個煙霧偵測器品牌打廣告。

　　(C) 鼓勵火災安全措施。　　　(D) 爲新的滅火設備辯護。

　　* reveal〔 rɪ'vil 〕v. 透露
　　　fire-fighting〔'faɪr'faɪtɪŋ 〕adj. 消防的；滅火的
　　　technique〔 tɛk'nik 〕n. 技術；技巧
　　　advertise〔'ædvɚ͵taɪz 〕v. 替…打廣告　　brand〔 brænd 〕n. 品牌
　　　encourage〔 ɪn'kɝɪdʒ 〕v. 鼓勵；促進
　　　measure〔'mɛʒɚ 〕n. 措施　　plead〔 plid 〕v. 爲…辯護
　　　equipment〔 ɪ'kwɪpmənt 〕n. 設備

3. (**A**) 作者可能會同意下列哪一種看法？

(A) 孩童的死亡其實是可以避免的。

(B) 這場公寓火警是因為抽煙所引起的。

(C) 救援隊本來可以救活那個孩子。

(D) 火災總是會導致悲劇。

* opinion〔əˋpɪnjən〕*n.* 意見；看法
result in 導致；造成

4. (**D**) 作者將房屋內缺少煙霧偵測器的責任怪罪於

(A) 高花費。　　　　　(B) 無法運轉。

(C) 難以安裝。　　　　(D) 無知。

* blame〔blem〕*v.* 怪罪　　***blame on*** … 將（責任）歸咎於…
failure〔ˋfeljɚ〕*n.* 失敗　　installation〔ˌɪnstəˋleʃən〕*n.* 安裝
ignorance〔ˋɪgnərəns〕*n.* 無知

5. (**C**) 這位作者用這則公寓火災的故事來_

(A) 證明滅火是很危險的。

(B) 說服讀者成為消防隊員。

(C) 當作支持煙霧偵測器的案例。

(D) 反對在公寓中抽煙。

* prove〔pruv〕*v.* 證明　　fireman〔ˋfaɪrmən〕*n.* 消防隊員
case〔kes〕*n.* 案例
argue〔ˋɑrgju〕*v.* 主張；爭論
argue against 反對

本書答題錯誤率分析表

本資料經過「劉毅英文家教班」閱讀測驗大賽 288 位同學實際考試過，經過電腦統計分析，錯誤率如下：

測 驗	題號	正確選項	錯誤率	最多人選的錯誤選項	測 驗	題號	正確選項	錯誤率	最多人選的錯誤選項
Test 1	1	D	3%	B	Test 10	1	B	9%	A / C
	2	C	14%	B		2	D	11%	A
	3	D	32%	A		3	D	22%	A
	4	B	70%	A		4	C	11%	D
	5	C	18%	D		5	B	44%	C
Test 2	1	A	21%	C	Test 11	1	C	21%	B
	2	D	10%	B		2	D	19%	C
	3	B	16%	C		3	A	24%	B
	4	A	32%	D		4	A	15%	C
	5	B	32%	C		5	B	16%	A
Test 3	1	A	12%	C	Test 12	1	B	69%	C
	2	C	5%	A		2	C	14%	D
	3	D	31%	A		3	B	42%	D
	4	D	44%	A		4	B	56%	C
	5	C	81%	A		5	D	45%	B
Test 4	1	B	8%	D	Test 13	1	C	35%	A
	2	A	21%	D		2	A	7%	C
	3	D	11%	B		3	B	10%	C
	4	A	3%	C / D		4	C	15%	B
	5	C	18%	A		5	D	18%	C
Test 5	1	B	54%	A	Test 14	1	A	16%	D
	2	D	33%	C		2	B	13%	A
	3	B	43%	A		3	C	29%	D
	4	B	55%	C		4	D	27%	C
	5	A	54%	D		5	B	21%	D
Test 6	1	D	7%	B / C	Test 15	1	B	27%	D
	2	A	28%	B		2	C	16%	B
	3	C	50%	A		3	D	11%	B / C
	4	B	48%	A		4	B	37%	A
	5	D	47%	C		5	B	33%	D
Test 7	1	B	33%	A	Test 16	1	D	16%	A
	2	C	15%	B		2	A	13%	C
	3	B	14%	A		3	C	57%	A
	4	D	22%	B		4	B	14%	D
	5	C	10%	B		5	D	57%	C
Test 8	1	D	41%	A	Test 17	1	D	12%	B
	2	B	24%	A		2	B	23%	A
	3	D	32%	C		3	C	9%	A
	4	C	70%	D		4	C	20%	A
	5	B	18%	A		5	A	43%	D
Test 9	1	A	14%	C	Test 18	1	B	53%	C
	2	C	21%	B		2	D	43%	C
	3	D	10%	B		3	B	51%	D
	4	C	14%	B		4	D	48%	A
	5	A	10%	B		5	C	57%	B

測 驗	題號	正確選項	錯誤率	最多人選的錯誤選項	測 驗	題號	正確選項	錯誤率	最多人選的錯誤選項
Test 19	1	D	39%	C	Test 30	1	D	32%	A
	2	B	33%	C		2	B	58%	D
	3	C	15%	D		3	C	48%	A
	4	C	60%	C		4	B	33%	A
	5	D	28%	A		5	A	47%	B
Test 20	1	B	15%	C	Test 31	1	B	31%	C
	2	C	14%	D		2	B	38%	C
	3	A	22%	D		3	C	32%	A
	4	D	28%	B		4	A	46%	C
	5	C	12%	C		5	A	43%	C
Test 21	1	B	27%	D	Test 32	1	D	50%	B
	2	D	24%	A		2	D	42%	C
	3	C	17%	B		3	C	42%	B
	4	A	42%	C		4	B	58%	A
	5	C	52%	A		5	B	68%	D
Test 22	1	D	15%	B	Test 33	1	D	28%	B
	2	B	12%	C		2	A	25%	C
	3	B	9%	D		3	B	23%	C
	4	D	47%	A		4	A	66%	B
	5	A	92%	C		5	D	28%	C
Test 23	1	B	31%	C	Test 34	1	B	24%	C
	2	B	20%	C		2	B	36%	C
	3	A	24%	C		3	C	28%	B
	4	D	33%	A		4	C	50%	B
	5	C	28%	D		5	D	42%	C
Test 24	1	C	31%	B	Test 35	1	A	72%	B
	2	B	55%	C		2	D	55%	C
	3	D	54%	B		3	C	53%	B
	4	A	45%	D		4	B	58%	D
	5	C	65%	B		5	D	75%	C
Test 25	1	D	36%	A	Test 36	1	B	29%	C
	2	A	24%	B		2	A	32%	C
	3	C	15%	B		3	A	55%	C
	4	B	37%	D		4	B	43%	B
	5	C	76%	A		5	C	30%	B
Test 26	1	B	30%	D	Test 37	1	A	50%	C
	2	D	14%	B		2	B	79%	C
	3	B	16%	A		3	C	42%	B
	4	B	30%	A		4	C	57%	B
	5	B	47%	C		5	D	68%	C
Test 27	1	D	60%	C	Test 38	1	C	28%	B
	2	C	37%	A		2	B	36%	C
	3	D	21%	C		3	C	39%	B
	4	A	38%	B		4	D	49%	C
	5	D	49%	C		5	A	49%	C
Test 28	1	B	18%	C	Test 39	1	B	31%	C
	2	D	21%	B		2	A	63%	D
	3	C	63%	D		3	C	42%	B
	4	A	31%	B		4	C	38%	B
	5	B	29%	D		5	B	37%	C
Test 29	1	B	31%	A	Test 40	1	B	40%	C
	2	D	26%	A		2	C	48%	B
	3	B	32%	A		3	A	59%	C
	4	C	27%	D		4	D	46%	B
	5	D	43%	A		5	C	50%	B